THE HISTORY OF
MYSTERY

"In memory of Bill DeAndrea"

Copyright ©2001 Max Allan Collins

For a free catalog write to:

COLLECTORS PRESS, INC.

P.O. Box 230986
Portland, OR 97281
Toll-free: 1 800 423 1848
or visit our website at:
www.collectorspress.com

Book design Drive Communications, New York
Copy editing Ann Granning Bennett

Printed in Hong Kong

First American Edition

9 8 7 6 5 4 3 2 1

Library of Congress Cataloging–in–Publication Data

Collins, Max Allan.

The history of mystery /

by Max Allan Collins.
        p.   cm. — (Art fiction series)
    Includes bibliographical references (p.   ) and index.
    ISBN 1-888054-53-0 (hardcover : alk. paper)
    1. Detective and mystery stories, American—History and criticism.
    2. Detective and mystery stories, English—History and criticism. I. Title.
        II. Series.
    PS374.D4 C59 2001
    813'.087209—dc21   2001001531
                                                              CIP

THE HISTORY OF MYSTERY

by Max Allan Collins

Research Associates: Matthew V. Clemens, George Hagenauer

PORTLAND, OREGON

TABLE OF CONTENTS

INTRODUCTION

With the help of George Hagenauer, my chief research associate on the Nathan Heller historical detective novels, my goal in writing this book was to explore the beginnings of the genre that other histories have downplayed or overlooked. In the Heller series, George and I often have uncovered new facts and developed new theories about famous crimes and we approached this material with a similar mindset. • Matt Clemens, my collaborator on a number of published short stories, is a more knowledgeable fan of the current mystery field than I and he helped me on that aspect of this book. He agreed with me, however, that covering the entire genre was hopeless. We have left people out; fans and fellow mystery writers might be annoyed with me on that account. But we wanted only to provide an overview of trends and notable sub-genres as well as sample some of the best, most interesting series in the history of the mystery. • Our focus here is strictly on sleuths. No cops, only crooks who also solve crimes, and very few one-shot mysteries. I have chosen ten authors to showcase, whom I consider to be the prime movers and shakers of the genre. These choices reflect my bias and I stand behind them unapologetically • Neither have I attempted to gather the most significant, the rarest book covers and movie posters, etc., for what is, in part, a picture book. I'll leave that to expert collectors like my buddy Otto Penzler for what might one day be the definitive book. Although we display a sampling of the significant material, I have leaned toward images that I found, well, fun. So you will see a disproportionate number of pulp covers and funky fifties and sixties paperback art. As a private-eye writer, I have a great fondness for the wonderfully sleazy, girls-and-gats paperback covers of that era. My high opinion of Mickey Spillane and his importance to the genre is also underscored, similarly without apology. • We have emphasized books and magazines, but we discuss TV, radio, and movies as well. I have been a mystery fan since childhood. This book is a valentine to a genre I love unreservedly and without shame. Sex and violence, after all, are love and death. And what subjects are of more interest to any of us? • **Max Allan Collins** *January 2001*

CHAPTER

1

MYSTERIOUS BEGINNINGS

Roots in Reality

The mystery story maintains its perennial hold on readers because, at its core, is crime — and death, those inevitable elements of society and life that so fascinate us. Unlike real life, however, in most mystery yarns injustice is redressed in fairly short order, and the conundrums of living and dying are resolved in a tidy, satisfying way, thanks to the efforts and skills of the hero or heroine: the sleuth. • Crime and death are always with us; but the sleuth of mystery fiction is a relatively recent creation. Though fanciful detectives thrived throughout the twentieth century, making it the first full century of American detective fiction, the pattern was set by Edgar Allan Poe only sixty years earlier. The reason is, as Holmes would say, elementary: in order for there to be fictional detectives, there first needed to be real-life detectives. • Detectives and police forces are relatively new inventions in Western civilization, an outgrowth of the birth of democracies in Europe and the United States in the late 1700s and early 1800s. As average citizens gained rights, the military lost part of its role in maintaining law and order, and local police forces were created. In England, Sir Robert Peel reorganized the Bow Street Runners into a modern force, following the lead of Napoleon's Gendarmerie, which included Le Sûreté Nationale, Europe's first real detective bureau. • The Sûreté's François Eugène

Vidocq provided the first modern detective tome when he published his *Mémoires* in 1828. Born in 1775, Vidocq spent his early life more on the wrong side of the law than the right. He served his country as a soldier, yes. But he deserted and was jailed after being convicted of a felony; that he had been trying to free an innocent man from prison indicates Vidocq's mixed agenda.

Renowned for numerous attempts, often successful, to escape from prison, Vidocq played on both sides of the law. Though an active criminal, he also served as a key police informer for the Paris police. His information proved so useful that he was that rare informer who was promoted to police officer. And, finally, he ascended to the "top cop" slot of his day, becoming chief of the Sûreté in 1812. Vidocq claimed to have solved more than a thousand crimes and hired ghost writers (scholars suspect notables such as Honoré de Balzac and Victor Hugo) to create his memoirs. These originally appeared in four volumes, shortly after he retired from the detective bureau. With their publication, Vidocq inadvertently created the first crime narrative, so fictionalized it can be classified as either fact or fiction, essentially making him the innovator of both mystery fiction and true crime.

Though Vidocq is seldom read today, his *Mémoires* proved enormously popular not only in France, but in America. Vidocq used them to promote himself as a speaker and later started Europe's first private detective agency. In both reality and fiction, private eyes frequently are former cops, and Vidocq's *Mémoirs* are solidly within the action detective genre.

In his fictionalized tales, Vidocq goes undercover in Holmes-like disguise, sets up elaborate traps for criminals, and ferrets out clues on the streets of Paris. His history as a criminal (as a police informer, he once simultaneously maintained three separate identities in Paris) is at the fore, thus creating the noir-style detective story in which the line between cops and crooks is thin at best.

Inspired Poe

The American popularity of Vidocq's *Mémoires* undoubtedly inspired Poe to create his detective short stories about Monsieur C. Auguste Dupin. Poe's narrator, Dupin's roommate, mentions Vidocq in "The Murders in the Rue Morgue," bemoaning the lack of sophistication in Vidocq's approach. Dupin, unlike Vidocq, was not a member of the police force, but an amateur. Dupin's cases were recorded by his roommate, setting the pattern for Sherlock's Dr. Watson, and many a Watson to come.

Unlike Vidocq who always depicted himself as a heroic figure, Dupin enjoyed a lifestyle far from heroic. In "Rue Morgue," Dupin's roommate describes a detective who would be comfortable in the dark alleys of film *noir*: "Had the routine of our life been known to the world, we would have been regarded as madmen.... Our seclusion was perfect. We admitted no visitors. Indeed the locality of our retirement had been carefully kept a secret from my former associates.... We existed among ourselves alone...enamored of the Night for her own sake.... At the first dawn of the morning, we closed all shutters of our old building; lighted a couple of tapers which, strongly perfumed, threw out only the ghastliest and feeblest of rays. By the aid of these we then busied our souls in dreams— reading, writing, or conversing, until warned by the clock of the true Darkness. Then we sallied forth into the streets...seeking, amid the wild lights and shadows of the populous city, that infinity of mental excitement which quiet observation can afford."

If Vidocq set a standard for the sleuth as a man of action, the languid Dupin is the first cerebral detective. What he thinks is far more important than what he does: he meticulously pieces together the clues surrounding the murders of two women—one beheaded, the other stuffed up a chimney. He then outperforms the police and identifies the killer as a great ape, specifically, an orangutan.

In this single story, Poe creates and develops numerous themes that continue in the genre to this day. His chief innovation, the amateur detective, sets the stage for countless eccentric sleuths. Poe also establishes the detective's partner (and chronicler), the somewhat less intelligent (than Dupin) sounding board who fills in for the reader; and his sleuth, of course, outwits the police, showing them to be ineffective crimefighters and problem-solvers. The approach is cerebral and deductive, obviously inspiring Doyle in his creation of Holmes. But, unlike Holmes, Dupin does not dress up in disguise or carry a pistol. All he needs to do to solve a crime is to think and deduct.

Poe's first detective yarn was written during a rare period of stability in his life. From 1839 through 1842, he was involved in various editorial positions at the *Gentleman's Magazine*. Magazines in the early 1800s differed from their modern counterparts: illustrations were scant and most periodicals lacked slick covers, instead resembling small-sized newspapers. Poe's editorial work at *Gentleman's*

EDGAR ALLAN POE

Drawing
December 1958

Edgar Allan Poe as depicted by Leo Morey, a prolific illustrator of early science-fiction magazines. From a Poe Biography by Sam Moskowitz in *Satellite Science Fiction*.

—and the publication of his first book of short stories in two volumes—provided his family with a steady income for the first time.

During this period of relative calm, Poe created "The Murders in the Rue Morgue," his first "tale of ratiocination," which had its horrific elements (a homicidal ape, for example), but remained a departure from his usual morbid horror yarns. With the onset of his wife's tuberculosis in 1842, however, Poe fell apart once again, turning to drink. Nonetheless, due to the unexpected popularity of his character, Dupin, Poe wrote two more stories featuring the eccentric detective: "The Mystery of Marie Roget" (1842) and "The Purloined Letter" (1845). In doing so, the tortured poet created the first detective series. A writer of Poe's stature writing in this form placed the genre firmly in the ranks of fine literature.

Unlike Great Britain, where the detective throughout the 1800s appeared in great literature by Dickens, Wilkie Collins, and Arthur Conan Doyle, in America the detective story after Poe's death in 1849 established itself firmly in the lowest levels of popular culture. The true roots of the modern mystery are found in the American dime novels and story papers of the 1800s, and this literary form would flourish and mature in the pulpy pages of cheap magazines in the early decades of the next century.

Pinkerton and the Birth of the Private Eye

Before the genre took hold as a significant part of popular culture, and the detective earned his (and her) status as an enduring modern mythic hero, Allan Pinkerton established the first American private investigation firm. The Pinkerton Agency was the model on which most of the next one hundred years of detective fiction would be based, as well as providing the field with one of its most influential and best writers, former Pinkerton agent Dashiell Hammett.

Born into extreme poverty in Scotland in 1819, Allan Pinkerton grew up to be a cooper, a maker of barrels. In his teens, he became a member of the Chartists, a radical organization fighting for universal suffrage and better living and working conditions for Scotland's and England's poor. The Chartists were divided between a nonviolent faction and the "physical force men," who felt violent revolt was the only way to gain their goals.

In 1839, when the tattered Chartist "Army" marched on Monmouth Castle armed with hammers, sledges, and the occasional musket, Pinkerton was among them. In Newport, the King's 42nd Foot soldiers met the army, firing on the Chartists from concealed positions, massacring the protestors. Pinkerton barely escaped with his life.

The future detective continued as an agitator and political activist for another three years, working not only on suffrage and justice issues, but also in labor unions, organizing and supporting strikes. During this exciting, dangerous period, he fell in love with Joan Carfrae, a singer with a Chartist choral group. In 1842, with a price on his head, Pinkerton married Joan, and the young couple left for America, narrowly eluding police bearing King's warrants for the groom's arrest.

The couple's respite from peril was short-lived: their ship crashed, sinking on the Nova Scotian coast. Weeks later, via rowboat, the Pinkertons finally arrived in America—specifically, Chicago, whose population numbered just more than one thousand. There, Pinkerton worked as a cooper and as a printer's assistant before moving to Dundee, a Scottish settlement about fifty miles away.

In 1847, while cutting wood for barrel staves, Pinkerton discovered a hidden camp on an island in the Fox River. His curiosity piqued, he returned several times to check on the campsite, only to discover that it harbored a band of counterfeiters. Pinkerton contacted the sheriff and helped the local law capture the gang.

As the story of how Pinkerton cracked the counterfeiting gang was spread by word of mouth and the local press, the cooper became a hero in rural Kane County. Soon two local storeowners approached Pinkerton about several counterfeit bills that had been passed in the village. Thirty-five miles away lived a reputed counterfeiter, Old Man Crane; but the sheriff had searched Crane's place without finding any counterfeit cash. A city slicker, John Craig, had come to town looking for directions to Crane's place, and the storeowners hired local celebrity "sleuth" Pinkerton to investigate the suspicious newcomer, as they were convinced the city boy was part of Crane's ring.

Pinkerton met Craig at the local saddle shop, where the city slicker was having his saddle repaired, and convinced Craig that he was looking for some easy money. Over time Craig took Pinkerton into his confidence, offering to sell him counterfeit cash, while Pinkerton arranged for the sale to occur in Chicago under the surveillance of a Cook County deputy.

The extra publicity from his most recent feat resulted in Pinkerton's appointment as part-time deputy for Kane County. Increasingly, though, Pinkerton's efforts were focused not on work, but again on radical politics. He became a controversial local leader for the abolition of slavery and ran for office as an Abolition Party candidate. The local controversies and battles caused Pinkerton to tire of small-town Dundee. As a result, in 1847 he accepted a job as a deputy sheriff of Cook County and moved back to Chicago.

Chicago was now a Western boom town, a center of commerce, and a critical link between the urban Eastern Coast and the opening rural frontier. In 1849, Pinkerton became the first detective of the Chicago police department. Known as an effective rough-and-tumble cop, Pinkerton narrowly escaped several attempts on his life. Frustrated by political interference with his police work, Pinkerton signed on as Special United States Mail Agent. He went undercover in Chicago as a postal clerk to investigate a series of mail thefts. As in the Craig case, Pinkerton discovered the thief, befriended him, and then set him up for an arrest by the local sheriff. Over $3,700 in stolen bills and bank drafts—a large amount in those days—was recovered.

By the early 1850s, with the expansion of the railroads, Chicago had become a major center for cross-country commerce. The local police, swamped with street crime and vice, beset with payoffs from criminals, pressured by elected officials, were unable to reduce the ever-increasing warehouse thefts and railroad robberies. Outside the city, law enforcement officials were few and far between, and spread too thin to provide any consistent protection against train and stagecoach bandits. Pinkerton saw an opportunity for a skilled detective to open his own private police service.

In partnership with attorney Edward A. Rucker, Pinkerton established the North-Western Police Agency in Chicago and offered its services to the business community. Pinkerton's was not the first private investigation agency: in addition to Vidocq's bureau in France, a small agency in St. Louis did private policing. Pinkerton's firm, however, soon became the largest and most successful.

"THE MYSTERY OF MARIE ROGET"

Illustration
1933

The only color illustration done for a Dupin story by famous Poe illustrator Harry Clarke.

"THE MYSTERY OF MARIE ROGET"

Illustration
1933

Irishman Clarke's black-and-white Poe illustrations show the influence of Aubrey Beardsley.

Logotype
The Pinkerton Detective Agency's corporate logotype is often cited as the source of the term "private eye."

ALLAN PINKERTON
Photograph
circa late 1870's

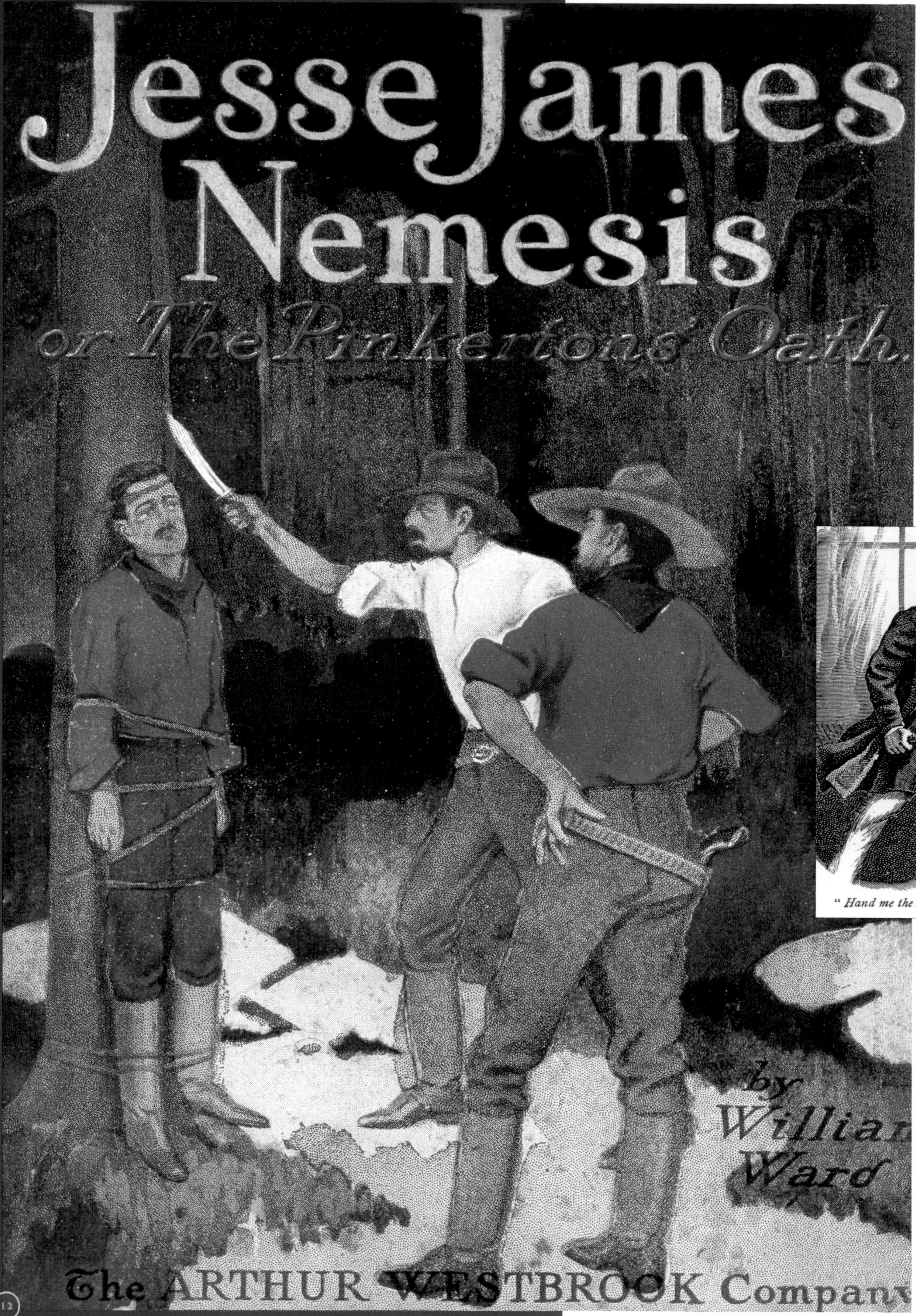

Jesse James Nemesis
or The Pinkertons' Oath

by William Ward

The ARTHUR WESTBROOK Company

JESSE JAMES NEMESIS OR THE PINKERTON'S OATH

Dime novel
undated

Typical of the fictionalized dime novel "histories" that caused Allan Pinkerton to begin his own casebook series. (Shown is a later reprint edition of an early Jesse James novel by William Ward.)

"Hand me the knife," I said, firmly, "or I will spatter the room with you..."

Illustration
1880
Earlie

Claude Melnotte as a detective, in one of Allan Pinkerton's casebooks.

With law enforcement primarily a local responsibility, inconsistent and haphazard at best, Pinkerton provided a valuable service. In many areas, the railroads were operating without benefit of local government. Pinkerton offered services to bridge the gap, not only detective work after a crime had been committed, but also skilled private guards to prevent crime from occurring.

Pinkerton soon had several contracts with major railroads out of Chicago. He set up a training program for operatives, and even hired the first female private investigator, Kate Warne, in 1856. The agency's logotype—an eye with the slogan "We Never Sleep"— inspired the term "Private Eye." Pinkerton established professional standards for his operatives, and, though his "dicks" were for hire, created an internal set of rules and ethics governing their conduct. As such, Pinkerton was selective about which clients he represented, and in the early days, his agency was set off from the usual guard services, which were basically thugs whose allegiance changed according to who paid the highest price.

In a time when literacy was rare, Pinkerton's operatives had to maintain case journals and documentation that became permanent records at the agency. The "Pinks" even created the first rogues' gallery or photographic archive of criminals. They also worked freely in the shadowy domain between the law and the underworld, developing a large network of criminal informants. The result was a skilled agency that delivered when local law enforcement failed.

Coverage by *The Police Gazette*, a national monthly magazine founded in 1845 and dedicated to covering crime stories, fueled the Pinkerton Agency's growth and fame. The exploits of Pinkerton agents frequently made the *Gazette*, and an even bigger boost came from Pinkerton's Abolitionist efforts. The late 1850s was a period of political strife, centering on the issue of slavery, and Illinois was a hotbed of that controversy. The state was torn apart, the northern portion strongly Abolitionist, while slaves were kept in many farms in Southern Illinois.

Pinkerton's Abolitionist activities brought him into contact with supporters of Illinois lawyer Abraham Lincoln. After President Lincoln's election, Pinkerton was hired to prevent possible attempts on the President's life. Pinkerton and his men went undercover in Maryland, then a swing state on the slavery issue. On the way to Lincoln's inaugural, Pinkerton and his operatives uncovered a plot to kill the President. Pinkerton's men spirited Lincoln out of the city before the plot could succeed.

After the start of the Civil War, the U.S. government contracted with Pinkerton to organize the Secret Service. Pinkerton's assigned goals were to gather intelligence regarding Confederate war efforts and to ferret out Confederate spies, particularly in Washington, D.C. When the Pinkerton Agency's war exploits made a splash in the press—sparking controversies about the Lincoln assassination attempt in Baltimore, among other issues—Pinkerton published the first short pamphlets on his agency's work.

By the war's end the agency was firmly established and well-known across the country, even prior to its most famous, headline-making cases: the investigation of the Molly Maguires, the smashing of the Jesse James gang, and the capture of notorious early Chicago serial killer H.H. Holmes. Pinkerton's men lived the themes that later became the core of detective fiction. They regularly used disguises and went undercover. They worked Raymond Chandler's mean streets following their own code of honor, but associating with criminals and law enforcement at will in order to fulfill their contract with their employer. Finally, they regularly outperformed the police in a series of high-profile cases.

Thus the first American private eye was born by way of a meager, rural counterfeiting case from which rose the great Pinkerton Agency. Real-life, backwoods petty crime had done what somehow Poe had not managed: set the stage for the growth of not only an American business—the private investigation agency—but an indigenous American mystery genre. Now it was up to a group of underpaid hack writers to excite the imagination of America with a new kind of hero.

Dime Novels

About the time businessman Pinkerton was accidentally inventing the private eye of reality, a major revolution was occurring in the business of fantasy. An American publishing phenomenon, the dime novel, was the television of its time. Reviled by the snooty, devoured by the sooty, dime novels were cheap paperback books introduced in June 1860 by Beadle's Publishing of New York. While "dime novel" has become the accepted description for the majority of American

as."—Page 213.

paperbound books published before 1920, it's a term more colorful than accurate. Most "dime novels" did not cost a dime, and many are not long enough to be considered novels.

Beadle's original series, begining with "Malaeska, Indian Wife of the White Hunter," did in fact cost a dime, and averaged 64 to 128 pages in a 4-by-6 inch format. As more publishers entered the field, however, the price and format varied; the price usually depended on the length of the story. Nickel libraries, home of most detective series, were usually twenty-six to forty pages in an 8-by-11-inch format. These thin nickel paperbacks averaged about twenty-five thousand to thirty thousand words, more novelette than novel. The Beadle dime novel format, smaller paperbacks, gave the reader about twice as much story but still could barely be termed novels. Longer stories usually were done in the Beadle format or a slightly larger 5-by-7-inch format but with twice the pages. These cost twenty cents.

For an incredible sixty year run, these proto-paperbacks were the dominant printed format for popular fiction. Two technical innovations led the way: the steam press, which allowed for quicker, higher volumes of printing, and the fabrication of cheap pulp paper made from wood pulp. These greatly reduced the cost of printing a paperbound book.

At the same time, the number of potential readers had been increasing due to the introduction of public schools; also influential in this new wave of literacy was a large influx of educated immigrants from Europe, as a result of the Napoleonic and other wars. The pocket-size Beadle format also flourished because of the Civil War, since a dime novel fit well into a soldier's pocket (much as comic books and paperbacks were the G.I.'s portable entertainment in World War II) and provided a cheap source of amusement, resulting in over four million dime novels sold during that four-year conflict.

Beadle's success prompted numerous other publishing firms—not a few of which had been founded by former Beadle employees—to start their own dime novel lines. Some were based in New York City, while others operated out of Chicago, Cleveland, and other Midwestern cities. By the 1870s, dime novels and so-called "story papers" were flourishing across the country with dozens of different series, hundreds of titles, and millions of readers.

So what was the first dime-novel detective series? That's difficult to pinpoint, chiefly because of the lack of distinction between detective and western fiction at this point in history. (Even now, the hard-boiled private eye is considered an extension of the frontier hero and western gunfighter.) In the 1870s, American Indians in tribal garb were regularly seen not only in western cities like Chicago, Cleveland, and San Francisco, but in Philadelphia, Washington, D.C., and New York City. Pinkerton's operatives spent as much time on horseback chasing train robbers as they did investigating crimes in major urban centers.

Westerns and frontier novels, of course, were a mainstay of the earliest dime novels, many of which had crime and detective aspects to their plots. Even in the late 1800s, however, the two genres frequently intersected, blurring into each other, with a major western hero like Deadwood Dick occasionally adventuring into the wilds of Coney Island or Detroit; meanwhile, urban detectives like Old King Brady or Cap Collier would suddenly set off in pursuit of western bandits like Billy the Kid or Jesse James.

As early as 1864, detective work with an urban setting reared its deductive head in a Beadle dime novel, *The Marked Bullet* by Edward Ellis. Seeley Register (pseudonym of Metta Fuller Victor) wrote *The Dead Letter* in 1867, now believed to be the first American mystery novel by a woman. In 1870, "The Bowery Detective" appeared in the *Fireside Companion*, a weekly story paper published by Beadle competitor, George Munro.

But the floodgates really opened in 1872, with the publication of "Old Sleuth Detective" as the first detective serial in *Fireside Companion*. While the stories were signed by "the Old Sleuth," they were the creation of Harlan Page Halsey, though by assigning their authorship to the popular character, Munro and later publishers were able to turn the character into the author/narrator of a wide range of different, non-Old-Sleuth detective stories.

The Old Sleuth was not old at all, rather a young and strapping detective who, often masquerading as a geezer, had merely dubbed himself the Old Sleuth. A master of disguise, the Old Sleuth infiltrated gangs, punching and shooting his way to the successful solution of any case. He was the first two-fisted, superhuman detective. Handsome, brilliant, and above all strong and tough, his

OLD SLEUTH WEEKLY #20

Dime novel
1908

An issue of the first and longest-running
dime novel detective series.

OLD SLEUTH WEEKLY #145

Dime novel
1911

The Tenderloin was a crime-infested area
of New York City at the turn of the century.

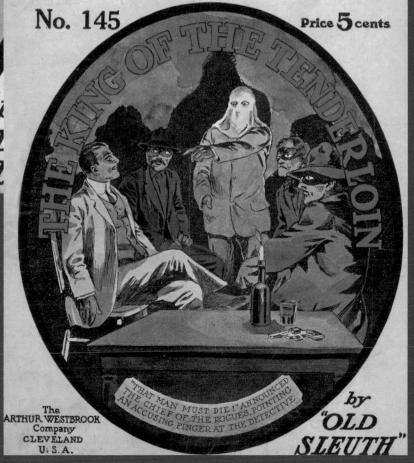

SECRET SERVICE WEEKLY #292

Dime novel
August 26, 1904

Bradys stories tended to be more realistic and darker than the average dime novel yarns. These detectives also weren't in the Secret Service!

SECRET SERVICE WEEKLY #216

Dime novel
March 13, 1903

The Bradys also traveled, investigating cases all over the world.

THE WOMAN OF DEATH

Dime novel
1908

Old Sleuth novels appeared in different formats and lengths. This book is 188 pages, while the weeklies usually featured a 28-page story.

SECRET SERVICE
WEEKLY #248

Dime novel
October 23, 1903

The division between westerns and urban-detective fiction was minimal in the dime novels. New York sleuths like the Bradys often went out west.

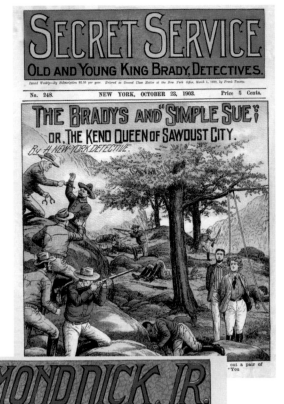

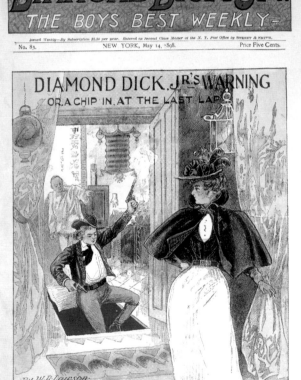

DIAMOND DICK, JR. #83

Dime novel
May 14, 1898

And western heroes like Diamond Dick Jr. also found themselves investigating cases in major cities.

descendants include the likes of Mike Hammer and James Bond. Starting in 1885, *Old Sleuth Detective Weekly* would continue in one format or another past 1910.

The Old Sleuth was rumored to have been based on Allan Pinkerton himself, and, while generalizing about dime novel detectives is difficult due to the thousands of different stories that appeared, the major series drew less upon Poe's Dupin and far more upon Pinkerton and Wild West fiction. The detectives are physically strong, and more heroic than cerebral. While they are a familiar mix of amateur sleuths, cops, and private eyes, the dime-novel detective is most often of the Pinkerton model. The major themes and fixtures of the modern private eye novel can be found in these slim, simply written stories that stress action over mystery.

The success of the Old Sleuth inspired Pinkerton to release his own casebooks in both hardcover and dime novel editions. The first book appears to be *The Bankers, Their Vaults and the Robbers* in 1873. Unlike the Buffalo Bill, Jesse James, and Wild Bill Hickok titles that passed off tall tales as "real life adventures," most of Pinkerton's casebooks actually were nonfiction accounts, erroneously listed in recent years as fictional dime novels. Pinkerton and his ghost writers wrote the books using agency case files (setting the pattern for Dashiell Hammett's Pinkerton-derived Continental Op tales).

While part of the motivation was additional publicity for the Pinkerton Agency, the books also brought the detective agency critical additional income during the cyclical recessions that affected America in the 1800s. The casebooks continued after Pinkerton's death in 1884 and many of these—under the authorship of various other Pinkertons (including several fictional Pinkerton pen names)—are less accurate and often based on cases in which the agency was not involved.

King Brady and Cap Collier

Beating the Old Sleuth to press in their own weekly editions were Old King Brady in 1882 and Cap Collier in 1883. Unlike the Old Sleuth, these were darker, more *noir*-ish series.

Old King Brady was far closer to Allan Pinkerton than any of the other major-dime novel detectives; and unlike the Old Sleuth, Brady really is an old sleuth—at sixty, the experienced head of a private investigation firm in New York. In his action-packed detective yarns, Brady continually gets into fights, trading shots with crooks, and falling through trapdoors with the best of them. Many of the Brady stories, however, invoke the real working life of the early private eyes. The criminals in Brady's world are not all pure evil—he had developed his own network of criminal informants—but rather a mix of personalities and motivations which Brady often plays against each other. To attract younger readers, the series later adds a Young King Brady, as well as female operatives, notably Alice Montgomery.

Somewhat surprisingly, strong heroines maintain a credible presence in the normally male-oriented dime novels. Alice Montgomery, unlike many of her counterparts in twentieth-century pulps and B-movies, is not in the stories merely to be saved by the hero. She works as a full operative of the agency, goes undercover, speaks Chinese, and shadows suspects. Strong female protagonists are not unique to the King Brady series, but rather a trend in many dime-novel titles, in particular westerns, where Calamity Jane, the Dalton Girls and others played leading roles. While this may seem strange during a period where women did not have the vote, the working class reality of readers included females performing physical labor on farms and toiling in sweatshops in the city.

King Brady, in numerous incarnations, proved popular and—like the Old Sleuth—his cases were chronicled well into the twentieth century. His rival, Cap Collier, began as a burlesque of a dime-novel detective, lampooning the likes of the Old Sleuth or King Brady. When that approach proved unpopular, the series turned gritty and serious. Cap was no clean-cut American hero. At a time when dime-novel heroes were the epitome of virtue, Cap not only smoked, but drank and gambled. Like the Old Sleuth, Cap is a master of disguise and quick with his fists or a pistol. Cap's popularity, however, did not extend into the twentieth century.

While these are the earliest and longest-running detectives, they are standouts in a large crowd: Bob Brooks, Millionaire Detective Dick Dobbs, Young Broadbrim, and many other sleuths starred in mysteries that ran a single up to hundreds of issues, littering the newsstands from the early 1880s through the first decade of the twentieth century. Series often ran for hundreds of weekly or monthly issues, and, since the stories were mainly written under work-for-hire agreements, the material could be reprinted endlessly, without further payment to the writers.

IVAN THE SERF, FLASHLIGHT DETECTIVE #16
Dime novel
Undated

The incredible popularity of Sherlock Holmes is reflected in this cover illustration. (The hero of the story bears no resemblance to the detective depicted.)

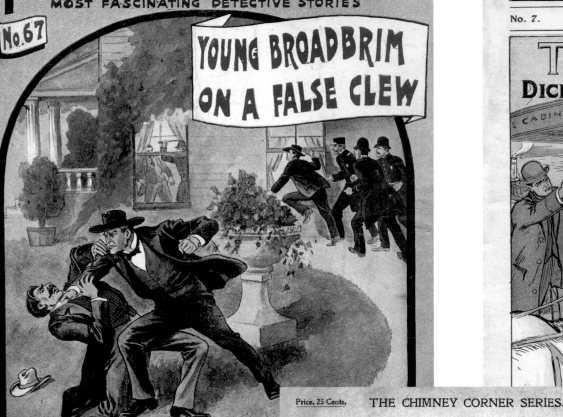

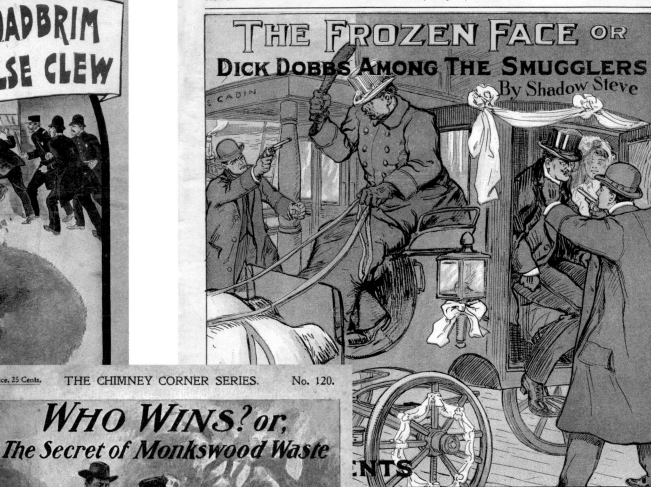

Broadbrim and Morello met in the garden and a fierce fight follo[wed]
long time and both fell to the ground exhausted. Meanwhil[e]
an entrance to the house and put the ruffians to [flight]

red the detective. "I'm damned if I do!" cried the other, reaching for his gun.
secured a grip on the count's collar and jerked him from the cab;
me time holding his gun steadily on the criminal.

YOUNG BROADBRIM WEEKLY #67

Dime novel
January 9, 1904

Dime novels appealed to children as well as adults, and publishers often created younger versions of their detectives to draw that market. The Young Broadbrim Weekly is a spin-off from the Old Broadbrim series.

MILLIONAIRE DETECTIVE DICK DOBBS #7

Dime novel
May 1, 1909

One of many short-lived series that attempted to capitalize on the success of Nick Carter and Old Sleuth.

WHO WINS? or, THE SECRET OF MONKSWOOD WASTE

Dime novel
Undated

Novels marketed to women usually were longer than those designed for men. In the time of suffragettes, women characters were also more traditional and less powerful than the two-gun female sleuths found in the shorter male-oriented novels.

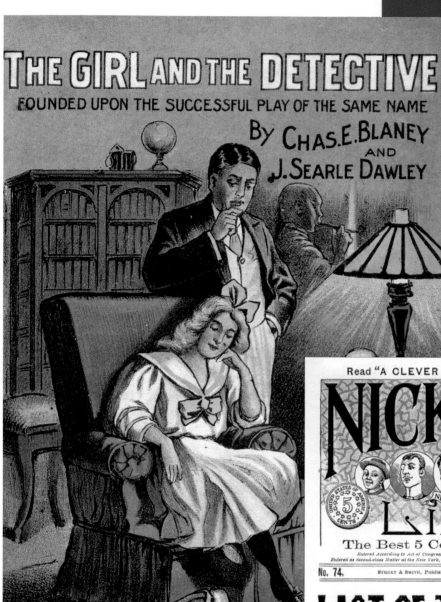

THE GIRL AND THE DETECTIVE

Dime novel
1908

Dime novels were often based on popular plays (as was this one) and, by the early 1900s, silent films.

NICK CARTER #79

Dime novel
1892

An early Nick Carter, with our hero being tossed into a furnace. Note the logotype with Carter in various disguises.

NICK CARTER #74

Dime novel
1892

Dime novels predated the invention of color printing and the early ones like this had black-and-white line drawings for covers.

As such, the same Old Sleuth or King Brady story might be reprinted every few years under its original or a new title. After all, the series were mainly written under generic authors like "A New York Detective" or the "Author of Old Cap Collier," and little is known about the mostly anonymous authors who weekly produced 25,000-word novelettes for the dime-novel industry. Their identities often were not revealed until obituaries credited them with creating major characters, and all too often ended with the words "died impoverished."

Foreshadowing comic books and rock 'n' roll, the dime novels attracted controversy. While tame by today's standards, the novels were the trash of their time, featuring mayhem and crime galore. Numerous Western titles glorified bandits like Jesse James or the Daltons into sympathetic leading characters. The crowded urban slums of the late 1800s swarmed with gangs, both adult and kid (i.e., the street Arabs of pedophile Horatio Alger's novels). Most schools and libraries banned dime novels, which—shades of the Twinkie Defense!—were used as evidence in several trials by criminals claiming this vile popular literature had caused them to turn to crime. As a result, the nickel libraries, aimed more at juveniles, began toning down the violence.

Enter Nick Carter

In 1886, Nick Carter, the most enduring of the dime-novel detectives, made his debut in "The Old Detective's Pupil or the Mysterious Crime of Madison Square." Carter proved so popular that several other stories appeared in Street and Smith's *New York Weekly* story paper. Street and Smith were latecomers to the dime novel trade. A family firm founded by Francis Scott Street and Francis S. Smith, the publishing company began when the two men took over a weekly New York paper where they had been employed. By the late 1880s, the firm was publishing not only weekly and monthly story papers, but a host of dime novels.

By 1889, after successful runs of Carter tales in their weekly papers, Street and Smith wanted to produce a full-length Nick Carter dime novel. The problem was that Nick Carter's creator John Coryell also wrote popular and highly profitable romance novels as one Bertha Clay. Frederick Marmaduke Van Rensselaer Dey was hired to continue the series; he wrote the first novel in the new series, *Nick Carter Detective*, and continued to produce an average of one 25,000-word novel a week for the next seventeen years, a staggering feat.

Virtuous to a saccharine degree, Nick Carter didn't smoke, curse, drink, or chase after women, and was scrupulously honest, not to mention well-groomed. He was also (sound familiar?) a master of disguise, able to transform himself into any identity in a matter of seconds by simply delving into his pockets and turning his coat inside out. Nick Carter's pockets must have been enormous, since in the average story he not only pulls out several disguises but guns, handcuffs, rope, and other assorted useful tools. Not until the advent of Batman's utility belt did any detective's wardrobe contain so many handy items.

Yet the formula worked: a virtuous hero—the likes of whom any parson could approve—fighting crime in tales crammed with enough action to satisfy the average unsophisticated reader. Nick Carter appeared in dime novel format through 1915, one of the last traditional dime novels to be published. Street and Smith was the only publisher who made the transition to other forms of publishing, surviving the death of the dime novel.

Their star Nick Carter also survived, appearing in Street and Smith pulp magazines, digests, paperback novels, and—starting in the 1960s!—a long-running paperback series, *Nick Carter—Killmaster*. This James Bond knockoff ran a remarkable 200 novels, a significant accomplishment by today's standards, if minor compared to the over 800 Nick Carter dime novels.

Carter also appeared in four French films (1909–1912), then a series of American silents, making his talkie debut in 1939 with Walter Pidgeon as Carter. In 1972, Robert Conrad—whose 1960s TV series, *The Wild Wild West* depicted a Bond-style character in the Old West, echoing the early days of dime novels when mystery and western blurred—played Carter in his correct historical period in an NBC-TV movie, *The Adventures of Nick Carter*.

Literally hundreds of writers tackled Nick Carter books over the character's one-hundred-plus year history, with the Killmaster series attracting notable mystery talents such as Michael Avallone, Robert Randisi, Sean Flannery, Dennis Lynds, and Martin Cruz Smith.

In Great Britain, following a path similar to Nick Carter, was Britain's Harry Blyth's Sexton Blake. After first appearing in the boys' paper, *The Halfpenny Marvel*, in December 1893, Blake got his own vehicle, *The Union Jack*, in 1894. By 1915, *The Sexton Blake Library* appeared and ran through the 1950s. Seven films were made and a television series as well. As time wore on, Blake became less of a detective and more and more James Bondian.

Dime novels survived into the early twentieth century. In the 1890s, due to improvements in printing technology, bright color illustrations replaced drab black-and-white covers. Publishers plumbed their huge files of back stories to continue producing series at a very low cost. New readers did not usually realize that the "new" Nick Carter, King Brady, or Deadwood Dick story actually had been written twenty years prior. Increased second-class postage rates, however, added costs that greatly reduced profit margins on dime novels.

Nor could the dimes compete with the dawning competition: thicker pulp magazines, priced the same, or only a nickel more; and—perhaps an even more devastating blow—detectives at the movies, fighting criminals in the flesh. Tired old plots and stories from the 1880s and 1890s guaranteed the disappearance of dime novels from newsstands. While most other publishers simply closed up shop, Street and Smith was smart enough to begin converting their dime novels into pulp magazines around 1915.

Even when the dime novels were still selling their pulpy mayhem—and exporting it to Europe, especially in the form of British "Penny Dreadful" editions—higher-end magazines were busy importing the better class of English and French detective fiction to America.

Magazines like *Harper's*, *Cosmopolitan*, *Collier's*, *Saturday Evening Post*, and *Scribner's* were printed on better quality paper, often generously supplied with well-drawn interior illustrations. Marketed to a more moneyed, middle-class readership, these magazines, later dubbed the "slicks" as they moved increasingly to using coated paper stock, benefited greatly from the birth of modern advertising in the late 1870s. Dime novels and nickel weeklies carried few ads and supported themselves mainly from the cover cost of the magazine. Advertisers wanted to reach the readers of the slicks, and so these magazines were able to lower their cover prices, as advertising picked up more and more of the publishing costs.

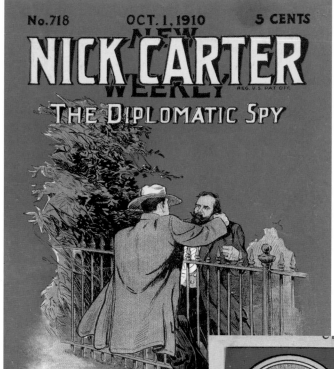

NICK CARTER #718

Dime novel
October 1, 1910

Nick Carter battles spies —a forerunner of the later Carter paperbacks that copied James Bond.

NICK CARTER #27

Dime novel
Undated

Dime novels had international appeal and many American ones were translated and sold in Europe.

No. 711   AUG. 13, 1910   5 CENTS

NEW NICK CARTER WEEKLY

REG. U.S. PAT. OFF.

A SECRET FROM THE PAST

STREET & SMITH.
PUBLISHERS.
NEW YORK.

He then turned his attention to the second dial, revolving it as he had done with the other one; to the right, to the left—to the right again.

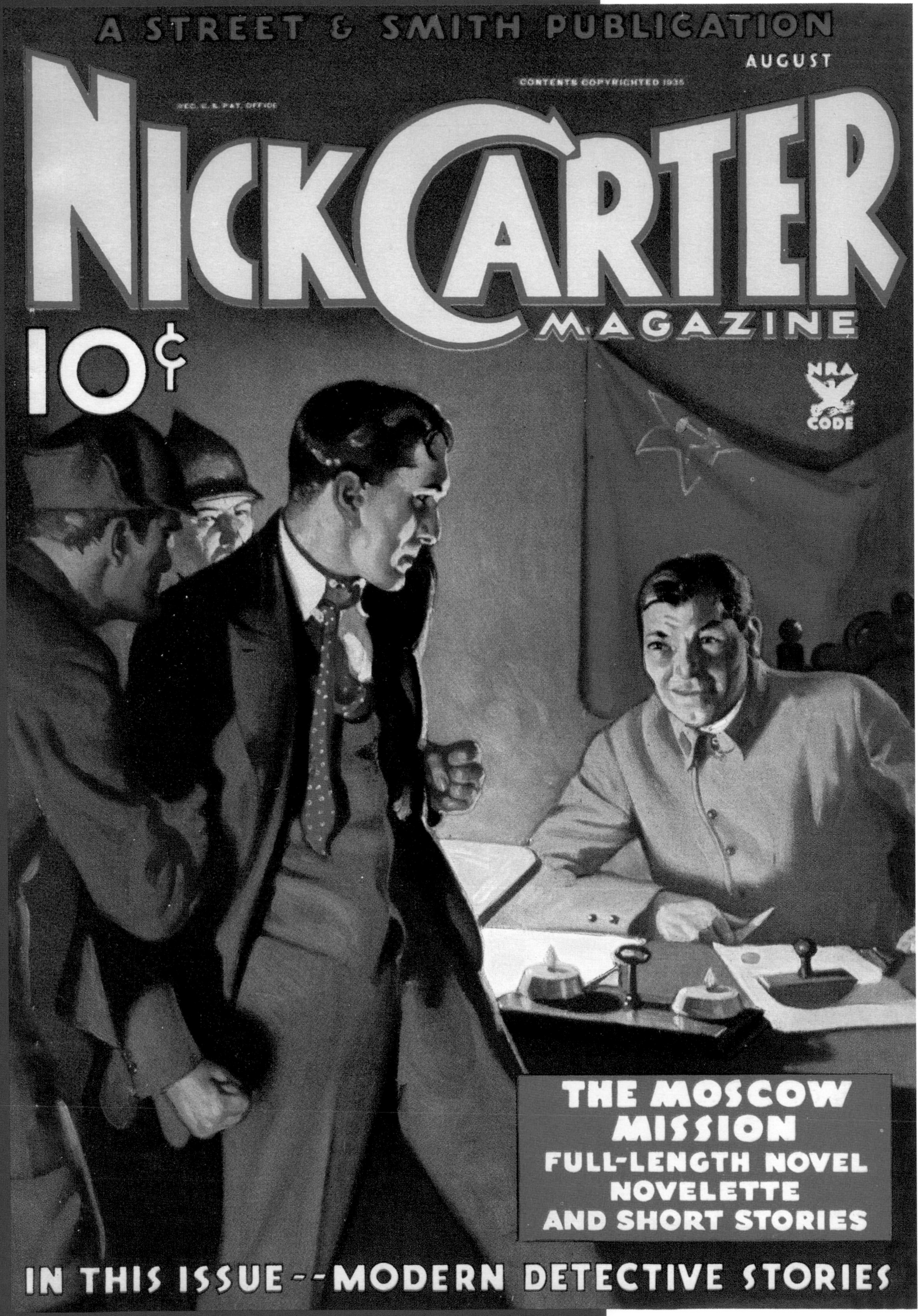

A STREET & SMITH PUBLICATION

AUGUST

CONTENTS COPYRIGHTED 1935

NICK CARTER

MAGAZINE

REC. U. S. PAT. OFFICE

10¢

NRA CODE

THE MOSCOW MISSION
FULL-LENGTH NOVEL
NOVELETTE
AND SHORT STORIES

IN THIS ISSUE--MODERN DETECTIVE STORIES

EMPIRE OF CRIME

Pulp/Paperback
1945, Vital Book

Starting in the 1940s, Nick Carter appeared in digest and standard-size paperback formats.

America's middle classes looked to Europe as the source of high culture, and the slicks, while publishing relatively few detective stories, nonetheless brought to America the fine work of Wilkie Collins and other British and French mystery writers. This fascination with European culture set the stage for the next major revolution in detective fiction in America, ushered in by the publication of Sir Arthur Conan Doyle's "The Sign of the Four" in *Lippincott's Magazine* in February 1890. While Doyle's Sherlock Holmes is a return to the tradition of Poe's Dupin, the first eccentric cerebral detective, Holmes is both a well-paid "consulting detective" and a two-fisted man of action, if an occasionally coked-up one.

Readers of the slicks took to the more genteel detective stories, so-called "drawing room mysteries," of authors such as Jacques Futrelle, Agatha Christie, and Mary Roberts Rinehart, who followed Doyle in the late 1890s up through about 1920. But a new style of American detective story—with its roots in the much reviled dime novels—was just around the corner...and not genteel at all.

NICK CARTER KILLMASTER: CHINA DOLL

Paperback
1964

In the 1960s Carter was revived as a competitor to James Bond.

ARTHUR CONAN DOYLE

(1859–1930)

Born on May 22, 1859, Sir Arthur Conan Doyle was the third child among ten siblings born to Charles Doyle and Mary Foley. Raised in a Catholic family, Conan Doyle studied under the Jesuits at Hodder, then Stonyhurst, followed by a year in Feldkirch, Austria, before returning to Edinburgh University to study medicine in 1876. There he met two men who would serve as inspiration for characters in his fiction.

Professor Rutherford's voice, beard, and manner could clearly be seen in Professor George Edward Challenger from *The Lost World* (1912) and Dr. Joseph Bell—for whom Doyle became surgeon's clerk—was the acknowledged model for Sherlock Holmes. Bell's amazing ability of deduction provided the modus operandi for the Great Detective.

Although Conan Doyle first published in 1879, Holmes didn't arrive on the scene until 1887, when *A Study in Scarlet* appeared in *Beeton's Christmas Annual*. In Holmes and Dr. John H. Watson, Doyle perfected what Poe had invented with C. Auguste Dupin: the brilliant, eccentric detective whose rather pedestrian associate serves as his Boswell. Once the two become flat mates (at perhaps the most famous address in fiction, 221B Baker Street), Watson is not merely a reporter, but the human filter through whom the sometimes outlandish plots are made to seem more plausible. And, whether battling

DR. JOSEPH BELL
Prototype of Sherlock Holmes.

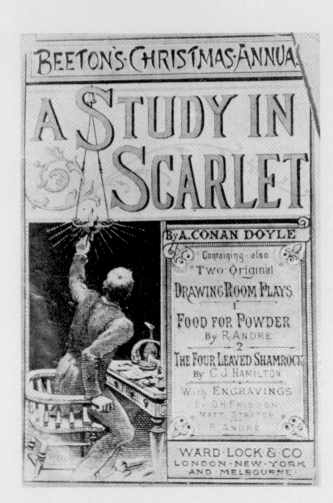

BEETON'S CHRISTMAS ANNUAL
Magazine
1887

Beeton's Christmas Annual, first publication of *A Study In Scarlet*, the debut of Sherlock Holmes.

a poisonous snake in "The Adventure of the Speckled Band," or wrestling atop Reichenbach Falls with his nemesis Dr. Moriarty in "The Final Problem," Holmes is the clear precursor of not just cerebral detectives, but the two-fisted hardboiled dicks.

In all, Conan Doyle penned sixty Holmes adventures. Fifty-six are wholly or partly narrated by Watson, two are third-person stories, and two more are first-person adventures told by Holmes himself: only four are novels. The sleuth's hawk-nosed, slender visage—and his wardrobe of deerstalker cap, Inverness cape and meershaum pipe—are indelibly pressed upon the collective consciousness, thanks in no small part to the work of illustrators like Sidney Paget and Frederic Dorr Steele, and actors William Gillette and Basil Rathbone, on stage and screen respectively.

Despite Conan Doyle's death in 1930—odd to think that Doyle and Dashiell Hammett were both writing detective stories in the 1920s—Holmes's career kept going. The target of more parodies and pastiches than any other fictional character, Holmes has been the subject of authors as diverse as August Derelth, Vincent Starrett, O. Henry, Stephen Leacock, and Mark Twain: Nicholas Meyer's *The Seven Percent Solution* (1974) spawned several sequels of its own and a film. Notable movies include Holmes's two encounters with Jack the Ripper—*A Study in Terror* (1965) and *Murder by Decree* (1979)—and Billy Wilder's underappreciated *The Private Life of Sherlock Holmes* (1970). But Rathbone's Holmes of the late 1930s and 1940s remains the quintessential big-screen version of the hero, while Jeremy Brett, in the PBS Mystery series, based faithfully on the canon, etches the finest small-screen interpretation.

SHERLOCK HOLMES

Laserdisc
1988

The screen's definitive Holmes and Watson
—Basil Rathbone and Nigel Bruce—in *The
Adventures Of Sherlock Holmes* (1939) and
The Voice Of Terror (1942). Purists find Bruce
too bumbling; others find him charming.

COLLIER'S

Magazine illustration
1953

Robert Fawcett's *Collier's* illustrations for a new
series of Holmes tales by Doyle's son Adrian
(sometimes in collaboration with John Dickson
Carr) are much admired but little seen.

Magazine illustration
1893

Artist Sidney Paget's magazine illustrations defined
Holmes in the public perception at least as much
as Doyle's prose.

"Most I remind you of your boast?" she asked. "Come, sir, admit you have failed to recover the ruby"

THE ADVENTURES OF SHERLOCK HOLMES

SHERLOCK HOLMES AND THE VOICE OF TERROR

Sherlock HOLMES

Basil RATHBONE Nigel BRUCE

CBS FOX VIDEO

Laser Videodisc

Extended Pla

**THE CASE
BOOK OF
SHERLOCK
HOLMES**

Paperback
1964

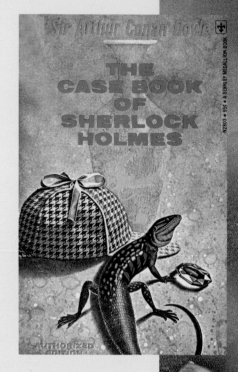

**THE HOUND
OF THE
BASKERVILLES**

Paperback
1976
Anderson

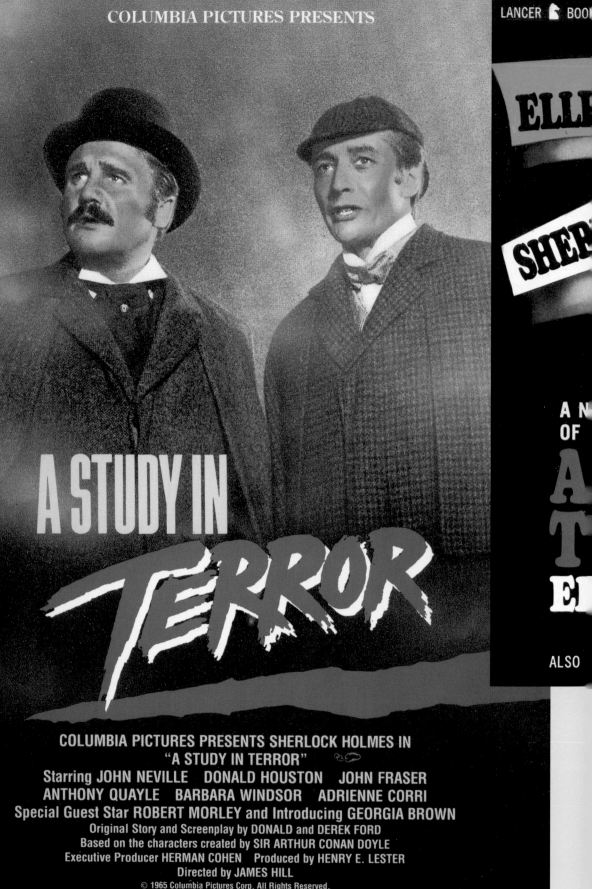

COLUMBIA PICTURES PRESENTS SHERLOCK HOLMES IN
"A STUDY IN TERROR"
Starring JOHN NEVILLE   DONALD HOUSTON   JOHN FRASER
ANTHONY QUAYLE   BARBARA WINDSOR   ADRIENNE CORRI
Special Guest Star ROBERT MORLEY and Introducing GEORGIA BROWN
Original Story and Screenplay by DONALD and DEREK FORD
Based on the characters created by SIR ARTHUR CONAN DOYLE
Executive Producer HERMAN COHEN   Produced by HENRY E. LESTER
Directed by JAMES HILL
© 1965 Columbia Pictures Corp. All Rights Reserved.

INTRODUCTION BY DON PENDLETON

A STUDY IN TERROR

Laserdisc
1987

John Neville's Holmes is the first to battle
Jack the Ripper in this fine 1965 thriller.

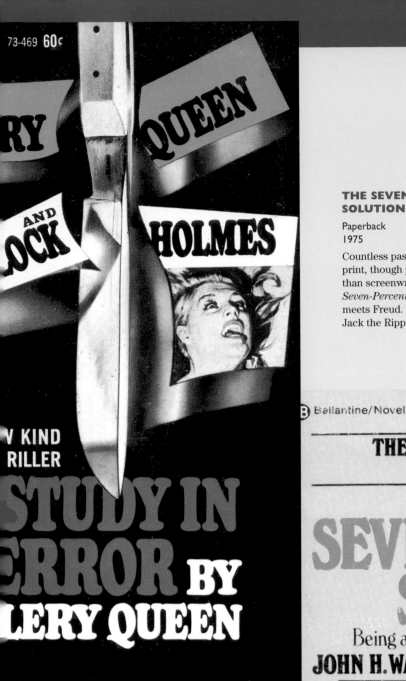

THE SEVEN-PER-CENT SOLUTION

Paperback
1975

Countless pastiches of Holmes have seen print, though perhaps none more successful than screenwriter/director Nicholas Meyer's *Seven-Percent Solution*, in which Holmes meets Freud. Meyer also has Holmes meet Jack the Ripper, in *The West End Horror*.

SHERLOCK HOLMES' GREATEST CHALLENGE...
IT BEGAN AS A CLASSIC LOVE STORY
—THE SERVANT AND THE DUKE—AND IT ENDED
IN A REIGN OF TERROR.

MURDER BY DECREE

A STUDY IN TERROR

Paperback
1966

A rare book—and a rare treat: in this unusual movie-tie in for *A Study In Terror*, Ellery Queen the author writes a Holmes story...involving Ellery Queen the character, as one famous sleuth uncovers the lost case of another.

Ⓑ Ballantine/Novel   24550/$1.95

THE SMASH **#1** COAST-TO-COAST
BESTSELLER!
THE
SEVEN-PER-CENT
SOLUTION

Being a Reprint from the Reminiscences of
JOHN H. WATSON, M.D. as edited by **NICHOLAS MEYER**

ADAPTED BY ROBERT WEVERKA
FROM THE SCREENPLAY BY JOHN HOPKINS

MURDER BY DECREE

Paperback
1979

Director Bob Clark—of *A Christmas Story* fame —directed a bigger-budget, all-star Holmes vs. Jack the Ripper film, the many strengths of which include James Mason's Watson.

PULP FICTION

Hardboiled Dicks

By 1915, the dime novel was struggling: costs were up due to changes in the postal rate, the slicks were cheaper and more accessible to the average worker, and an innovation called the pulp magazine was taking over the working-class fiction market. • In 1896, Frank Munsey took a struggling story paper he owned, *The Golden Argosy*, and clipped its title down to *Argosy*, reformatting the paper into a thick 7-by-11-inch magazine printed on cheap pulp paper. The 192-page magazine resembled the higher-priced slick magazines like *Century* and *Harper's*, yet only cost a dime. Better still, *Argosy* wasn't filled with high-class, high-toned fiction; instead it carried the adventure, western, and other action yarns found in dime novels. • *Argosy's* success made Munsey a multimillionaire and inspired several imitators — thick, pulp-paper magazines featuring several serials, short stories, and "short novels" or novelettes in every issue. For the price of a weekly dime novel, the reader got eight to twelve times the reading material. Street and Smith felt the pressure and started *Popular* magazine in 1903 with the breakthrough of a full color painting on its cover, often by the young N.C. Wyeth. • In 1915, Street and Smith decided to pull the plug on their long running *Nick Carter* dime novel weekly. Since a full-length dime novel ran as long as a novelette in the new pulps, savvy circulation manager Henry William Ralston suggested converting the *Nick Carter* dime novel weekly into *Detective Story Magazine* as of October 5, 1915. To keep the Nick Carter fans happy, or at least somewhat fooled, Nick himself was initially listed as editor, and Nick Carter yarns, albeit often in a short story format, continued appearing in the new pulp.

Street and Smith attracted several well-known British authors from the hardcover field to their new venture, including the best-selling, wildly prolific Edgar Wallace, and further insured *Detective Story Magazine's* success as the first pulp magazine devoted to just one genre. In 1920, however, Street and Smith found itself with a new competitor: *Black Mask*, perhaps the most famous and certainly the most respected pulp magazine of all...the birthplace of hard-boiled mystery fiction.

The term "hardboiled" had been around since World War I, during which it was an adjective applied to the tough drill sergeants who made men out of boys, and soldiers out of civilians. When the Great War ended, those soldiers turned back into civilians, popularizing the term "hardboiled" into something referring to any person, or action, that reflected a tough, unsentimental point of view.

Perhaps it was natural that the term became applied to the tough strain of American mystery fiction that emerged between the two World Wars. From its beginnings in *Black Mask*, the hardboiled crime story (not always a mystery per se) seemed immediately as American as a Wild West shoot-out.

Which is precisely what the earliest practitioner of the art, Carroll John Daly, was writing about: his heroes, notably Mike Hammer's precursor, private eye Race Williams, were two-gun kids riding an urban range, delivering death and justice via the same hot-lead route as dime-novel gunfighters, but with a modern edge Nick Carter or the Old Sleuth never attained. These action stories had scant mystery elements, updating the western tale and adapting it to a big-city setting.

The writer who defined hardboiled in the sense that still prevails was, of course, Dashiell Hammett, that former Pinkerton op whose bad health led him into popular literature. The writer who in the eyes of many elevated the tough mystery to art also began in the pulps: Raymond Chandler, whose Phillip Marlowe remains for many the definitive hardboiled private eye. Of the major pulp-derived private eyes, only Mickey Spillane's Mike Hammer—and this is ironic, considering the pulpy reputation of both author and character—was born in the pages of reputable hardcover fiction.

Spillane brought pulp fiction full circle, because his favorite writer as a youth had been Carroll John Daly, who saw the private eye as a western hero walking the streets of Manhattan, not Dodge City. As the private eye who emerged after the *next* war, Pacific vet Mike Hammer would further define hardboiled, making the violence grittier but the tenderness more overt as well.

What separates the American hardboiled detective/crime novel from the British (and American) drawing-room mystery is not, as some would have it, that the former is more "realistic" than the latter. The traditional mystery has a cooler head, is more intellectual, generally, with a more detached view of its puzzle. The hardboiled mystery deals more overtly with the real concerns of life—specifical-ly, love and death, a. k. a. sex and violence—but *not* in a particularly more realistic fashion.

Both forms present a view of life unrealistically linear, creating a place where problems are invariably solved, solutions are convoluted but tidy, where justice is usually done. In other words, a place no living human recognizes as his own.

The hardboiled detective novel is concerned with the heart, not the head; emotions churn at the center of this supposedly "unsenti-mental" beast. It can be surreal (for example, Spillane's *One Lonely Night*); but almost never *real* real. And it all began with *Black Mask*.

Black Mask was born when H. L. Mencken and George Jean Nathan, co-editors of the sophisticated *Smart Set* magazine, decided they needed a low-end cash cow to make up the losses on their high-toned literary monthly.

Originally *Black Mask* was just another all-genre pulp magazine, westerns and adventure stories mingling with detective fiction. The pulp's sales were strong, and Mencken soon sold it for $100,000 to another publisher. George Sutton, the new editor, moved the magazine firmly into the detective/mystery field, publishing the first of what was to become the new hardbolled private-eye fiction—by the aforementioned Carroll John Daly.

ARGOSY

August 5, 1933
Paul Stahr

Detective stories regularly appeared in *Argosy* and the other anthology pulps. This issue features Madame Story, an early female sleuth created by Hulbert Footner.

NICK CARTER STORIES #158

Dime novel
September 18, 1915

One of the last Nick Carter dime-novel weeklies.

DETECTIVE STORY MAGAZINE

Pulp Magazine
October 5, 1915

The first issue of the detective pulp magazine that replaced *Nick Carter*.

DETECTIVE STORY MAGAZINE

Pulp magazine
December 25, 1920
John A. Coughlin

This issue features Christmas mysteries by Zorro creator Johnston McCulley and others.

DETECTIVE STORY MAGAZINE

Pulp magazine
November 30, 1920

Artist John A. Coughlin created exceptional conceptual cover images like this one, a rare occurrence when the true-fact editorial is the lead cover story.

DETECTIVE STORY MAGAZINE

Pulp magazine
September 5, 1916
John A. Coughlin

Despite later Street and Smith dime novels having used full-color paintings for covers, the first year of *Detective Story* often had simpler covers drawn in pencil or litho crayon like this one.

DETECTIVE STORY MAGAZINE

Pulp magazine
October 16, 1917
John A. Coughlin

The Secret Six in this story was a band of criminals; less than ten years later, that same term would be used to denote the secret group of Chicago businessmen who backed Eliot Ness's war against Al Capone.

DETECTIVE STORY MAGAZINE

Pulp magazine
October 11, 1930
John A. Coughlin

Note the "Magazine on the Air" blurb next to the woman in the trap. *Detective Story Magazine* was now on radio.

BLACK MASK

Pulp magazine
September 1929
H.C. Murphy, Jr.

By the mid-1920s, Street and Smith had competition from *Black Mask*, home of hardboiled private-eye fiction by Dashiell Hammett, Carroll John Daly, and others.

DETECTIVE STORY MAGAZINE

Pulp magazine
November 29, 1924
John A. Coughlin

Most of the American authors in this issue are long forgotten—but a strong cover image nonetheless.

DETECTIVE STORY MAGAZINE

Pulp magazine
February 23, 1929

Another strong John A. Coughlin cover.

DETECTIVE STORY MAGAZINE

Pulp magazine
April 25, 1931
John A. Coughlin

A number of Street and Smith's most popular authors were British, like Edgar Wallace.

As we have seen, despite what previous histories have indicated, *Black Mask* and Carroll John Daly did not invent the private-eye story, merely the hardboiled variety. *Black Mask's* writers updated the genre to include the realities of the 1920s, though many elements of hardboiled fiction could be traced to the old dime novels. Still, the most familiar and longest-lived dime novel detective was that goody-two-shoes Nick Carter. If King Brady or Cap Collier had still been around, Race Williams, while still innovative, would have seemed less of a jarring change.

True Detectives

What *Black Mask* writers brought to the genre was their visceral response to the realities of life under Prohibition. In 1890s dime-novel fiction, police were depicted as ineffectual rather than corrupt; villains included Asian tong lords, ruthless rural bandits, slick upper-class crime lords, and Mexican dope dealers. Under the Volstead Act, however, almost everyone—anyone—could be a criminal. After all, the average pulp reader broke the law every time he entered a speakeasy or blind pig and had a beer or a shot. In the 1920s, as huge bootleg profits poured into the pockets of police, corruption boomed, a reality visible to the average citizen who watched pay-offs at speaks and saw cops-on-the-beat suddenly able to afford the "better things."

Even the Pinkerton organization had changed with the times, and, in the eyes of many, not for the better. In an economy that every few years cycled into a recession or depression, the Pinkerton agency, founded by a radical leftist, had, ironically enough, maintained itself by taking on more and more industrial clients. To many readers of pulps, Pinkerton private eyes weren't heroes catching serial killers and bandits; they were strongarms cracking skulls on the picket line.

In general, violence in society was on the rise. The street gangs of the 1890s wielded baseball bats, and vicious knife rings gouged out the eyes of their marks. But the gangs of the 1920s were better financed, driving in "speedsters," brandishing Thompson submachine guns that spewed hot lead, firing off hundreds of rounds in minutes. While low by modern standards, cities saw murder tallies jump into the hundreds, as rival gangs battled for bootleg profits. Men coming back from the horrors of war in Europe found themselves in a different battleground at home.

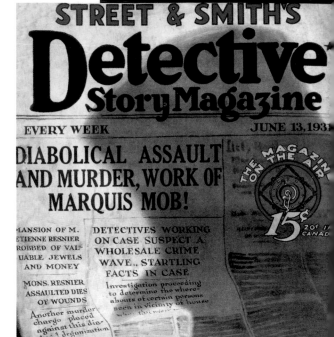

DETECTIVE STORY MAGAZINE

Pulp magazine
June 13, 1931
John A. Coughlin

The Shadow—*The Detective Story* radio program's "host"—proved so popular that a Shadow motif was often used on the cover.

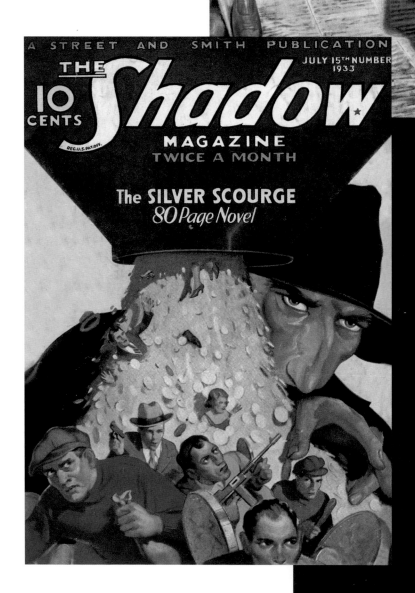

THE SHADOW

Pulp magazine
July 15, 1933
George Rozen

By 1931, the Shadow had his own magazine, which in a short time was appearing semi-monthly.

The Shadow

A STREET & SMITH PUBLICATION

TWICE A MONTH

10¢

FEB · 1 · 1942

THE SHADOW

Pulp magazine
May 15, 1935
George Rozen

Unlike most hero pulps, author Walter Gibson often wrote his Shadow stories as standard mysteries; the clue to this one lies on the cover.

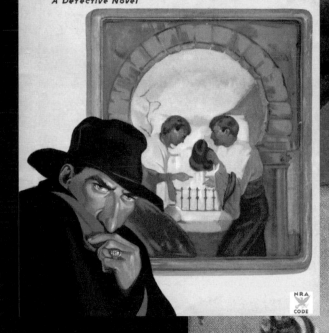

A STREET & SMITH PUBLICATION

10 CENTS

MAY 15th NUMBER

The Shadow

MAGAZINE
TWICE A MONTH

THE THIRD SKULL
A Detective Novel

THE SHADOW

Pulp magazine
February 1, 1942
George Rozen

In Gibson's mysteries, opportunities abound for good old-fashioned two-gun mayhem.

Flowing red blood of innocent people dulled the brilliant lustre of these

DEATH DIAMONDS

A great mystery novel

COMPLETE IN THIS ISSUE

TRUE DETECTIVE

True crime magazine
March 1949
Richard Cardiff

Physical Culture publisher Bernarr MacFadden started True Detective in 1924, the first detective magazine to exchange fiction for fact-based articles.

REAL DETECTIVE TALES

Pulp magazine
June 1930
A. Redmond

Pulp purists tend to scorn *True Detective* magazines, but many pulps featured both true crime and detective fiction, including this early *Real Detective*.

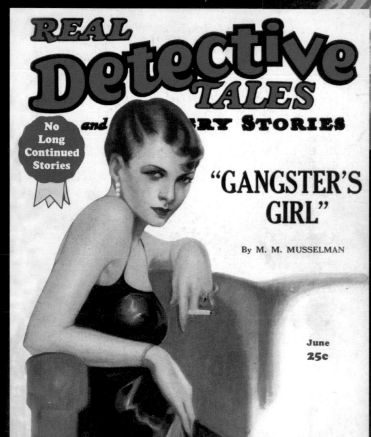

STARTLING DETECTIVE ADVENTURES

True crime magazine
June 1930
R. A. Glass

Startling featured a mix of fact and fiction until switching to an all true-crime format in the early 1930s.

DETECTIVE STORY MAGAZINE

Pulp magazine
September 12, 1931
John A. Coughlin

Another intense cover by Coughlin.

DIME DETECTIVE

Pulp magazine
October 1, 1933
William Reusswig

Street and Smith's real competition came from the *Popular* pulp line, whose titles cost a dime and whose covers featured unclothed ladies in peril.

DETECTIVE STORY MAGAZINE

Pulp magazine
November 10, 1932
John A. Coughlin

Coughlin provides a fantastic cover, complete with a memorable snake.

DIME DETECTIVE MAGAZINE

Pulp magazine
April 1936
Walter Baumhofer

Dime Detective had some of the worst and best writers, the latter group including Raymond Chandler and Erle Stanley Gardner. This pulp features Carroll John Daly's Race Williams.

SCIENTIFIC DETECTIVE MONTHLY

Pulp magazine
March 1930
Ruger

Detectives weren't limited to the traditional mystery pulps. *Scientific Detective*—edited by Arthur Reeve, creator of Craig Kennedy—offered a mix of detective and science fiction; and *Scientific Detective* featured articles on detective science, classic detective fiction by writers like S.S. Van Dine and straight science fiction.

WEIRD TALES

Pulp magazine
June 1938
Margaret Brundage

One of the most popular series in *Weird Tales* featured occult detective Jules de Grandin, written by Seabury Quinn.

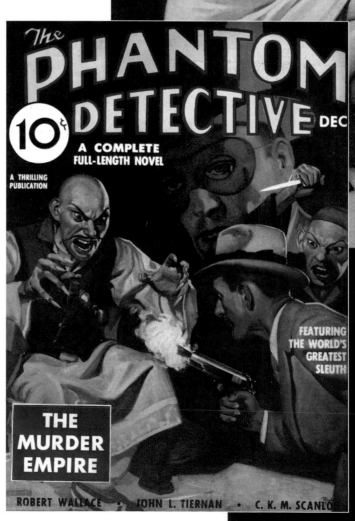

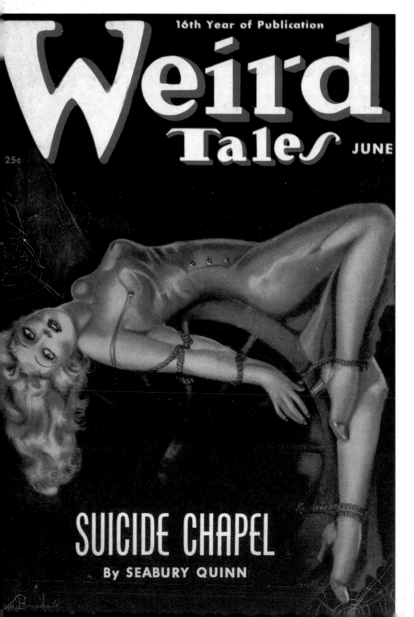

THE PHANTOM DETECTIVE

Pulp magazine
May 1948

Pulp magazine
December 1935
Rudolph Belarski

The first competitor of *The Shadow*, *The Phantom Detective* was the longest-running detective hero pulp.

King Brady and Cap Collier dealt with criminals as informants
and allies, but Brady and Collier were "good guys." In their world, it
was easy to tell who was on the side of the angels and who ran
with devils. In the 1920s the average good guys were no longer so
sure, and *Black Mask* writers reflected an often amoral world. The
gloves came off, blood flowed, and sex was no longer a strictly
taboo subject; the nights got darker, and so did the knights. Detectives themselves broke the law or anyway took it into their own
hands; even now, few fictional detectives are as morally ambiguous
as Hammett's Sam Spade. Thanks to *Black Mask* and writers like
Daly and especially Hammett, detective fiction had grown up.

While often characterized as "fiction factories," the pulps were
far less ghettoized than the dime novels. Thanks to Arthur Conan
Doyle, Jacques Futrelle, Mary Roberts Rinehart, and other mainstream mystery writers, detective-fiction novels were appearing
between respectable hard covers. Many dime novelists had toiled
anonymously, and on a work-for-hire basis; most pulp writers—
with the exception of those ghosting company-owned characters
like Nick Carter or the Shadow, under "house" bylines—wrote under
their own names and owned the rights to their stories. The more
successful writers were rewarded with hardcover editions of their
works and movie contracts.

THE WHISPERER

Pulp magazine
April 1941
Hubert Rogers

Starting as a short-story series in the back of *The Shadow, The Whisperer* was Street and Smith's own (unsuccessful) attempt to duplicate the *Shadow's* success.

THE AVENGER

Pulp magazine
September 1939
H.W. Scott

Another master of disguise, the Avenger's dead white skin could be molded into a duplication of almost anyone's face.

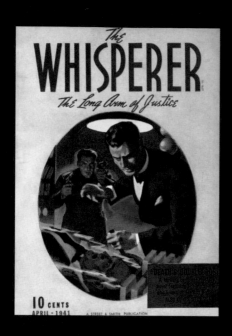

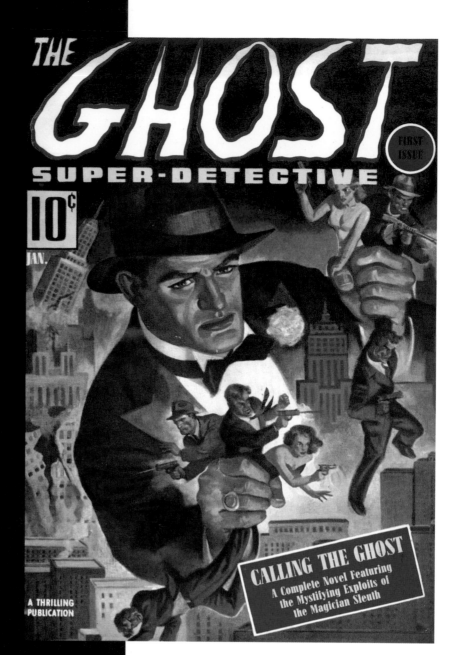

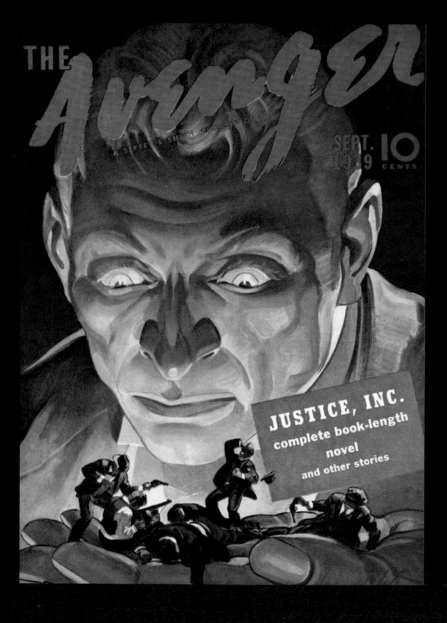

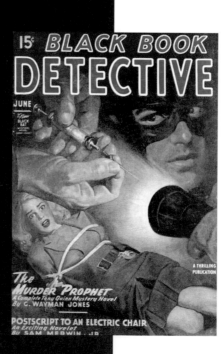

THE GHOST

Pulp magazine
January 1940
Raphael De Soto

One of a number of pulp series about amateur-detective magicians, the Ghost series was written in the first person and signed with the name of the fictional Ghost's alter ego George Chance.

BLACK BOOK DETECTIVE

Pulp magazine
June 1947
Rudolph Belarski

This long running pulp—featuring the Black Bat, a blind detective—provided typically garish covers, as the hypodermic needle and bondage elements here indicate.

DETECTIVE FICTION WEEKLY

Pulp magazine
February 26, 1938

As the depression continued, many pulp private eyes—like their real-life counterparts, the Pinkertons—were embroiled in stories about unions and industrial conflict.

DETECTIVE FICTION WEEKLY

Pulp magazine
August 17, 1940

As World War II began, many pulp private eyes and amateur detectives began battling saboteurs and Axis agents. Here the Park Avenue Hunt Club takes on the Nazi-like Green Shirts.

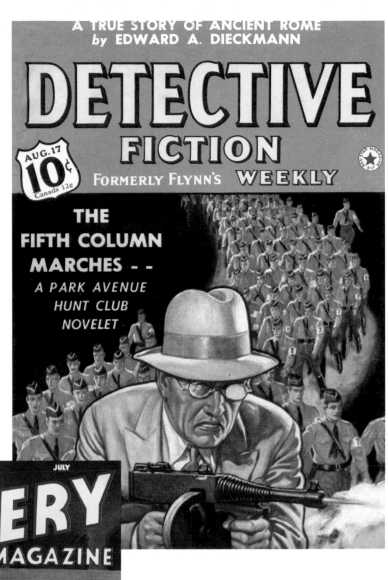

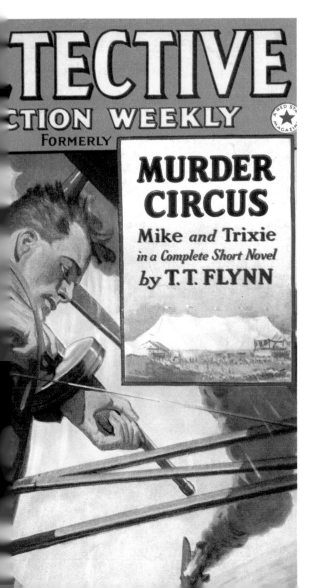

DIME MYSTERY MAGAZINE

Pulp magazine
July 1940
Raphael De Soto

Nothing like a group of rapacious midgets to gum up a case!

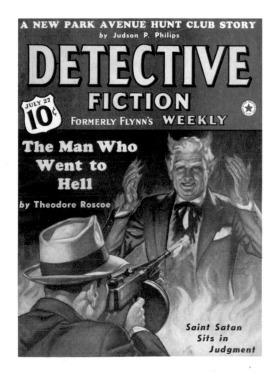

DETECTIVE FICTION WEEKLY

Pulp magazine
May 21, 1938

Rudolph Belarski provides a standard air-war pulp cover, enlivened by the presence of a Thompson submachine gun.

DETECTIVE FICTION WEEKLY

Pulp magazine
July 27, 1940

Detective Fiction Weekly was home to a number of detective series including Satan Hall, the Park Avenue Hunt Club, and Mike & Trixie.

TEN DETECTIVE ACES

Pulp magazine
December 1933

Lester Dent also wrote
the Doc Savage yarns.

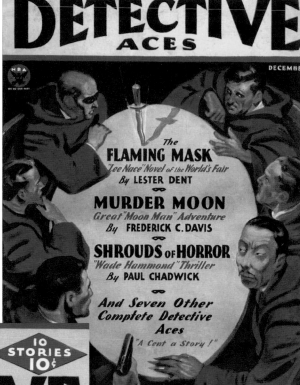

TEN DETECTIVE ACES

Pulp magazine
March 1936

Aces offered ten detective stories for a dime, with series ranging
from "Lee Nace Private Eye" to police procedurals, as well one
of the strangest masked detectives—Moon Man, who masked
himself by placing an opaque fish bowl over his head!

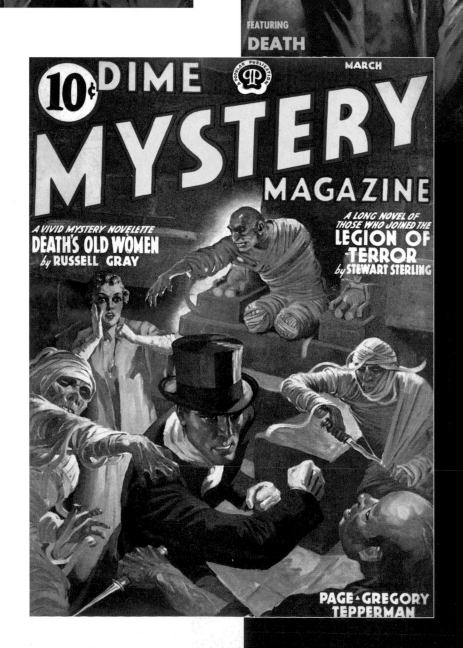

POPULAR DETECTIVE

Pulp magazine
February 1937

Popular Detective had some
of the wildest covers of the
1930s; witness this one, on
which a peg-leg cripple shoots
a man in an unenviable spot.

DIME MYSTERY
MAGAZINE

Pulp magazine
November 1940

Popular pulps—who incidentally
did not publish *Popular Detective*
—offered private eye stories
that could have just as easily
been published in their sister
magazine, *Terror Tales*. Norval
Page (listed as a contributor on
this cover) also wrote The Spider.

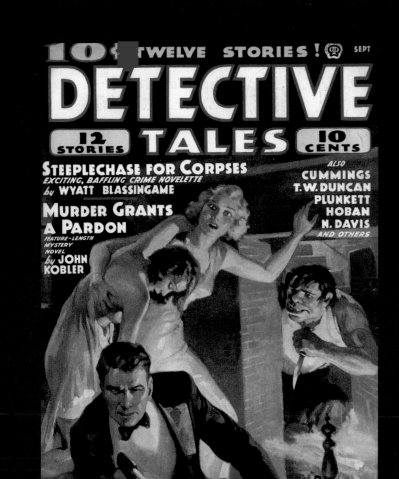

DETECTIVE TALES

Pulp magazine
September 1938
Rafael De Soto

Another Steeger title which featured beautiful women in peril, and the mandatory subhuman degenerate threatening them—this time with a knife.

STRANGE DETECTIVE MYSTERIES

Pulp magazine
November 1938

Here in the home of the defective detectives, the heroic amateur detective on the cover is as likely to be the blind dick as the guy in the top hat!

DIME MYSTERY MAGAZINE

Pulp magazine
March 1941

Dime Mystery's amateur sleuths not only had to fight gangsters, but mummies as well.

NEW DETECTIVE

Pulp magazine
March 1948
Rafael De Soto

Many pulp artists used their wives as models; here, Mrs. De Soto finds some surprises in her filing cabinet!

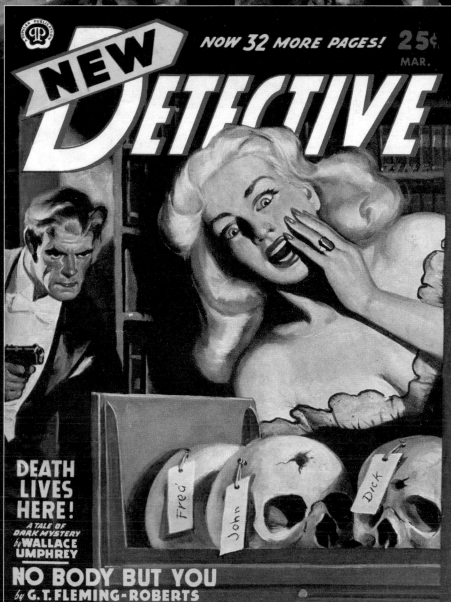

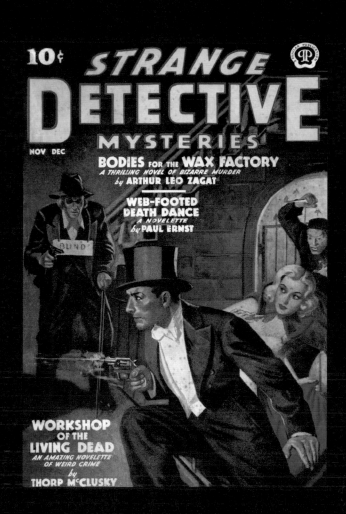

THRILLING DETECTIVE

Pulp magazine
May 1944

Fredric Brown wrote dozens of
pulp private-eye short stories
before cracking the big time.

Black Mask was followed in 1924 by *Flynn's Detective Weekly* from Street and Smith's competitor, Frank Munsey. The most important innovation of the same year pertained not to fiction, but nonfiction. In 1919, health food guru and *Physical Culture* magazine publisher Bernarr MacFadden had launched *True Story*, probably best described as a full-size slick magazine with pulp sensibilities. Aimed mostly at women, the magazine predictably featured "true" stories of love and adventure, many of which were actually fiction, illustrated with verisimilitude-inducing photos, many shot on site in MacFadden's own studios.

Following up this incredible hit in 1924, MacFadden started *True Detective*, using a *True Story* format for a few issues, mixing fiction with fiction labeled as fact. Soon MacFadden found that fact sold better than fiction; also, in the roaring twenties, true crime stories were plentiful: every newspaper crime reporter had files filled with stories and photos available for sale—cheap. *True Detective* focused totally on the true—actually true, in most cases—and became a big seller.

True Detective affected detective fiction in a number of ways, including fostering a generally increased interest in detectives. Both *Detective Story Magazine* and *Flynn's* featured short sidebars of true crime stories, the latter especially running long fact features. *True Detective's* larger "slick" magazine size inspired several new pulp publishers to try a similar large format; two of *True Detective's* longest-running competitors—*Startling Detective* and *Real Detective*—both started out as oversize pulps mixed equally of factual articles and detective-fiction yarns, before later settling on an all-fact format.

The true-crime magazines raised the ante on cover and story content, setting a new standard for sex and violence in the pulps. As nonfiction, the true-crime magazines could show gory crime-scene photos, and even shots of scantily clad rape victim's bodies, usually staged in studios, without facing many objections from vice and obscenity groups. By the 1930s, the true-crime magazines had prepared an audience and laid the groundwork for material far rawer that what was found in the average pulp of the 1920s.

POPULAR
DETECTIVE

Pulp magazine
June 1945

The circus made a
lively setting for a
mystery—or the
cover of a pulp.

THRILLING
MYSTERY

Pulp magazine
March 1943

This pulp mixes
standard private-
eye stories with
"The Green Ghost"
(The Ghost Super
Detective hero
written in the
third person).

10 STORY DETECTIVE

Pulp magazine
October 1944
Norman Saunders

Ace publishing, which produced this pulp, later became Ace Paperbacks, known for its Ace Double books, single paperbacks with a novel on each side.

LONE WOLF DETECTIVE

Pulp magazine
April 1940
Norman Saunders

A short-lived private-eye pulp with a great title and cover art from the early 1940s; no connection to the Louis Joseph Vance character.

DETECTIVE SHORT STORIES

Pulp magazine
November 1937
H. W. Scott

The publisher also published Marvel Comics, and some issues featured art by the young Jack Kirby (future co-creator of Caption America).

MAMMOTH DETECTIVE

Pulp magazine
May 1946
Arnold Kohn

Ziff Davis's major asset was editor Howard Browne, who wrote some of its best novels (albeit under pen names). *Halo for Blood* is from his Paul Pine series.

DIME DETECTIVE

Pulp magazine
November 1935
Walter Baumhofer

The amateur detective in this pulp is a medical student.

SPICY DETECTIVE

Pulp magazine
September 1934
H.J. Ward

While tame today, *Spicy* pulps were often sold under the counter.

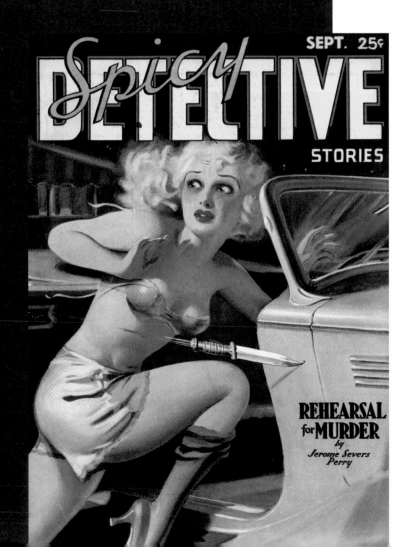

SPICY DETECTIVE

Pulp magazine
July 1941
Alan Anderson

Spicy was home to tongue-in-cheek Dan Turner, Hollywood Detective and lots of women tied up nude or in their scanties.

SPICY MYSTERY

Pulp magazine
December 1936

In the 1930s artist H.J. Ward's women usually wore only the bare essentials.

Masked Detectives

Before the 1920s ended, however, the pulps gave rise to another innovation that would shape American (and international) popular culture: the masked detective hero, who later developed into the modern superhero of comics, television, and film.

Since the days of Vidocq, disguise had been a mainstay of dime-novel detectives, with Nick Carter's masthead depicting the sleuth in various disguises. In the late teens and early 1920s, disguise became for many pulp heroes not just a tool of investigation, but their defining identities. Probably the best known hero from this period is not a detective but Johnston McCulley's enormously influential western hero, Zorro, who first appeared in 1915. Little read today, McCulley was a strong pulp-style writer who also wrote detective stories. His Zorro rivals Edgar Rice Burroughs's Tarzan in impact upon popular culture; yet Burroughs is still read while McCulley is forgotten.

In *Street and Smith Detective*, taking the masked avenger theme of Zorro into the world of mystery, Frank Packard's Jimmy Dale disguised himself as the Grey Seal, and in a similar chromatic theme, Herman Landon's Grey Phantom also fought crime. Both series were so popular that they had their novels reprinted in hardcover.

Before long, pulp magazines faced new competition—and detective fiction found a new home—in the burgeoning medium of radio. In 1930, Street and Smith responded to an ad agency's inquiry and turned the new enemy into an ally. On July 31, 1930, *The Detective Story Hour* first aired. Each program featured a story from the current weekly issue, initially not dramatized, merely read aloud. The show promoted *Detective Story Magazine* and the magazine sported a cover slogan, "On the Air," to promote the radio program.

In time, the narrator of these stories was given a name, and script writer Harry Charlot, who had a history of mental problems, came up with the mysterious sounding, "The Shadow." The narrator, actor James LaCurto, began reading the stories in a deep, spooky voice, ending each program with the enigmatic tagline, "The Shadow knows...."

The Shadow quickly captured listeners' imaginations and soon Henry Ralston of Street and Smith discovered that instead of asking at newsstands for *Detective Story* readers were requesting that "Shadow" magazine. Ralston suggested a separate Shadow title be developed to address the demand. In the meantime, *Detective Story* started sporting "Shadow" covers, and began a contest for readers and listeners to figure out what the mysterious Shadow looked like.

Amateur magician Walter B. Gibson had just sold a story to Street and Smith, and Ralston suggested that an unpublished Nick Carter story be rewritten with the Shadow replacing Carter as the hero. The editor assigned to the new magazine, Frank Blackwell, discussed the suggestion with Gibson, and they wisely scrapped that plan. Instead, Gibson created a whole new story, drawing on his experience related to magic, escape artists, illusion, and mysticism. The result was the ultimate detective superhero—the Shadow—trained in the Orient to cloud men's minds, a master of disguise, maintaining several secret identities during the long run of the magazine.

The Shadow debuted in the April 1931 issue of *The Shadow Magazine*, with Gibson using the Street and Smith house name, Maxwell Grant. The Shadow appeared in 325 novels in the pulps, 283 written by Gibson himself. Though the Shadow used the identity of Lamont Cranston, that was not the Shadow's true self. A real Lamont Cranston allowed the Shadow to use his name since Cranston constantly traveled the world and was seldom around. Using his vast network of operatives, the art of disguise, his ability to "cloud men's minds" and, at some point usually, his trusty pistols, the Shadow overcame any criminals stupid enough to take him on.

In 1936, Orson Welles took over the role on the radio for a year, and the show reached the zenith of its popularity, remaining on the Mutual Network until 1954. Though several movies tried, only the 1940 serial *The Shadow* featuring Victor Jory in the title role seemed to come close to capturing the magic of the characters, at least until 1994's under-appreciated *The Shadow* with Alec Baldwin starring as the cloaked hero with Penelope Ann Miller as the lovely Margo Lane.

Meanwhile, back in the 1930s, the Shadow proved immensely popular, going from quarterly to twice-monthly publication, and spawning its own radio program, comic books, and fan clubs. A legion of superhero imitators arose in the Shadow's wake—the Spider, the Phantom Detective, the Whisperer, the Avenger, Black Bat (whose costume resembles Batman's), and a host of others. Many of these heroes were masters of disguise; *The Spider* magazine alone featured three such heroes.

PRIVATE DETECTIVE

Pulp magazine
November 1947
Allan Anderson

No Dan Turner, Private Eye,
but plenty of public leg.

SPEED DETECTIVE

Pulp magazine
March 1943
H. J. Ward

To get Army PX distribution, *Spicy* became
Speed and the girls got more dressed up,
though they were still fit to be tied.

HOLLYWOOD DETECTIVE

Pulp magazine
July 1946
Allan Anderson

Robert Leslie Bellem's prose was among the funniest
in the pulps, but he benefited from great cover art by
Anderson, Ward, and others.

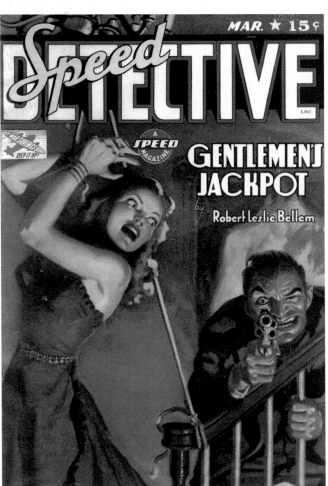

PRIVATE DETECTIVE

Pulp magazine
September 1942

Cover artist Allan Anderson did some great "sexy girl"
covers for both the Spicy and Fiction House pulps.

HOLLYWOOD DETECTIVE

Pulp magazine
October 1950

With Sally the Sleuth cartoonist Adolphe Barreaux as editor, *Hollywood Detective* was shrunk to paperback size, a unique experiment that failed.

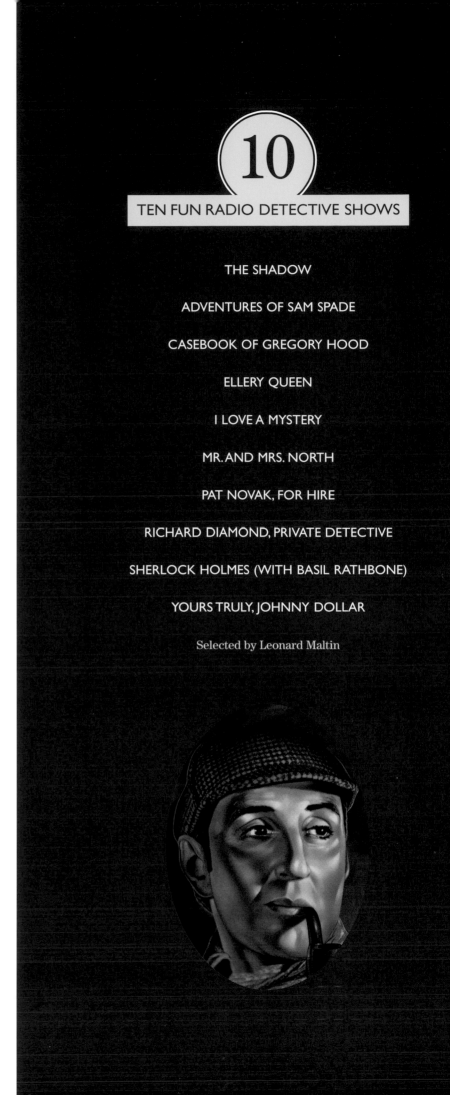

10
TEN FUN RADIO DETECTIVE SHOWS

THE SHADOW

ADVENTURES OF SAM SPADE

CASEBOOK OF GREGORY HOOD

ELLERY QUEEN

I LOVE A MYSTERY

MR. AND MRS. NORTH

PAT NOVAK, FOR HIRE

RICHARD DIAMOND, PRIVATE DETECTIVE

SHERLOCK HOLMES (WITH BASIL RATHBONE)

YOURS TRULY, JOHNNY DOLLAR

Selected by Leonard Maltin

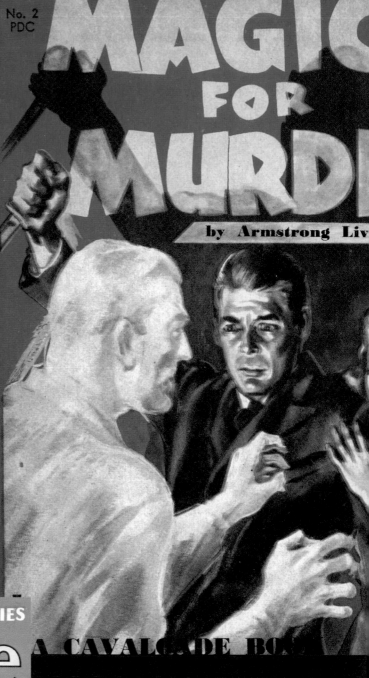

MAGIC FOR MURDER
Digest magazine
1945

Hit by paper shortages, the pulps also faced stiff competition from paperbacks and pulp-style digest books that better fit into soldiers' knapsacks. Many —like this one—were reprints of old pulp novels.

DETECTIVE BOOK MAGAZINE
Pulp magazine
Fall 1942
George Gross

A pulp reprinting of *The G-String Murders*—reportedly ghosted for stripper Gypsy Rose Lee by Craig Rice.

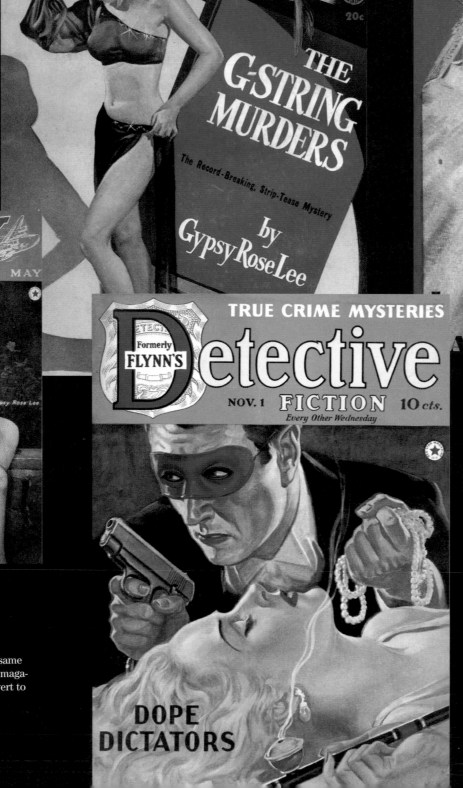

ARGOSY
Magazine
May 1942

The G-String Murders was re-packaged the same year by Argosy to look like a true-fact men's magazine. *Argosy* was the first major pulp to convert to a slick men's magazine format.

DETECTIVE FICTION
Pulp magazine
November 1, 1941
Emmett Watson

While "fiction" is in the title, true-crime stories get equal billing as the former *Flynn's* attempts to move away from the mainstream pulp market.

BLUEBOOK
Pulp magazine
March 1954
Glenn Grohe

By 1954, *Argosy* was a slick, and most of the pulps were long gone. *Bluebook* was the last holdout as a large-format pulp—half fiction and half fact stories. Soon after this issue, *Bluebook* became a men's adventure magazine.

MANHUNT

Digest Magazine
July 1953
Lou Marchetti

The digest format proved popular and magazines like *Manhunt* continued the legacy started thirty years earlier by *Black Mask*.

THE MYSTERIOUS TRAVELER #1

Digest magazine
November 1951
Norman Saunders

This digest magazine was based on a popular mystery radio program.

The superhero detectives at times only marginally qualify as mystery or detective stories, though—at least when written by Gibson, Theodore Tinsley, and other top Street and Smith writers—Shadow tales regularly feature deduction and a very good mystery. In many others, notably the Spider, mayhem takes priority over plot, with fewer mystery elements—a secret villain often ends up the only secondary character left alive at story's end. Other series, featuring the likes of Captain Satan and the Moon Man, as well as various G-Man/FBI series, fall more properly inside the noir-ish crime genre, not detective fiction; the same is true of many 1920s gangster and underworld pulps.

More than any other type of pulp fiction, the hero pulps required an incredible output from their writers. Nick Carter's writers in the dime novels wrote 25,000 words a week; an average Shadow, Spider, or Avenger novel ran more than 80,000 words. On the magazine's semi-monthly publishing schedule, a new Shadow novel had to be produced in, at most, fifteen days.

The Decline of the Pulps

The 1929 stock market crash made the dimes and quarters required to buy pulp magazines a scarce commodity. New publishers entering the field approached the problem by pushing the envelope.

Harry Steeger's Popular Publications began with a series of pulps with the word "Dime" on the cover, including *Dime Mystery* and *Dime Detective*. Steeger's formula was simple: sadistic extreme violence, usually combined with depiction on the cover of a sexy half-dressed woman in peril. Steeger's cover girls usually wore strapless gowns, torn and falling off the shoulder, or sprawled nude on slabs with large leather bands covering the areas most likely to offend the various city vice commissions. As the decade progressed, the stories underneath these garish covers also became more extreme. *Dime Mystery* featured more horror than mystery, and spawned *Horror* and *Terror Tales*. Steeger's superhero pulp, *The Spider*, saw New York destroyed in almost every issue.

With the Production Code clamping down in 1932, sex in movies was heavily censored, and male readers had to return to paper media for cheap thrills. While sex-oriented pulps like H.L. Mencken's *Saucy Stories* and *Parisienne Tales* had existed since the late teens the *Spicy* line of the 1930s first mixed sex with common pulp themes. *Spicy Detective* and *Spicy Mystery* were the line's detective genre

MIKE SHAYNE
MYSTERY MAGAZINE

Digest magazine
May 1980

Starting with Ellery Queen, various authors licensed their own magazines, as Brett Halliday did with his character Mike Shayne.

CHARLIE CHAN
MYSTERY MAGAZINE

Digest magazine
May 1974

Charlie Chan—more famous for movies than the excellent Earl Derr Biggers novels—also had his own magazine for a brief period.

ALFRED HITCHCOCK'S
MYSTERY MAGAZINE

Digest magazine
March 1969

Legendary film director (and TV host) Alfred Hitchcock lent his name—and frequently his image—to the still-running magazine. He also sponsored a popular series of paperbacks and even a detective series for young boys.

ED McBAIN'S MYSTERY
BOOK #3

Digest magazine
1961

Author Ed McBain did the same, for an excellent short run.

56

offerings. On *Spicy* covers, the women in peril often went bare-breasted and, if their breasts did happen to be covered, nipples inevitably poked at the sheer cloth. The simple pen-and-ink interior illustrations were often even more direct—bare breasts predominated. Stories were filled with description after description of silky thighs and rounded breasts as the heroines or villainesses regularly lost their clothes. Probably in deference to the literacy level of their audience, the *Spicy* pulps also featured a four-page black-and-white comic-book sequence of a female heroine, Sally the Sleuth, in similarly unclad perilous circumstances.

Detective pulps flourished through the 1930s and early 1940s, with close to fifty titles hitting the stands. As with any glutted market, every effort was made to distinguish one detective from another; mysteries were solved by dwarf detectives, blind detectives, magician detectives, female sleuths, occult investigators, and scientific P.I.s. The "gimmick" detectives of recent years have nothing on the pulp dicks—a whole sub-genre in the Steeger pulps featured "defective detectives," hemophiliacs, cripples, etc., whose disabilities did not prevent them from solving crimes.

World War II paper shortages greatly restricted the pulp magazines' numbers, and even their size. Street and Smith depended on strong story content, rather than lurid covers, and reduced its entire pulp line to a digest format, similar to the twenty-cent dime novels of the turn of the century (or the still popular *Reader's Digest*). In terms of paper use, four digests were equivalent to one pulp. The experiment worked well since, like the dime novels, digest magazines fit easily into a serviceman's backpack or duffel bag.

New publishers often began publishing in digest format. The enduring *Ellery Queen's Mystery Magazine* after a disastrous attempt to do a Queen pulp in the 1930s, successfully debuted in the 1940s, as did Lawrence Spivak's line of *Best Seller* mystery digests—dull-looking volumes with only the author's name and book title on the cover. *Ellery Queen* inspired other publishers to build a digest around a famous genre name, with such characters as Mike Shayne, Charlie Chan, and the Saint inspiring magazines, as well as authors like Rex Stout and Ed McBain; only *Alfred Hitchcock's Mystery Magazine* (now sister publication of *Ellery Queen's Mystery Magazine*) has endured.

In January 1953, touting a new serialized Mickey Spillane novel, *Manhunt* began an impressive run, lasting into the 1970s, picking up *Black Mask's* mantle. Most major hardboiled mystery and crime writers of the 1950s and 1960s appeared in those pulp pages, including Spillane, Richard S. Prather, William Campbell Gault, James M. Cain, W.R. Burnett, and many more.

The pulps were essentially replaced—not so much by their smaller, digest variation, which never earned more than a modest market niche—but by the wave of new, small paperback books... initially reprints of hardcover novels, but later original, more overtly sex-and-violence-oriented material (after Spillane's phenomenal success in the early 1950s). Ironically many pf the new "paperback originals" were first published as serials in the pulps. Also, large numbers of comic books—with similar violent, sexy subject matter, the medium never as overtly kiddie-oriented as some would have it—flooded the market from the late 1930s on.

While the pulps suffered, their publishers didn't. Most of the pulp magazine publishers simply produced other products. As the pulps waned, A. A. Wynn's *Ace Pulp* magazine line was supplanted by a comic-book and paperback novel line. Likewise, Popular Pulps became Popular Publishers of paperbacks; and Dell pulps were survived by both Dell comics and paperbacks. Scratch a comic or paperback publisher and find a former pulp publisher.

Thus, the pulp legacy lived on, as the new publishers needed large amounts of material to publish and drew heavily on the pulps for genre novels that could be produced as paperbacks; and pulp writers became paperback writers, just as the same artists whose lurid style attracted readers to the pulps found themselves painting covers for the paperbacks.

The death blow, of course, was television, and by the mid-1950s all of the detective pulps were either gone or reduced in size to a digest. That late 1950s television was dominated by pulpy private-eye shows—*Peter Gunn, 77 Sunset Strip, Perry Mason, Phillip Marlowe, Mike Hammer*, et al.—was both final indignity and fitting irony, since those shows had such strong pulp roots—Mason's creator Erle Stanley Gardner and Marlowe's creator Raymond Chandler were, after all, former "*Black Mask* boys."

DASHIELL HAMMETT

(1884–1961)

Born in St. Mary's County, Maryland, on May 27, 1884, Dashiell Hammett grew up on the streets of Philadelphia and Baltimore. In 1915, he joined the Baltimore branch of the Pinkerton detective agency; his mentor was one James Wright, a hardnosed fireplug of a "dick" who became the role model for Hammett's fictional detectives. In 1918, Hammett enlisted in the Army, where he contracted tuberculosis. He returned to the Pinkertons, but his health worked against him; so did his leftist philosophies, which came in conflict with the new Pinkerton union-busting style. With a family to support, he became a jewelry-store clerk and ad copywriter.

Then in 1922, Hammett placed a short story with *Smart Set*, and later that year in *Black Mask* began a long regular run with the magazine, where his Continental Op stories, based on his Pinkerton days, changed mystery fiction forever. Hammett's diamond-hard prose, and his deadpan understatement, added to his own real-life P.I. background, lent his pulp tales a credibility his chief rival Carroll John Daly lacked.

As Ellery Queen pointed out, under Hammett's realistic surface was romance—the cynicism represented by the failed quest for the Maltese falcon does not diminish the jeweled bird's larger-than-life allure. Sam Spade was not a realistic depiction of an op, but Hammett's romantic notion of what a real-life op would have *liked* to be.

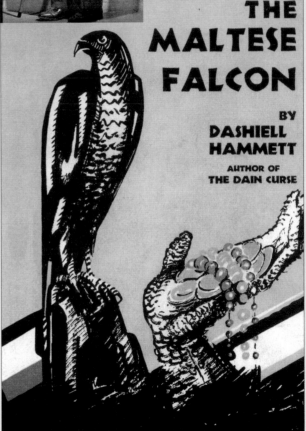

THE THIN MAN

Hardcover
1934

By his fifth—and final (though no one would have guessed that fact)—novel, Hammett was famous enough…and slim enough …to appear on the front jacket of *The Thin Man*. Of course, detective Nick Charles was not the title character, though the later film series would imply that.

THE MALTESE FALCON

Hardcover
1930

Hammett revised his text from the serialized version that appeared in *Black Mask*.

Hammett defines, perfects, and abandons the perfect private eye in one masterpiece. In *The Maltese Falcon* (1929), all the accouterments of the tough P.I. are in place: the unrequited loving secretary, the one-man agency, the private eye's cop pal, the private eye's cop adversary, the untrustworthy female client, Mr. Big, "gunsels" (in both senses of the word), and all the rest.

In his four other novels, Hammett defined, perfected and abandoned most of the other sub-genres of the tough crime fiction form, as well. In *Red Harvest*, he improves upon Carroll John Daly and prefigures Mickey Spillane in a wild, bloody tale of vigilante justice. In The *Dain Curse*, he leads the way for Raymond Chandler and Ross MacDonald in a complex yarn of family skeletons in closets. In *The Glass Key*, he abandons the private eye for an amoral anti-hero in a story of big-city politics that set a pattern followed by countless writers, including John D. MacDonald and Elmore Leonard. In *The Thin Man*, he presents the mystery as the novel of manners and sets the pattern for husband/wife detective teams from Mr. and Mrs. North to television's *Moonlighting*.

Sadly, in five novels (and scores of short stories), Hammett had said everything he—and, arguably, anybody else—could say about the tough mystery. His alcoholic's life —as lap dog to Lillian Hellman, with periodic attempts to write again, and one oasis of self-respect in his World War II service in the Aleutians—was blandly tragic, highlighted by persecution in the McCarthy era that saw Hammett stick to his code, going to jail before he would betray a friend.

RED HARVEST
Paperback
1943

THE CONTINENTAL OP

Paperback
1945

HAMMETT HOMICIDES

Paperback
1947

THE ADVENTURES OF SAM SPADE

Hardcover
1944

A MAN CALLED SPADE

Paperback
1944

This inexpensive (at the time, that is) Tower Books edition is the same collection of the only three Sam Spade short stories (filled out with other Hammett tales) as the differently titled Dell Books paperback. The moody, hardcover jacket closely apes the description of Spade in Hammett; Robert Stanley, on the Dell cover, uses his usual favorite model: himself.

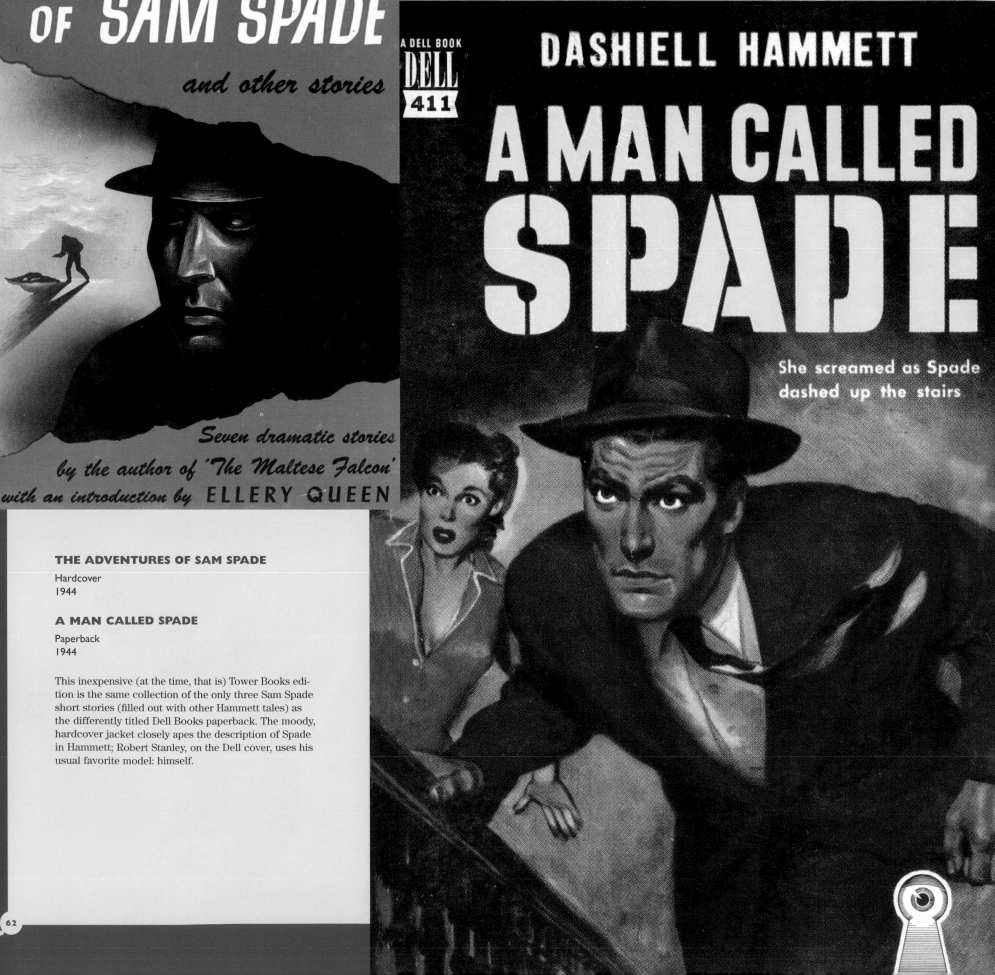

BLOOD MONEY

Paperback
1943

Possibly the work of Gregg, this wonderfully garish air-brushed deco design is the cover to the first book publication of a Continental Op novel Hammett serialized but never chose to collect as a hardcover.

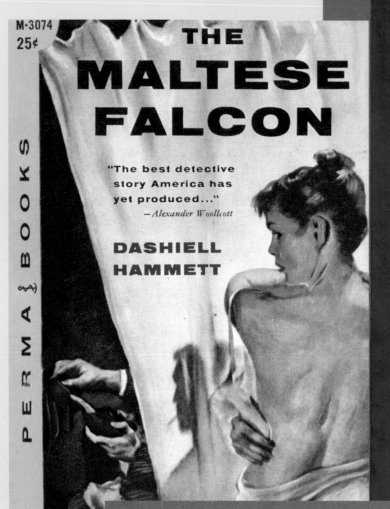

M·3074
25¢

THE MALTESE FALCON

"The best detective story America has yet produced..."
—*Alexander Woollcott*

DASHIELL HAMMETT

PERMA BOOKS

THE COMPLETE BOOK

35¢
PERMA BOOK

RED HARVEST

A city torn apart by gamblers, gunmen and crooked police

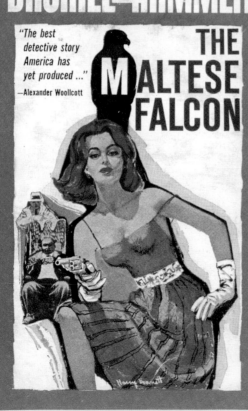

35¢
PERMA BOOK
M 4200

DASHIELL HAMMETT

"The best detective story America has yet produced ..."
—Alexander Woollcott

THE MALTESE FALCON

THE COMPLETE BOOK

THE MALTESE FALCON

Paperback
1957

THE MALTESE FALCON

Paperback
1961

RED HARVEST

Paperback
1961

THE THIN MAN

Paperback
1961

Stanley Meltzhoff—one of the most respected of the 1950s paperback artists—contributes a great Spillane-era cover for *The Maltese Falcon*, depicting the one major scene John Huston had to leave out of the Bogart film. Uniform, sharply modern designs from Harry Bennett were used by Pocket Books in 1961 to introduce Hammett's five classic novels to a new audience.

35¢
PERMA BOOK
M 4202

DASHIELL HA

THE THI

The mystery classic sta
Nick and Nora Charle

THE COMPLETE BOOK

THE MALTESE FALCON

Sam Spade's Greatest Radio Adventure

THE MALTESE FALCON

Radio Show LP

1978

Featuring art from the film, this Radiola album gathered two radio versions of Hammett's tale, both featuring Bogart, Mary Astor, and Sydney Greenstreet: September 20, 1943; and July 3, 1946.

HAMMETT

Hardcover

1975

One real-life private eye writes about another: Joe Gores—a pioneer in period P.I. fiction—uses Dashiell Hammett as the detective in this strong fictional mystery, which inspired an interesting, underrated film (1983). Lovely jacket art by Honi Werner.

HAMMETT

a novel by JOE GORES

ERLE STANLEY GARDNER

(1889–1970)

Man's man Erle Stanley Gardner wrote numerous non-fiction books about his nature-oriented travels in the American Southwest.

Born in Malden, Massachusetts, in 1889, Erle Stanley Gardner became a young roughneck who made good. His father, a mining engineer, took the family west, and Gardner grew up in mining towns from Oregon to the Klondike. A boxer and a wrestler, Gardner got kicked out of school for punching out a professor—the perfect background for a future pulp writer.

Without ever going to law school, Gardner passed the bar in 1911 after a three-year stint as a legal typist. In addition to establishing a reputation for wild court-room maneuvering, he became known as a champion of the underdog, defending penniless Mexican and Chinese clients. This thirst for justice would inspire his founding of the Court of Last Resort, which sought to overturn unjust convictions.

In the 1920s, in Ventura, California, he was a lawyer by day, at night pursuing a new career: fiction writing. Perhaps the most successful pulp writer of all time, Erle Stanley Gardner wrote millions of words for *Argosy*, *Black Mask*, *Detective Detective*, and many others. In 1932, he earned $20,000 writing at a rate of a cent or two a word.

Turning to better-paying markets, Gardner combined his penchant for action and suspense with his legal knowledge, publishing *The Case of the Velvet Claws* (1933), introducing the most famous fictional attorney of all, Perry Mason. Gardner's style was heavily influenced by his fellow *Black Mask* contributor, Dashiell Hammett.

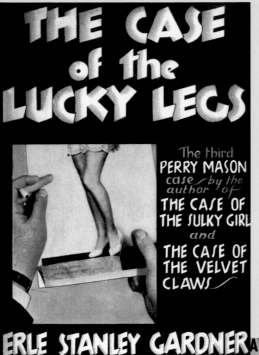

THE CASE OF THE LUCKY LEGS

Hardcover
1934

Perry Mason's early cases showed the strong Black Mask heritage of Erle Stanley Gardner.

LIBERTY

Magazine
1935

Gardner's dream was to use Perry Mason to trade in the penny-a-word pulps for the better-paying world of the slicks, and it didn't take him long to make the transition, as this *Liberty* cover attests.

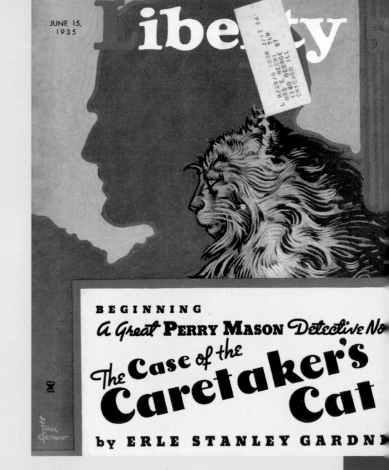

**THE CASE OF THE
PERJURED PARROT**

Paperback
1947

**THE CASE OF THE
BAITED HOOK**

Paperback
1946

**THE CASE OF THE
LAZY LOVER**

Paperback
1952

**THE CASE OF THE
BAITED HOOK**

Paperback
1956

**THE CASE OF THE
CURIOUS BRIDE**

Paperback
1956

**THE CASE OF THE
SUN BATHER'S DIARY**

Paperback
1963

**THE CASE OF THE
SHOPLIFTER'S SHOE**

Paperback
1986

Times change, but Perry Mason endures, as these paperbacks over the decades indicate. From the hysterical *Perjured Parrot* to the masked beauty of the 1946 edition of *Baited Hook*, early Pocket Books afforded their star mystery performer with striking covers. The early 1950s show the Spillane/Prather influence in the deadly dames of *Lazy Lover* (art by Clyde Ross) and the 1956 version of *Baited Hook* (art by *Esquire* pin-up artist, Al Moore). Designs including photos and the distinctive signature of the author enliven late 1950s Pocket Books covers (i.e., *Curious Bride*), and by 1963, such typical yet exquisite mystery-cover fare as the Robert McGinnis sunglasses-wearing blonde of *Sun Bather's Diary* attempts to make these adult but not terribly sexy books seem salacious. A Jayne Mansfield bubble-bath bottle (a collectible item in its own right!) spices up the 1986 Ballantine edition of *Shoplifter's Shoe*.

PERRY MASON solves

THE CASE OF THE

BAITED HOOK

ERLE STANLEY GARDNER

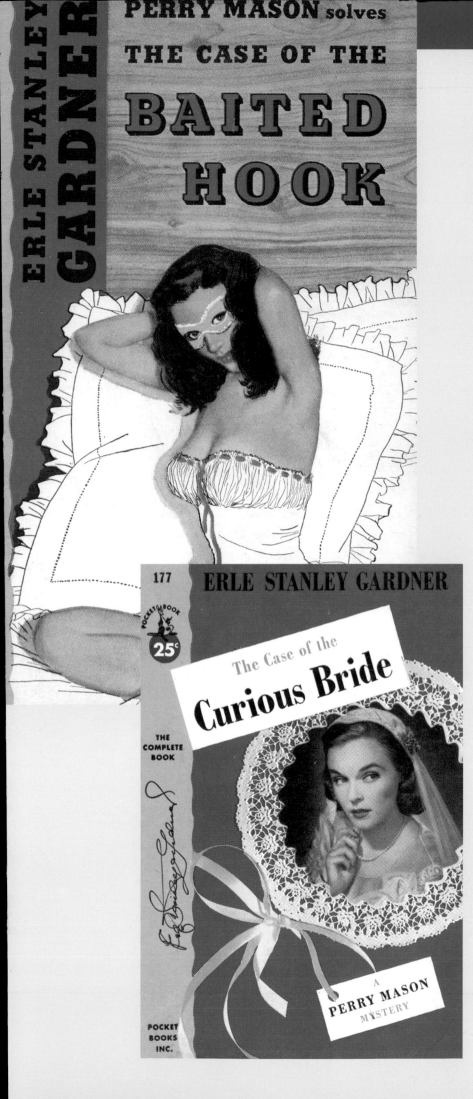

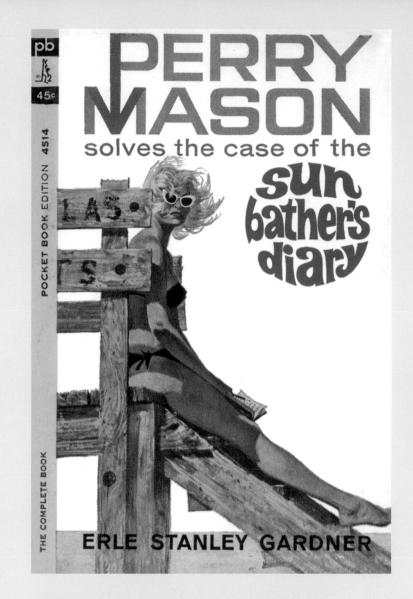

PERRY MASON solves the case of the sun bather's diary

POCKET BOOK EDITION 4514

45¢

pb

THE COMPLETE BOOK

ERLE STANLEY GARDNER

177

ERLE STANLEY GARDNER

POCKET BOOK 25¢

THE COMPLETE BOOK

The Case of the Curious Bride

A PERRY MASON MYSTERY

POCKET BOOKS INC.

THE WORLD'S BEST SELLING MYSTERY WRITER

ERLE STANLEY GARDNER

A PERRY MASON MYSTERY

THE CASE OF THE SHOPLIFTER'S SHOE

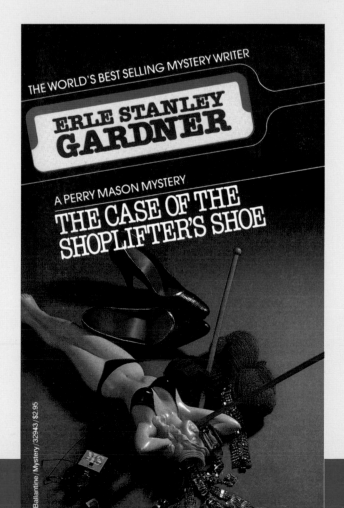

Ballantine / Mystery 32943 $2.95

Throughout his career, Gardner's writing was lean, with crackling dialogue James M. Cain might have envied. Nonetheless, Gardner is often accused of poor characterization, scant description, and formulaic writing.

Such critics apparently have not read much Gardner. No two of his logical yet convoluted plots resemble each other, and his characters and descriptions are achieved with deft, telling strokes; and like Cain, Gardner's most common topics were designed for grown-ups: adultery and big business.

The Mason novels often had showy courtroom scenes, echoing Gardner's own experience; sometimes as much as a third of a Mason novel takes place in court—and no one wrote such scenes better. At heart, the Masons, slicked up as they were for the *Saturday Evening Post* crowd, remained *Black Mask*-style stories, with Mason and his private eye, Paul Drake, racing from one clue, one situation, to another. Mason, Drake, secretary Della Street, Lt. Tragg, and hapless D.A. Hamilton Burger are timeless detective characters, thanks in part to Gardner's resistance of topicality.

Mason fared well on the radio (1943–1955, a rare mystery soap opera which evolved into the radio version of *The Edge of Night* when Mason moved to television).

But the movies were a lackluster affair, Warren William and others starring in a number of 1930s Warner Brothers films. The definitive portrayal, of course, was by former screen heavy Raymond Burr on the CBS series (1957–1966) in scripts faithfully based on Gardner's novels.

Gardner's tough, comic series featuring female P.I. Bertha Cool and diminutive lawyer Donald Lam, written as by A.F. Fair, was well-regarded though never any competition to Perry Mason.

Promotional postcard
1984

Raymond Burr so defined Perry Mason in the 1957 -1966 series that serializations in slick magazines used his image in their illustrations.

PERRY MASON

A. A. FAIR now admitted to be an alias of **ERLE STANLEY GARDNER**

The Bigger They Come

"How big was this man who tried to strangle you?"

THE BIGGER THEY COME
Paperback
1952

FOOLS DIE ON FRIDAY
Paperback
1951

TOP OF THE HEAP
Paperback
1959

The critics and a considerable cult of readers preferred Gardner's work as A.A. Fair to the Mason novels, but sales were a distant second (Gardner's D.A. series just hobbled along). P.I. Donald Lam frequently appears on the paperback covers, but heavy-set partner Bertha Lam does not, as the Robert Stanley art for *Fools Die On Friday* demonstrates. (A later printing tones down the décolletage of the damsel, modeled by Stanley's wife Rhoda.) Maurice Thomas supplies another provocative cover for *The Bigger They Come*, but no one can top Robert McGinnis in his delightful *Top Of The Heap*.

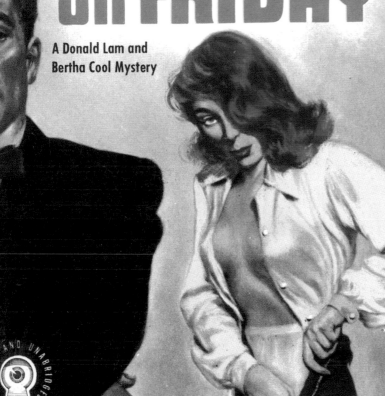

25¢ **DELL BOOK 542**

"Get your clothes on — just enough to cover yourself, and get out of here."

A. A. FAIR

FOOLS DIE on FRIDAY

A Donald Lam and Bertha Cool Mystery

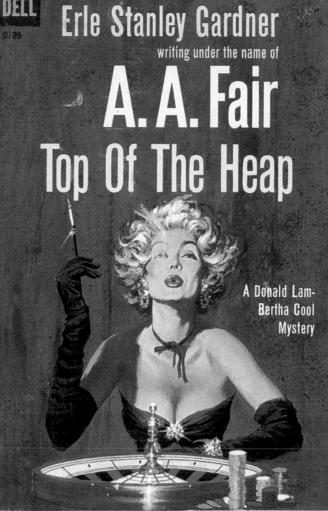

DELL D-109

Erle Stanley Gardner writing under the name of

A. A. Fair
Top Of The Heap

A Donald Lam-Bertha Cool Mystery

CHAPTER
3

DECTECTIVE COMICS

Silly Sherlocks

In the early days, American comics were comic: humorous full-page, full-color gag strips appearing in Sunday "funnies" sections; so it's no surprise that the first detective comic strip was a spoof. In 1912, midwestern artist Sidney Smith, who would later create the enormously popular, influential *Gumps* strip — began *Sherlock, Jr.* After all, "Sherlock" was already a slang term meaning detective, thanks to the popularity of Conan Doyle's character. Though humorous, Smith's pioneering strip, which lasted about a year, did include humorous adventures as well as gags in a feature chronicling the adventures of a young detective in rural America. • More directly inspired by Holmes, and far more successful, was Gus Magers's *Hawkshaw the Detective*. Originally appearing as *Sherlocko the Monk* (in a Magers spoof in which monkeys played human roles), *Hawkshaw* parodied not only Holmes but other detective-story conventions. Sporting a deerstalker cap and puffing a meerschaum pipe, Hawkshaw caricatured Holmes, though his adventures often resembled those of Nick Carter, or the new melodramatic serials just beginning to appear at the "flickers." • In spite of Magers's crudely exaggerated, so-called "big foot" drawing style, *Hawkshaw* proved extremely popular, running from 1913 to 1922, revived in the early 1930s for another almost twenty-year run. In 1917, a large paperback book collected *Hawkshaw* strips in an early forerunner of current comic books.

Hawkshaw had few competitors in its early days. While detective or mystery stories would occasionally appear in comic strips, none had a detective hero. Ed Wheelan's *Minute Movies*, a comic strip with a cast of actors who put on serialized stories or movies, did periodically feature serio-comic stories with mystery themes. Wheelan might do a twelve-week detective serial, however, only to follow it with a tale of King Arthur's knights or a pirate yarn.

Then in the late 1920s, the comic pages were intruded upon by the serious, or at least the melodramatic: adventure strips had arrived, *Little Orphan Annie*, *Tarzan*, *Wash Tubbs*, and *Buck Rogers* forever making misnomers out of the terms "comics" and "funnies." In 1930, the first real *Sherlock Holmes* strip appeared; the work of artist Leo Omealia for a small syndicate, "Holmes" quickly died not at the hands of Professor Moriarty, but from lack of interest, possibly due to the artist's decision to load the strip with dense blocks of text as opposed to using the more popular device, word balloons.

Plainclothes Dick

The breakthrough came in 1931 with Chester Gould's *Dick Tracy*. Prior to this, Gould had written and drawn *Fillum Fables*, a copycat of Wheelan's *Minute* movies. But *Tracy* was not a gentle parody of current silent-film trends. Gould's hardhitting, unprecedented strip featured raw stories of crime and deduction right out of the wild Chicago headlines of the roaring twenties. A handful of adventure strips preceded *Tracy*, assuredly—but none of them contained merciless torture, blazing machine guns, and cold-blooded murder. *Tracy* did, though he was not an amateur sleuth or a private eye, even though his creator envisioned the character as a modern-day Sherlock Holmes, substituting a fedora and trench coat (still the standard uniform for tough detectives) for Sherlock's deerstalker cap and Inverness cape. Like Joe Friday, Dick Tracy was a cop. As such, an in-depth discussion of the strip really belongs more in a history of crime fiction than mystery.

Still, *Tracy* succeeded where a *Sherlock Holmes* strip had failed because the world Gould depicted was the real one of his readers' experience. In 1931, the year *Tracy* debuted, Eliot Ness left his undercover role and openly battled the Capone gang in the streets and on the front pages of Chicago dailies. The rough-and-tumble world of gangsters and bandits also translated better to the visual medium of comics than the more cerebral stories of Conan Doyle.

That *Tracy* opened the door for detective and mystery strips cannot be denied.

G-Men and Cops

Virtually all of the comic strips introduced in the five years after the phenomenal success of *Dick Tracy* featured cops, G-men, and other government agents. Private eyes and amateur detectives were conspicuously missing in action. *Red Barry*, *Radio Patrol*, *Secret Agent X-9* (written first by Dashiell Hammett and later by the *Saint's* Leslie Charteris), *War Against Crime*, *Inspector Wade*, and others were cops-and-robbers strips, though all were heavily influenced by the private-eye fiction published in *Black Mask*.

The absence of traditional P.I. or amateur sleuths in the comics pages of the 1930s seems puzzling, at first, considering the wide success of such characters in books and movies. But in comics—a visual medium with very limited text—a story with more action and violence was not only easy to tell, but the stuff of compelling melodrama. That ruled out the cerebral sleuths.

And in a venue like a family newspaper, a policeman or FBI agent as the leading hero rationalized the violence better than a private eye. Also, a police-versus-the-mob approach made for a clear delineation between right and wrong, good and evil, as opposed to the *noir*-ish, gray-toned private eye's world of the *Black Mask*, filled as it was with moral ambiguities.

Though "kids" of all ages read the funnies, newspaper comic strips were viewed by many as children's literature; syndicates could get away with injecting adult subject matter and violence into their comic strips in the context of good cops versus the evil underworld.

Detective Comics

While Dick Tracy and his sidekicks changed the face of newspaper comic strips with real-life bullets and bloodshed (courtesy of Chester Gould's brilliant surreal artwork), another comics revolution took place at the same newsstand.

In 1933, entrepreneur M. C. Gaines invented the modern comic book by securing the rights to reprint comic strips in magazine form, first to be given away as premiums, then distributed as monthly periodicals sold on newsstands. Early comics like *Famous Funnies* were anthologies, reprinting runs of various comics features; in time, publishers produced comics showcasing a single strip character. *Dick Tracy* had the distinction of inaugurating two early series of comic books from two rival publishers—appearing as the first Feature Book from David McCay in 1937 and the first Dell Four Color Comic in 1939.

In 1933, Humor Publishing produced two large black-and-white comic books containing all new material. The first of these, *Detective Dan*, was a Dick Tracy clone. Scripted and drawn by Norman Marsh, the feature re-emerged several months later as the syndicated strip *Dan Dunn*, becoming perhaps the most popular of *Tracy* competitors, lasting well into the 1940s. Humor Publishing's second book was a bona fide private-eye comic: *The Adventures of Detective Ace King, the American Sherlock Holmes*. Both detective comic books were aimed at adults, featuring stories rife with dope dealers, torture, gangsters, and gun molls.

Humor Publishing closed up shop before publishing second issues of either detective publication. This groundbreaking company has one further distinction; Humor was the first publisher to turn down a certain outlandish comics feature: Jerry Siegel's and Joe Shuster's "Superman."

While the comic-book field was still dominated by comic-strip reprints, the pulp magazine *Spicy Detective* introduced the first successful original detective feature to appear in comic-book format. Sexy *Sally the Sleuth* began in 1934 and ran in pulps and/or comic books through the early 1950s. The two-to four-page *Sally* comics condensed racy stories previously published in the *Spicy* pulp line. Unlike the *Spicy* pulp stories, however, where several pages of text and snappy patter were required before the heroine exposed "her milky breasts and creamy thighs encased in silken panties," the comic-book Sally would be down to her undies by the third panel, usually with the obligatory stray dots indicating her nipples.

By 1934, the four-color comic-book publishers were running out of newspaper strips to license and began looking for new material. Copying the standard genres found in newspaper strips, these new comic books—including *New Comics*, *More Fun*, and *Funny Pages*—all featured detective series...cops, of course, but also masked sleuths and private eyes.

DICK TRACY AND THE WOO WOO SISTERS

Paperback
1947

Novel and cover artwork attributed to Chester Gould (but ghosted in both cases). Dick Tracy not only appeared in the comics but in several novels written for both the children's book and, as in this case, adult paperback market.

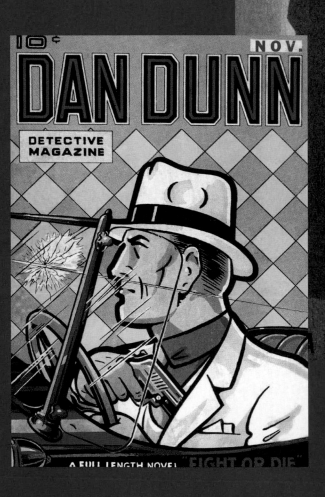

DAN DUNN

Pulp magazine
November 1936

Early Tracy imitator Dan Dunn also briefly appeared in text stories in this pulp magazine.

ACE KING #1

Comic book
1933
Martin Naydel

The second comic book and the first to feature a private detective.

DETECTIVE COMICS #1

Comic book
March 1937
Vincent Sullivan

Detective Comics proved the most successful of the early detective titles, and is still running.

DETECTIVE PICTURE STORIES

Comic book
1936
William Allison

The first all original detective anthology comic book.

Joe Shuster and Jerry Siegel, whose great success with *Superman* would come later, contributed such features as *Federal Men* and *Radio Squad*; George Brenner created the first masked detective, *The Clock*. The stage was set for the first anthology comic book devoted to a single genre—and detectives again led the way. Comics Magazine Company published *Detective Picture Stories* in December 1936, later continued as *Keen Detective Funnies*. A few months later, *Detective Comics* began, the title that became the "D.C." in famed DC comics. *Detective Comics* introduced Siegel and Shuster's *Slam Bradley*, the first successful private-eye feature in four-color comics.

The dominance of private eyes and G-men in comic books was short-lived, ending with the birth of Superman in *Action Comics* and Batman in *Detective*. Costumed heroes and superheroes soon dominated covers with their garish presence, and the lead-story slots quickly went to the men in capes; the plainclothes detectives moved to the back pages—when they appeared at all.

Meanwhile ...

Back on the comics page, sleuths were starting to turn up. With the continued success of Dick Tracy and such imitators as Dan Dunn and Hammett's Secret Agent X-9, syndicates approached mystery writers, seeking to license their famous characters to the comics medium. The estate of Edgar Wallace licensed Inspector Wade to King Features in 1935; Earl Biggers's *Charlie Chan* appeared in 1935 drawn by Milton Caniff's protege, Alfred Andriola. While in the Earl Derr Biggers novels, Chan was ostensibly a Honolulu policeman, he behaved in the strips (as in the movies, from which the strip drew its primary inspiration) more like an amateur sleuth, as the stories shifted from Honolulu to Hollywood and various other locales.

In spite of attractive, Caniff-style art by Andriola, *Chan* did not generate enough sales to justify its licensing fees, and in the early 1940s, Andriola launched *Kerry Drake*, a cop strip whose grotesque villains mirrored the bizarre rogue's gallery of Gould's *Tracy*. Chan went on to several later appearances in comic books, notably five issues in the 1940s by *Captain America* creators, Joe Simon and Jack Kirby. DC Comics took a crack at Chan with Sid Greene as the artist in the late 1950s; and Frank Springer drew two issues for Dell

KERRY DRAKE #2

Comic book
1944

Andriola's next strip was *Kerry Drake*, a detective who started out as a private investigator but soon joined the police.

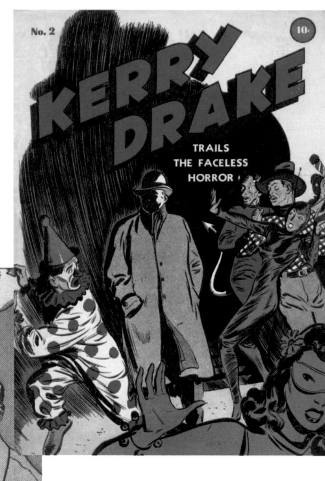

KEEN DETECTIVE FUNNIES

Comic book
May 1939

Detective Comic's success spawned several short-lived imitators, including this revival of *Detective Picture Stories*.

CHARLIE CHAN

Comic strip
January 22, 1939

Alfred Andriola's Chan owed more to the movie version than the original Biggers novels.

BLACK BOOK DETECTIVE

Pulp magazine
Fall 1945

The Black Bat bore an uncanny resemblance to Batman, but since the pulp started the same month as Batman's first appearance, the two coexisted for over a decade.

RIP KIRBY

Comic book
Unknown, patterned
after Alex Raymond

Raymond's *Rip Kirby*
established the private
eye comic strip in
America. It was so
popular that it was
reprinted all over the
world, including this
British edition.

VIC FLINT #2

Comic strip
October 1948

A moderately successful private
eye comic strip, *Vic Flint* had a
long run in his own comic book,
and as filler material in various
St. John crime comics.

5

FIVE BEST COMIC-STRIP DETECTIVES

DICK TRACY

RIP KIRBY

VIC FLINT

PETER SCRATCH

THE SAINT

Selected by George Hagenauer

5

FIVE BEST COMIC-BOOK DETECTIVES

JOHNNY DYNAMITE

MS. TREE

THE HUMAN TARGET

MAZE AGENCY

MIKE DANGER

Selected by George Hagenauer

Comics in the 1960s. In spite of Biggers's successful novels, which remain in print, and a very popular series of B-movies, Chan's low-key sleuthing eluded successful translation to the comics medium. Sherlock Holmes had his stories adapted into two issues of *Classics Comics/Classics Illustrated* (*The Adventures of Sherlock Holmes* and *A Study in Scarlet*), and a Holmes strip appeared for several years written by Holmes radio program scribe Edith Meiser in the 1950s. In addition to Holmes, *Classic Illustrated* adapted other public-domain mysteries by Poe and Wilkie Collins.

Perry Mason turned up in two 1940s Feature Books adaptations of Gardner novels, as well as a short run as a comic strip in the 1950s. Mason returned in the 1960s in two comics based on the popular TV series. In the mid-1950s, the *Nero Wolfe* comic strip ran slightly more than a year, and Ellery Queen made repeated attempts at producing comic books, with no real success. Dashiell Hammett's Sam Spade had a bit more success—albeit as a strip spinning off from the radio show...and advertising Wild Root Hair Cream. Spade also was seen in a Feature Book version of *The Maltese Falcon*.

The exception to all this floundering by sleuths on the funny pages was Leslie Charteris's the Saint, whose comic strip began in 1948 and ran through the 1960s, spawning a comic-book series that lasted several years, including both strip reprints and original material. Charteris didn't just license his character away to a syndicate to do with as they wished but actually wrote many of the scripts himself. After all, the Saint's creator had written *Secret Agent X-9* after Hammett left in the 1930s.

Charteris knew how to present his character in comics and created an interpretation that kept the Saint true to the spirit of the original novels. Also, the Saint had an action/adventure aspect—perfect for comics—that most amateur sleuths lacked.

The Saint also rode the coattails of a major postwar comic strip success story—the private-eye strip, *Rip Kirby*. *Flash Gordon* creator Alex Raymond returned from the war, but not to his very popular science-fiction strip; tired of space opera, Raymond proposed instead a sophisticated private-eye series. No gritty cops-and-robbers yarn populated with grotesque villains, *Rip Kirby*, debuting in 1946, dealt with the country-club set, i.e., the rich and the beautiful. With a funny/stuffy British butler, lovely fashion-model-esque women,

and sophisticated story lines, *Rip Kirby* was an instant hit, proving cops and mayhem weren't always necessary ingredients for a mystery strip. *Kirby* outlasted Raymond's tragic young death in 1957, ending in the 1990s, long after most story strips had disappeared.

Rip Kirby was just one of a group of new, more sophisticated strips emerging in the late 1940s, including *Mary Worth*, *Rex Morgan*, *MD*, and *Steve Canyon*. The success of *Kirby*, however, made it easier for Charteris to market his *Saint* strip. Who could imagine, before the war, selling the family funny pages a feature starring an amateur sleuth who was also an unreformed criminal? But after Kirby and The Saint, a number of other private eyes found a home in the comics section, including Vic Flint and Lou Fine's brilliant Peter Scratch, among others.

Since several companies publishing pulps also issued comic books, pulp detectives frequently showed up in comics, not surprisingly including such masked superhero detectives as The Shadow, The Ghost, and The Phantom Detective. Even everyday dicks occasionally sleuthed in four colors, like the venerable Nick Carter and zany Hollywood detective Dan Turner—even if the costumed detectives inevitably received top billing.

Crime Does Not Pay

The 1940s saw comic books embracing the mystery and crime genres. Lev Gleason was one of the most violent of the new superhero publishers, his characters fighting mass murderers, blood flowing across the pages. When church groups protested this lurid material, Gleason joined a comic-book association that produced its own code of approval. A gory Gleason cover depicting a man impaled on a stake would also include a seal of approval consisting of an open Bible and the word "integrity" placed near the pool of blood.

In 1942, when American males went off to war, a huge comic-book market in the military was created. Gleason editors/artists Charles Biro and Bob Wood converted their *Silver Streak* superhero title into a comic-book version of the popular new true-detective magazines. *Crime Does Not Pay* began in June 1942 with a narrator introducing the stories — the ghoulish Mr. Crime.

Gleason's books, filled with densely written morality tales, had more words per page than any other 1940s comic. The average story consisted of eight to twelve pages of mayhem, as the real-life story of a dangerous criminal unfolds, with the final page presenting the moral as the sociopathic lead character is captured or executed by the police. While *Crime Does Not Pay* featured a regular private-eye series, *Chip Gardner*, as well as a series of whodunit-style mysteries, the garish, gore-splattered covers emphasized bloody scenes of gangland murder.

Crime Does Not Pay began selling one to two million copies per month and transformed the comic-book field into an adult market for the next decade and a half. The short-story format became the norm, and by the 1950s the comics scene was littered with crime, horror, or romance titles, without any continuing characters.

Dangerous Comics

Mickey Spillane had written comic books prior to the war and on his return from the service turned out short crime and romance stories for Timely (now Marvel) Comics. Spillane had created a private-eye character just prior to his enlistment, and now he pitched the character—Mike Danger—as a continuing series to several publishers. With no takers, Spillane rewrote the concept into a novel—*I, the Jury*—changing Mike Danger into Mike Hammer. In the late 1940s *I, the Jury* outsold almost every book except the Bible, and comic-book publishers suddenly were interested in private eyes.... Only now they couldn't afford Mickey Spillane.

Vic Flint and The Saint were quickly reprinted in comic-book form. Chip Gardner occasionally even pushed the gangsters and ice picks off the cover of *Crime Does Not Pay*, and these sleuths were soon joined by a host of others—Ken Shannon, Mike Barnett, Casey Crime Photographer, Johnny Danger, Sam Hill, Gregory Gayle Gunmaster, Pete Webb, Mr. & Mrs. Chase, Roy Raymond, Martin Kane, and many others; some had their own books, others starred in anthology titles. Even Spillane's Mike Danger finally saw print in the pages of the short-lived *Crime Detector*, apparently utilizing file copies of Spillane's original proposed material (without the writer's approval). Mike Hammer briefly appeared as a newspaper comic strip in the early 1950s, until the tough, racy subject matter caused its cancellation.

The best of these series was *Johnny Dynamite*, written by various hands but usually drawn (beautifully so) by artist Pete Morisi. On the cover of *Dynamite #3* (1953), tough P.I. Johnny Dynamite came at the reader with a broken bottle, and neither he nor Morisi ever let up; the Spillane imitative stories breathed tension, employing some of the strongest hardboiled language in comics, with sex and violence rivaling any paperback of the era and boldly dramatic art where black shadows enhanced the *noir* effect.

The new crop of comic-book detectives included women sleuths whose ample charms were a major benefit in a visual media marketed primarily to men. Joining Sally the Sleuth (whose four-adventures were slightly more clothed) were Toni Gayle, Starr Flagg, and others, solving crimes in spite of a continual threat by strong winds ready to lift their skirts and expose their garter belts (which sometimes sheathed knives or guns).

Several publishers responded to the popularity of detective comics by experimenting with graphic novels—one-hundred to two-hundred-page paperback books. Richard Fletcher moonlighted from his *Chicago Tribune* comic strips to draw an adaptation of George Harmon Coxe's *Four Frightened Women*; Ben Raab created *The Case of the Winking Buddha*. None of the 1950s graphic novel experiments proved profitable, however, and decades would pass before original graphic novels were again attempted.

Seduction of the Innocent

In 1950, during the first Senate Hearing on Organized Crime, Senator Estes Kefauver led the charge to expose America's organized crime syndicates. Soon many of the most popular subjects of the "true crime" comic books—gangsters like Frank Costello and Willie Morretti—were squirming on TV under flood lights dodging questions from senators. Within four years, the publishers of mystery, crime and horror comic books would join the hoods under the hot lights.

Anti-comics crusades were nothing new in American politics. In the 1920s, illustrator Joseph Pennell's wife contended that the four-color funnies were a major threat to American culture and morals. The anti-comics crusades of the 1940s and early 1950s benefited from a different type of leadership and expertise, however; Dr. Frederic Wertham was the senior psychiatrist for the New York

THE MALTESE FALCON, FEATURE BOOK #48

Comic book
1946
Rodlow Willard

Dashiel Hammett's popular novel is adapted into a lively comic book.

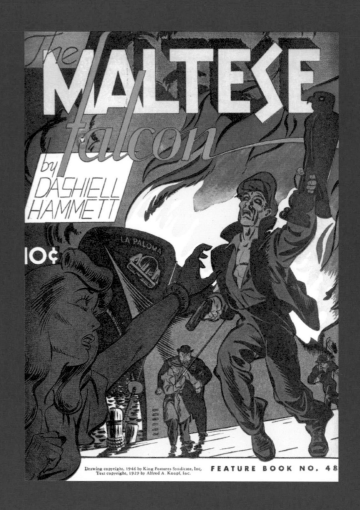

THE SAINT #9

Comic book
1950
Mike Roy

Leslie Charteris's The Saint —from his long-running novel series—appeared for more than twelve years as a successful syndicated comic strip, which was reprinted by Avon Comics.

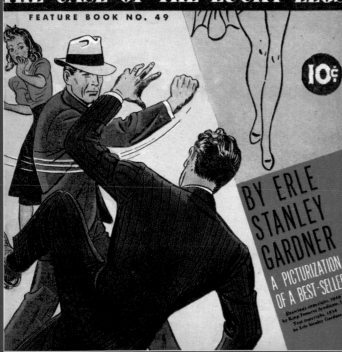

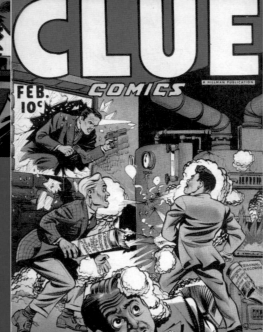

CLUE COMICS #12

Comic book
February 1947

Gunmaster Gregory Gayle saves the district attorney's records.

PERRY MASON: THE CASE OF THE LUCKY LEGS, FEATURE BOOK #49

Comic book
Vernon Greene

The first appearance of Erle Stanley Gardner's famous lawyer in a comic book. The detective later appeared in a syndicated comic strip, and a series of comic books was based on the popular TV series.

YOUNG KING COLE, VOL. 2, #4

Comic book
February 1947
Jack Harmon

In addition to Young King Cole, this comic book was home to female sleuth Toni Gayle.

PRIVATE DETECTIVE STORIES

Comic book
February 1949

A late appearance of *Spicy Detective's* Sally Sleuth, this time fully clothed.

SAM SPADE

Advertisement (comic strip)
1950
Johnstone Cushing

Hammett's famous private eye had a long career as a comic-strip pitchman for Wildroot Cream Oil (one of the Spade radio show's prime sponsors).

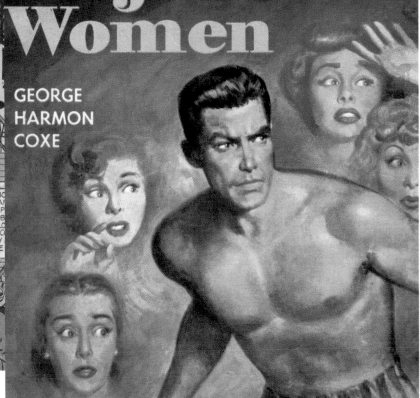

FOUR FRIGHTENED WOMEN

Paperback
1950

While it looks like a standard paperback, this is actually a comic-book-style adaptation of George Harmon Coxe's novel by Chicago Tribune artist Richard Fletcher.

AMERICA'S HARD-BOILED, WISE-CRACKING SLEUTH

Sam Hill

ANC

NO. **4** "PRIVATE EYE" 10¢

HE'S ASLEEP, ALL RIGHT... ONLY IT'S PERMANENT!

CALL SAM HILL TO THE STAND!

CAREFUL WHAT YOU SAY, SAM! MY BOYS WILL BE WATCHING YOU!

TELL 'EM TO LISTEN REAL CLOSE, TOO! THEY'LL HEAR T WHOLE TRUTH... AND NOTHING BU

IF WE DO, YOU'LL NEVE LEAVE THAT WITNESS CHA ALIVE!

'OU'RE BEAUTIFUL, ABY.. BUT YOU'LL 'RY THE SAME AS ANY MURDERER!

ALLING ALL CARS! CK UP SAM HILL... WANTED FOR MURDER!

TRUE TO LIFE NSIDE STORIES FROM SAM HILL'S PRIVATE FILES

HARRY Lucey

JULY NO. 100 10¢

CRIME DOES NOT PAY

A FULL-SIZE 52 page MAG!

LEV GLEASON, PUBLISHER · CHARLES BIRO AND BOB WOOD, EDITORS

CHIP GARDNER, Private Eye in THE CASE OF THE JITTERY PATIEN

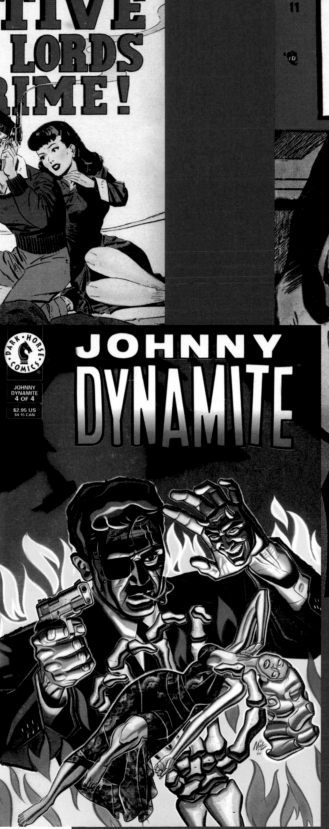

BOY DETECTIVE #2

Comic book
1951

Every boy's dream—a gat
and a long-legged doll!

JOHNNY DYNAMITE #4

Comic book
1994
Mitch O'Connell

A revival/revision of *Dynamite*,
adding elements of horror,
appeared in the 1990s.

JOHNNY DYNAMITE #11

Comic book
1955
Pete Morisi

Johnny Dynamite was the toughest
and best of the 1950s P.I.s.

Department of Hospitals. In that role, Wertham founded the La Fargue Clinic to deliver free psychiatric services in New York's inner city (Harlem) in 1946.

There, Wertham counseled children with a history of violent criminal behavior; there, for the first time, he was exposed to crime comics. Wertham believed in the innate goodness of his charges and felt that their violence stemmed from social conditions around them, including violence in the media, most specifically comic books whose easy reading levels made them very accessible to young children.

Possibly Wertham considered comic books an easier target than poverty. Nonetheless, Wertham was a skilled writer and organizer—a mental health professional who had been active in numerous civil rights and health campaigns. His articles deftly intertwined case histories of the troubled children he counseled and the gruesome crimes they had committed with equally gruesome examples of gory and sadistic stories from comic books. For many comic-book collectors, his book *Seduction of the Innocent*—a national best seller and Book of the Month Club selection—serves as an unwitting guidebook to finding the most extreme examples of sex and violence in early 1950s comics.

Wertham didn't just write: He worked with New York and other legislatures to create laws to control the sale and distribution of crime comics to children. He assisted hundreds of PTAs and women's groups in organizing anti-crime comic crusades in their communities. Finally, the proactive psychiatrist helped convince the Senate in 1954 to broaden its investigations from organized crime into juvenile delinquency, including the role crime comics had in creating young criminals.

That Wertham's young charges had often grown up in a climate of poverty, neglect, and often extreme physical abuse was largely ignored. Mainstream Americans, who normally thought of comic books as Mickey Mouse, Archie, and patriotic superheroes, were shocked to learn that comics were just as likely to include scenes of torture by hot pokers, syringes in the eyeball, and graphic examples of cannibalism...not to mention scantily clad damsels who were often the subject of the above.

Faced with national pressure, local boycotts, lost sales, and potential legislation, comic-book publishers set up the Comics Code Authority—a private independent regulatory agency that still screens comic books before they are published. The original code set strict guidelines that included banning the words "crime," "terror," and "horror" from comic-book titles. Within a few months, all crime and private eye titles disappeared from the market, and by 1960 all that remained were a number of tame minor back-up series, like *Roy Raymond, TV Detective*, in *Detective Comics*.

Two publishers—Classics Illustrated and Dell Comics (the majority of whose comics were licensed funny animals and TV series)—refused to sign the code. Classic's mystery adaptations stayed in print, and Dell became the sole source for occasional private eye and mystery comics—most often based on such popular TV shows as *Burke's Law*, *77 Sunset Strip*, and *Peter Gunn*. The latter were tamer not only than their 1950s predecessors, but even the shows and movies from which they were adapted.

In the 1960s and early 1970s several small companies took advantage of a certain loophole—the Comics Code only covered full-color fare—and published magazine-size black-and-white crime and horror comics, like *Crime Machine* and *Murder Tales*. Some contained new stories, others reprints of 1950s stories, and occasional English-language editions of gruesome adult Mexican or Spanish comic books.

The 1960s also saw the development of a collectors' market for old comic books. Used bookstores that traditionally sold back-issue comics at half-cover price were soon placing them in plastic bags and moving them inside glass display cases, with prices up to hundreds of dollars for older, rarer issues. The market became so big that stores specializing in old comics opened in many major cities. These stores often wanted to carry new comics as well.

Comic-book fan Phil Seuling dealt with the major publishers and set up a distribution system that sold new comics directly to comic-book stores on a non-returnable basis. One of the limitations originally faced by comic-book stores was the difficulty in finding enough back issues to sell. With access to new comics, that barrier was removed. The number of comic-book stores mushroomed in the 1970s and early 1980s.

PETER SCRATCH

Comic strip
1966

Artist Lou Fine had lost all of his celebrated detailed fantasy linework by the time he did this gritty *noir* detective comic strip.

NERO WOLFE

Comic strip
March 21, 1957
Mike Roy

Nero Wolfe went through three artists in its first and probably only year of syndication.

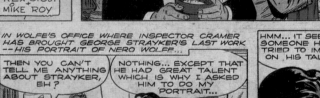

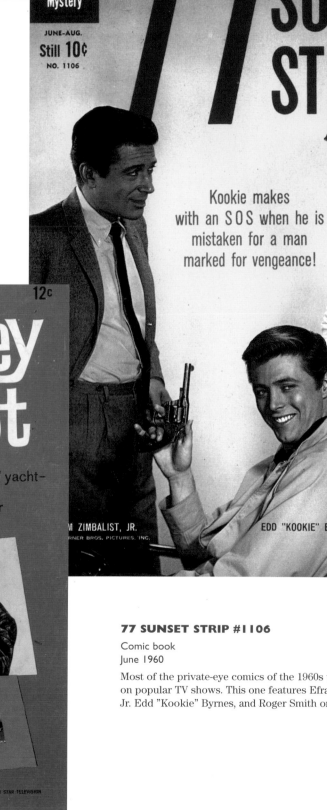

HONEY WEST #1

Comic book
1966

Dell produced most of the TV-related comics. Here's Anne Francis, perfect as P.I. Honey West.

77 SUNSET STRIP #1106

Comic book
June 1960

Most of the private-eye comics of the 1960s were based on popular TV shows. This one features Efram Zimbalist, Jr. Edd "Kookie" Byrnes, and Roger Smith on its cover.

As the comic-book store market grew, a number of writers, artists, and small publishers decided to make an end run around major newsstand comic-book companies, most of whom were restricted by the comics code. Thousands of comics could be sold on a lower risk nonreturnable basis through the direct-sale market. While science fiction and superheroes still predominated in the offerings of these new publishers, mystery writer Max Allan Collins—author of this book—and artist Terry Beatty convinced Eclipse Comics to publish *Ms. Tree*.

One of the first of the new wave of hardboiled female private eyes, Ms. Michael Tree was the daughter of a hardboiled LA cop; she inherited her husband's agency when he was killed, and her first case was to solve his murder. The series enjoyed a cult following and became the longest continually published comic book about a private eye created specifically for the medium. A hardboiled series in the Mickey Spillane mold, *Ms. Tree* ran sixty issues and outlived several of its publishers.

In spite of the new flexibility offered by the direct-sales market, few mystery comics were offered, and many of the titles that did appear were—like the 1950s variety—more often crime-oriented than focused on private eyes or amateur sleuths. *The Maze Agency*, created by former *Batman* writer Mike Barr, appeared five years after *Ms. Tree*, and again featured a female private eye, though the stories were in more an Ellery Queen style. In the 1990s, the sleuth that started the 1950s revival returned, as *Mickey Spillane's Mike Danger* reappeared for a two-year run in a series of private-eye stories mixed with science fiction.

The 1990s also saw the publication of numerous European and Japanese detective and crime comics and graphic novels. DC comics created its adult Paradox Press and Vertigo line, offering several crime and detective graphic novels and mini-series including adult revivals of *Johnny Double* and *The Human Target*. Independent publishers like Cleveland's Joe Zabel and Gary Dumm also periodically publish mystery comic books. While still a small section of the comics market, private-eye and amateur-detective comics entered the twenty-first century alive if not quite well.

Batman

One comic-book detective—a costumed hero—has outlasted and outperformed them all: Batman, who first appeared in the May 1939 issue of *Detective Comics*. The feature was created by young Bob Kane, who signed *Batman* for years, though drawing relatively little of it, and never writing.

Wealthy Bruce Wayne grew up scarred from seeing his parents gunned down before his eyes. Having spent years training and studying, Wayne took the secret identity of Batman and made it his personal mission to wipe out crime. For almost a year, Batman single-handedly fought crime, until *Detective #38*, when Bruce Wayne took in a ward, Dick Grayson, a young aerialist whose experience mirrored Bruce's. Bruce, too, had seen his parents gunned down. Wayne trained the young man in the same manner as himself and Grayson assumed the identity of Robin, the Boy Wonder, Batman's partner. The feature, initially grim, took on a lighter touch with the kid sidekick aboard.

In January 1966, Batman moved into the arena of television, with Adam West and Burt Ward as the Caped Crusader and the Boy Wonder; though savaged by critics, the ABC show not only garnered a large audience, but increased sales of the comic book as well. Actors like Cesar Romero, Julie Newmar, Victor Buono, and dozens more lined up for the possibility of playing a villain on the popular series. Hardcore comic-book fans of several generations, however, tended to hate the show, because it spoofed a detective feature they took (perhaps too) seriously.

With this in mind, writer/artist Frank Miller rekindled interest in Batman with his gritty 1986 graphic novel, *The Dark Knight Returns*. Following Miller's schematic, Tim Burton brought Batman to the big screen in 1989 with Michael Keaton in the title role. Keaton reprised the role in 1992's *Batman Returns*, but was willingly replaced by Val Kilmer in 1995s *Batman Forever*. The final episode in the series to date, *Batman and Robin*, featured George Clooney as the Caped Crusader and returned somewhat to TV's campy mode...angering purists and inspiring disappointing box office.

Batman should never be counted out, however...stay tuned... same Bat Time...same Bat Channel....

BATMAN ANNUAL #11
Comic book
1987

Most of the detecting, after the mid-1950s, was done by superheroes, most notably DC's Batman, the Dark Knight Detective.

MS TREE #34
Comic book
November 1986
Terry Beatty

The longest-running private-eye comic was Collins and Beatty's *Ms. Tree*.

Suchet's meticulous performance brings humanity and humor to the role. Ironically, the brilliant Suchet's first encounter with Poirot was as the sleuth's dull adversary, Inspector Japp, in a Ustinov "Poirot" TV movie, *Thirteen at Dinner* (1985).

Though Christie despised the films, a series of British-lensed, mid-1960s Miss Marple comedies starring the irrepressible Margaret Rutherord brought the spinster of St. Mary Mead into greater public awareness. More faithful screen Miss Marples have included Angela Lansbury (in a dry run for Jessica Fletcher) in 1980's fine *Mirror Crack'd*. In two unfortunate telefilms, Helen Hayes mugged shamelessly as the sleuth, but a BBC series (1985–1992), starring Joan Hickson, rivaled the Suchet *Poirot* in faithfulness and excellence.

MURDER ON THE ORIENT EXPRESS

Hardcover
1934

Christie invoked the Lindbergh kidnapping in this, Poirot's most famous case.

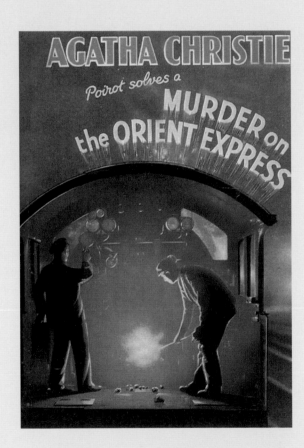

Commemorative program (back cover)
In 1983 Christie's record-breaking *The Mousetrap* celebrated its 30th year.

Agatha Christie

EVIL UNDER THE SUN

Hercule Poirot finds a quiet seaside hotel the setting for blackmail, voodoo and MURDER!

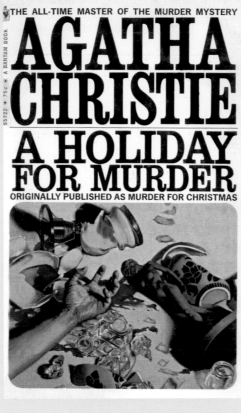

THE ALL-TIME MASTER OF THE MURDER MYSTERY

AGATHA CHRISTIE
A HOLIDAY FOR MURDER

ORIGINALLY PUBLISHED AS MURDER FOR CHRISTMAS

AGATHA CHRISTIE'S
MURDER ON THE ORIENT EXPRESS

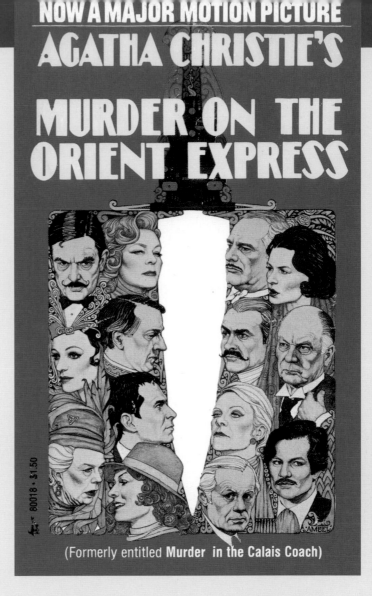

(Formerly entitled **Murder in the Calais Coach**)

Agatha Christie
The Big Four
featuring Hercule Poirot

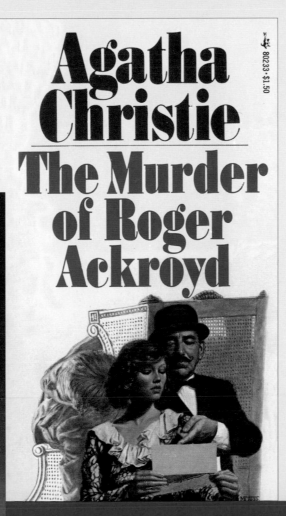

Agatha Christie
The Murder of Roger Ackroyd

EVIL UNDER THE SUN Paperback 1957	**MURDER ON THE ORIENT EXPRESS** Paperback 1975
A HOLIDAY FOR MURDER Paperback 1972	**THE MURDER OF ROGER ACKROYD** Paperback 1975
THE BIG FOUR Paperback 1978	

In paperback, Christie and Poirot bounced from eager publisher to eager publisher over the years. The 1957 Pocket Books edition of *Evil Under The Sun* sports a splendid sexy cover from James Meese (who also did Spillane covers!). The dramatic tableau of Bantam's *A Holiday For Murder* was typical of its era, but Mara McAfee's art for the 1975 Pocket Books edition of Christie's famous *The Murder Of Roger Ackroyd* depicts Poirot, who was starting to make his presence felt on the big screen. In 1978, Dell was back to striking designs (a format going back to the 1950s). But nothing could beat the movie poster art of the 1975 tie-in of *Murder On The Orient Express* by masterful Amsel.

APPOINTMENT WITH DEATH

Laserdisc
1996

After appearing in a trio of contemporary TV movies as Poirot, Peter Ustinov returned in 1930s period for a final big-screen mystery.

MURDER AHOY AND MURDER AT THE GALLOP

Laserdisc
1999

Christie disliked Margaret Rutherford's four mid-1960s Miss Marple films, but the public loved the venerated actress's outrageous mugging.

AGATHA

Laserdisc
1998

Agatha Christie's real-life disappearance in 1926, as her first marriage was breaking-up, was never addressed by the author. In 1979, this fictional film — directed by Michael Apted, starring Dustin Hoffman and (as Agatha) Vanessa Redgrave —provided a compelling, if fanciful, answer.

BLACK COFFEE

Hardcover
1998

Several posthumous Christie novels are actually Christie theater pieces novelized by Charles Osborne. BLACK COFFEE was Christie's only Poirot play.

THE WORLD OF AGATHA CHRISTIE

Hardcover
1999

Christie has inspired numerous books about her life and work. The cover of this one prominently features David Suchet, possibly the definitive Poirot.

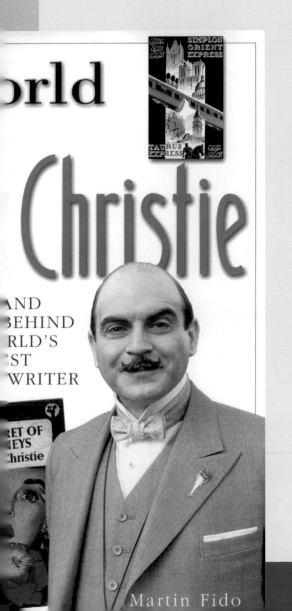

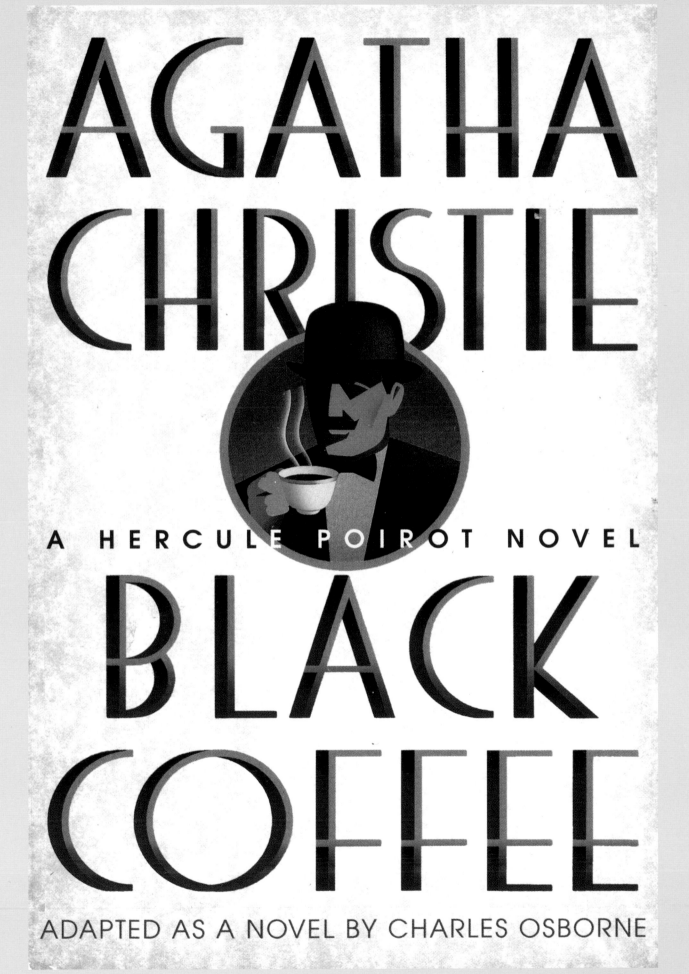

DILETTANTE DETECTIVES

Dupin's Descendants

From Miss Marple to Jessica Fletcher, from the Saint to Scooby Doo, the amateur sleuth comes in all shapes, sizes, ages, occupations, and social strata. No matter what these unpaid sleuths do to make their real living, their perilous avocation is the engine of their existence. And whomever they might visit while on vacation, or whatever other circumstance they might find themselves in, one thing is certain: wherever our favorite amateur sleuths turn up, somebody is going to get murdered. Try as they might, these greenhorn gumshoes cannot avoid homicide…and, despite their protestations, that's just how they like it. Amateur sleuths are forever stepping right in the middle of an unsolved mystery, and — as the great Maxwell Smart said — loving it. • They themselves represent a mystery of sorts. What is an amateur sleuth? The amateur is sometimes difficult to separate from his or her professional counterpart. Though many of these characters seem to do nothing but solve mysteries — and some are independently wealthy and can afford devoting their lives to their homicidal hobby — they are not primarily professional investigators. That is, they do not derive their incomes from the solving of crimes. • Poe's C. Auguste Dupin, Jacques Futrelle's Professor Augustus S.F.X. Van Dusen, and even retired

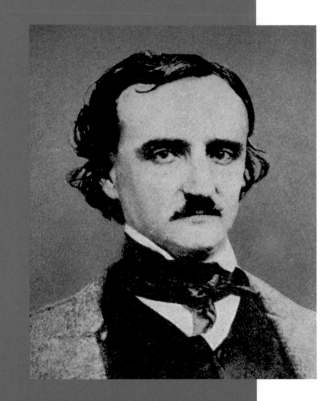

EDGAR ALLAN POE

Daguerreotype

The dignified, mysterious persona of Edgar Allan Poe makes him a fitting father to the detective story.

JACQUES FUTRELLE

Frontispiece photo
1909

THE DIAMOND MASTER

Hardcover
1909

Jacques Futrelle's non-Thinking Machine story, *The Diamond Master*, has elements of science fiction. Had he survived the Titanic tragedy, Futrelle might have endured as more than just an interesting foot-note in the genre.

professional detectives like Agatha Christie's Hercule Poirot and Dashiell Hammett's Nick Charles fall into this category. Contemporaries of these characters, Sherlock Holmes, Nero Wolfe, and Sam Spade are true private detectives and will be discussed later. Just deciding into which category our favorite fictional sleuths fit—amateur or professional—is a mystery not always easily solved. For the sake of discussion, lines had to be drawn...sometimes, somewhat arbitrarily.

That said, let's take another brief look at where the genre began. In 1841, when C. Auguste Dupin made his memorable first appearance in "The Murders in the Rue Morgue," life in both America and Europe was considerably different than today. Not only did a vast gulf exist between rich and poor, but between the literate and illiterate. Nearly a quarter of the American people were still unable to read, most of those in the lower-income brackets.

Hardcover books were purchased by well-educated, affluent readers; and the middle-class, themselves a fairly well-educated group, borrowed books from libraries. The settings for many mysteries were the very places that well-off readers frequented, and their environments represented a life style to which middle-class readers aspired. These drawing-room murders were among the upper crust, and so were the detectives who solved them. The fact that the caste system was so much in evidence also played a role in why the detectives in these stories were so seldom representatives of the police.

Though they depended on the police to protect their belongings and keep them safe, many of the rich looked down upon such common public servants as mere working men doing a dirty job. When it came to the art of detection, many times the police in these stories are made out to be inept bumblers, only a half-step above the criminals they seem unable to catch.

Although Dupin lives in poverty, the reader is made immediately aware that the great sleuth had suffered "untoward events" and, in fact, hailed from "an illustrious family." Even poverty, however, could not keep Dupin in check, by visiting the scene of the crime, reading accounts of the case, and deducing what really happened to the pair of women in the locked room, Dupin cleared an acquaintance accused of the murders and managed to show his clear disrespect for the police along the way.

After Dupin opened the door, many a disdainful detective slipped through after him. Among the more famous of these was Professor Augustus S. F. X. Van Dusen, known as "The Thinking Machine." Hardly a strapping physical specimen, the multi-degreed Van Dusen flaunted his mental capabilities to the point of arrogance. Although he first appeared briefly in *The Chase of the Golden Plate* in 1906, Van Dusen garnered far greater attention starring in the 1907 anthology, *The Thinking Machine*. A story from that collection, "The Problem of Cell 13," has become one of the most anthologized of all mystery stories. Only one other Thinking Machine collection, *The Thinking Machine on the Case* (1909), appeared before Van Dusen's creator, American Jacques Futrelle, went down aboard the *Titanic* in 1912, taking advance foreign royalty payments and several new Thinking Machine stories with him. Two more collections, *Best Thinking Machine Stories* (1973) and *Great Cases of the Thinking Machine* (1976), inspired a mild resurgence in interest in both Futrelle and his impressive creation.

Considered among the most scientifically accurate of the "thinking" detectives, R. Austin Freeman's Dr. John Evelyn Thorndyke was introduced in 1907's *The Red Thumb Mark*. Both physician and barrister, Thorndyke still found time to solve crimes with the assistance of his "biographer," Dr. Christopher Jervis, and his assistant, Nathaniel Polton. The trio lived at 5A Kings Beach Walk in a house that also held Thorndyke's considerable lab. Thorndyke always carried with him a smaller version of the lab in a green case.

Little read today, the series ran for thirty-five years, gaining popularity in both Britain and the United States. In a Thorndyke short story, "The Case of Oscar Brodsky," Freeman was credited with inventing what has become known as the "inverted" mystery, a story in which the reader knows who the killer is from the beginning and the question becomes not whodunit but how the perpetrator would be apprehended. (A modern example of this is the *Columbo* television series created by the gifted, award-winning team, Richard Levinson and William Link in their failed play, *Prescription: Murder*, filmed in 1967.)

Following Dr. Thorndyke was Dr. Lancelot Priestley. Created by John Rhode (pseudonym of Major Cecil John Charles Street), the doctor made his first appearance in *The Paddington Mystery* (1925).

In that debut volume, the former mathematics professor cleared a man named Harold Merefield of a false murder charge, after which Merefield married the doctor's daughter and stayed on to be Priestley's assistant. Hinging cases on obscure scientific facts (not unlike Thorndyke), Dr. Priestley's thirty-six year career included seventy-two books, making him one of the longest-running characters in the genre. Rhode also had success writing the Desmond Merrion series as Miles Burton. That series, beginning in 1930, ran for thirty years and included nearly sixty books. Merrion, a private eye, frequently teamed up with Scotland Yard's Inspector Henry Arnold.

Nigel Strangeways, also very much a thinking detective, was created by distinguished poet/novelist Cecil Day-Lewis, writing as Nicholas Blake. An Oxford graduate, Strangeways frequently solved cases for Inspector Blount of Scotland Yard, among others. The series began with 1935's *Question of Proof* and ran through 1966's *The Morning After Death*. In all, Strangeways starred in sixteen novels and the detective aged naturally over the course of the series, something some of his contemporaries managed to avoid. Day-Lewis is also remembered as the father of actor Daniel Day-Lewis.

Enter Philo Vance

Debuting in 1926 in *The Benson Murder Case*, S. S. Van Dine's Philo Vance proved to be both resourceful and detestable. Willard Huntington Wright hid his identity by writing the books under the name of Vance's chronicler, fictional New York lawyer S. S. Van Dine, and the latter stood mute as Vance outwitted—then punished—the criminals. Through eleven novels, the sidekick never spoke, making him the genre's most passive Watson character. His job was merely to pass on to the reader the legend of Philo Vance.

With the introduction of talkies, Vance found a new home on the silver screen. Future "Thin Man" William Powell played the successful art critic who moonlighted solving murders for D. A. John Markham, and the Powell characterization—really, all of the screen Vances— proved less irritating than the character of the novels. In 1929, the second book in the series, *The "Canary" Murder Case*, became the first of three films to feature Powell.

In 1929 Basil Rathbone (pre-Sherlock Holmes) played Vance in *The Bishop Murder Case*. Though the last novel, *The Winter Murder*

Case, appeared in 1939, this didn't slow down Philo Vance. Sometimes turning the character into a standard private eye, Vance films continued through the end of World War II. José Ferrer portrayed Vance on radio in 1945, and Jackson Beck played him in 1948. Pretentious art critic Vance infuriated most who crossed his path, but his deductive abilities always kept him in demand.

S.S. Van Dine and his Philo Vance were a publishing phenomenon, and the lack of staying power these novels have displayed reveals the vagaries of popular culture and the winds of changing times. That an imitation of Vance—Ellery Queen—became an enduring character might reveal popular culture's capriciousness, if the Queen novels weren't so clearly superior to the Van Dines.

At the other end of the spectrum from the disdainful detective was E. C. Bentley's Philip Trent. In the wake of pretentious, brilliant amateur detectives, Bentley described his desire "to create a detective who was recognizable as a human being." An artist, Trent also found himself hired by British newspapers to investigate crimes on their behalf. Initially appearing in, ironically, *Trent's Last Case* (1913), the all-too-human detective fell in love with the leading suspect, also the widow of the deceased, and conducted an investigation that led him to the wrong conclusion.

Though intended as a satire, the novel showed the emotional depth that could be achieved within the genre and put forth not one but two possible solutions to the crime. Over the years, Trent appeared in three more novels, although there was a twenty-three-year lag between the first and second books. Three different screen adaptations were made of *Trent's Last Case*, in 1920, 1929, and 1952, the latter featuring Michael Wilding as Trent.

Clerical Collarers

A lifelong friend of Bentley's, G. K. Chesterton—although the eminent author of more than one hundred books—is probably best remembered as the creator of Father Brown. The priest and part-time detective debuted in 1910 in a short story, "The Blue Cross." The next year, the unassuming priest returned in a collection of a dozen cases, *The Innocence of Father Brown*.

Chesterton, describing his famous character, said, "His commonplace exterior was meant to contrast with his unexpected vigilance

and intelligence; and that being so, of course, I made his appearance shabby and shapeless, his face round and expressionless, his manners clumsy, and so on."

The umbrella-toting Father has proven so popular over time that besides the fifty or so stories of Chesterton's, the cleric has in addition appeared in movies (both Walter Connolly and Alec Guinness portraying the priest), a radio series, and a BBC television series in the 1970s with Kenneth More as Father Brown.

As for Chesterton, who died in 1936, not only is he remembered as a superior writer, but also as the inspiration for John Dickson Carr's Dr. Gideon Fell. Both Chesterton's appearance and manner were hijacked by Carr for his portly, mustachioed detective. Dr. Fell first appeared in 1933, in *Hag's Nook*.

Created because Carr desired writing about a "likable" detective, Dr. Fell starred in more than twenty books. Equally well-known under his pseudonym Carter Dickson, John Dickson Carr, master of the "locked room mystery," created no less than four well-respected detective characters: Dr. Fell and French police chief Henri Bencolin (writing under his own name); Colonel March (writing as Dickson); and Merrivale, a more comic detective, appearing in more than twenty books. In a career spanning some forty years, Carr garnered multiple Edgar awards from the Mystery Writers of America and in 1962 was named a Grand Master by that organization.

Chesterton certainly wasn't the only writer intrigued by the melding of religion and mystery. Like Chesterton's Father Brown, Harry Kemelman's amateur detective was also a man of the cloth. First appearing in 1964's Edgar-winning *Friday the Rabbi Slept Late*, Rabbi David Small served the synagogue in Barnard's Corner, Massachusetts. Rabbi Small received assistance from his wife, Rachel, and his police contact, the Catholic Chief of Police Hugh Lanigan. The series lasted twelve books, marching through the days of the week, with Small aging accordingly along the way, ending with *That Day the Rabbi Left Town* in 1996, the year Kemelman died. A short-lived 1977 TV series, *Lanigan's Rabbi*, played down the Judaism, shifted the setting to California, and gave the Irish cop top billing.

Also grounded in a religious setting is Ellis Peters's Brother Cadfael series. Though Peters (pseudonym for Edith Pargeter) first published in 1938, her famous character Brother Cadfael didn't

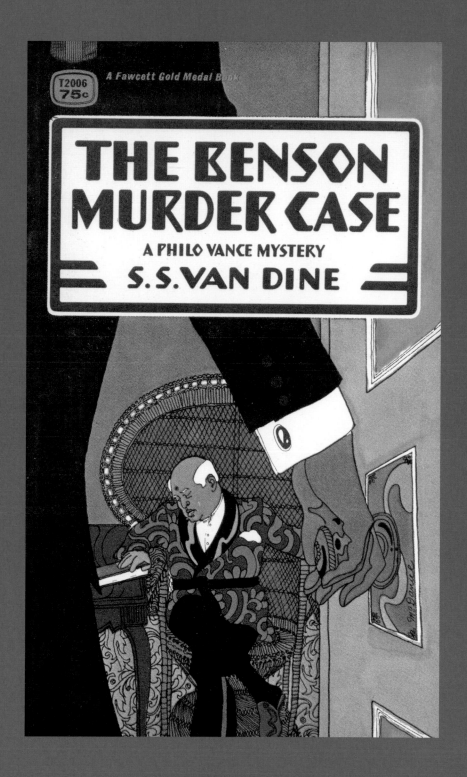

THE DRAGON MURDER CASE

Hardcover
1934

Van Dine felt that even the best mystery writers only had six good novels in them; *Dragon* was his seventh, and another five would follow, leading critics to agree with the author's assessment.

FOR THE DEFENCE, DR. THORNDYKE

Hardcover (British)
1934
Leslie Stead

Though Freeman—the inventor of the "inverted" mystery—was a leisurely, old-school writer, even Raymond Chandler admitted the Thorndyke yarns achieved "an even suspense that is quite unexpected."

THE BENSON MURDER CASE

Paperback
circa 1969

Despite this lovely Peter Max-ish deco cover, the effort by Gold Medal Books to introduce Philo Vance to a modern audience was, like all other such efforts to date, a failure.

TRENT'S LAST CASE

Paperback
1945

Journalist, poet and humorist Bentley's masterpiece received an evocative, typically deco Pocket Books cover by H. Lawrence Hoffman.

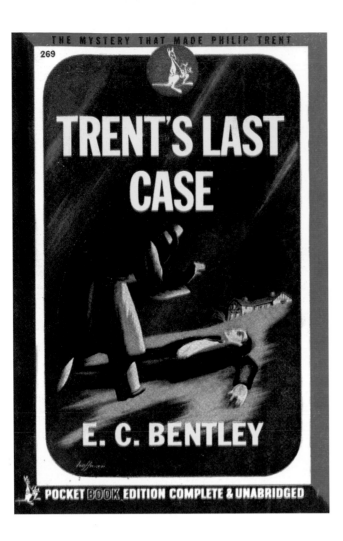

THE SCANDAL OF FATHER BROWN

Paperback
1967

Like too many ambitious writers who have occasionally "slummed" in mystery fiction, Chesterton's lasting literary works turn out to be his mysteries.

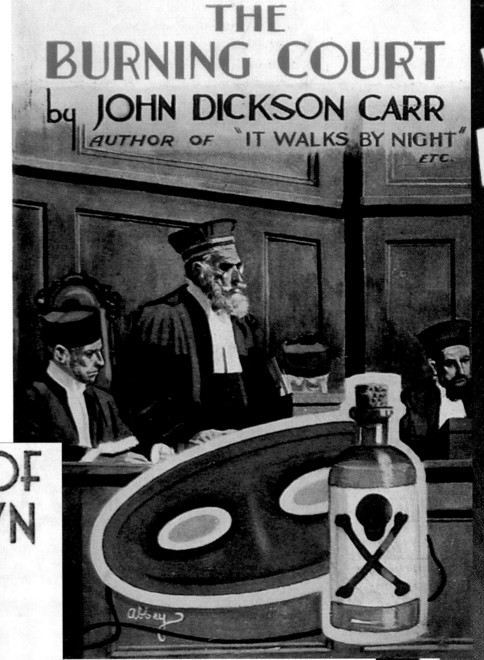

THE BURNING COURT

Hardcover (British)
1937

A master of historical detective fiction, John Dickson Carr occasionally ventured into the contemporary mystery, as in this particularly fine example. Cover art by J. Abbey.

NINE AND DEATH MAKES TEN

Paperback
1945

Another moody deco Pocket Books cover enlivens this Sir Henry Merrivale "impossible" mystery.

…INE ND DEATH MAKES TEN

Carter Dickson

POCKET BOOK

BOOK EDITION COMPLETE & UNABRIDGED

5

FIVE BEST AMATEUR SLEUTH TV SERIES

LORD PETER WIMSEY

ELLERY QUEEN

KOLCHAK: THE NIGHT STALKER

MURDER, SHE WROTE

THE SAINT

Compiled by John Javna and Max Allan Collins
from a survey of mystery writers and fans.

MURDER, SHE WROTE

Paperback

1996

Angela Lansbury (the erstwhile Mrs. Lovett
of *Sweeney Todd*) portrays a character equally
informed by Agatha Christie's Miss Marple
and Dame Agatha herself.

HARRY KEMELMAN

THE NINE MILE WALK

By the author of
**FRIDAY THE RABBI
SLEPT LATE**
and **SATURDAY THE
RABBI WENT HUNGRY**

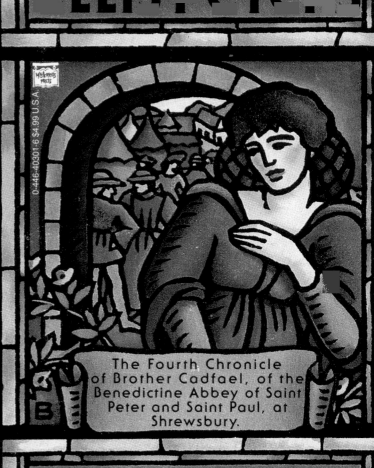

ELLIS PETERS

0-446-40301-6 $4.99 U.S.A.

The Fourth Chronicle
of Brother Cadfael, of the
Benedictine Abbey of Saint
Peter and Saint Paul, at
Shrewsbury.

ST. PETER'S FAIR

"Each addition to the series is a joy. Long
may the Chronicles continue." —USA Today

CHARTER | 75947-5 | $1.95

THE SEVENTH STATION

"His second novel
could be one of the ten or
twenty best crime novels anyone
will read this year...the man's a
winner" —*Washington Star*

THE NINE MILE WALK
Paperback
1968

ST. PETER'S FAIR
Paperback
1981

THE SEVENTH STATION
Paperback
1977

THE SAINT MAKER
Paperback
1961

A GENTLE MURDERER
Paperback
1982

DELL
R104

In the tradition of G.K. Chesterton's Father Brown, a superb mystery thriller

40c

THE SAINT MAKER

by Leonard Holton

The man (or woman) of faith who plays amateur sleuth has been an enduring sub-genre since Father Brown. Priests are the usual sleuths, but Kemelman's Rabbi David Small is one of the most successful. Ellis Peters's Brother Cadfael (so memorably portrayed on the PBS Mystery series starring Derek Jacobi) takes the sub-genre into history. The Father Dowling of Ralph McInery's popular series has little to do with the TV version; like many clerical sleuths, Dowling has a Watson in the form of a police detective. Leonard Holton's Father Breeder is well-depicted by artist Bob Abbett (abandoning the bosomy babes of his other mystery covers) on this paperback edition. The much-admired Dorothy Salisbury Davis—who admitted her success was hampered by her failure to develop a strong recurring character—came up with a masterful premise for Father Duffy, who must track down the murderer who confessed to him (pre-dating Hitchcock's *I Confess* by several years).

DOROTHY SALISBURY DAVIS

Author of A DEATH IN THE LIFE

AVON
60715
$2.50

A GENTLE MURDERER

"MASTERLY"
Saturday Review

A QUIET MAN CONFESSES TO A BRUTAL MURDER. THEN DISAPPEARS...PERHAPS TO KILL AGAIN.

enter the scene until 1977's *A Morbid Taste for Bones*. A twelfth-century Benedictine monk, Brother Cadfael was the herbalist at the monastery of St. Peter and St. Paul; over a seventeen-year run, he investigated cases in twenty novels and a volume of short stories. His last adventure, *Brother Cadfael's Penance*, appeared in 1994. Peters, an Edgar award winner for best novel and winner of both the Silver and Diamond Daggers presented by the British Crime Writers Association, passed away in 1995. Derek Jacobi portrayed the monk on television beginning in 1994.

William X. Kienzle, a former Detroit parish priest himself, began the series featuring Father Robert Koesler with 1979's *The Rosary Murders*. A mystery fan, Father Koesler touched on the methods of classic fictional detectives early in the series. Over twenty years and more than twenty books later, Kienzle still remains popular. A 1979 film of *The Rosary Murders* featured Donald Sutherland and Charles Durning.

Ralph McInerny, a Notre Dame University faculty member and a Fulbright Scholar in 1959, has two religion-themed detective series under his belt. Writing as Monica Quill, he has authored nine novels featuring Sister Mary Teresa Dempsey, better known either by her initials "Emtee" Dempsey or as "Attila the Nun." One of only three surviving sisters from the Order of Martha and Mary, Sister Mary Teresa lives in Chicago with Sisters Kim and Joyce. Together they solve mysteries as they attempt to add recruits to their Order. The series started in 1981 with *Not a Blessed Thing!* and has continued through 1997's *Half Past Nun*.

Far more famous is McInerny's other series, the Father Dowling mysteries, which premiered in 1977 with *Her Death of Cold*. Father Roger Dowling, a recovering alcoholic, worked in the Chicago suburb of Fox River and bore little resemblance to the Father Frank Dowling as portrayed by Tom Bosley on television, but whose origin was this series of more than a dozen novels. Father Dowling solved the cases and tried to deal with the soul of the perpetrator, while his police contact, Lieutenant Phil Keegan, an old seminary buddy, took it from there.

Leonard Holton created Father Joseph Bredder, a Los Angeles priest who occasionally assisted Lieutenant Minardi of the LAPD. The two knew each other because Father Bredder served as chaplain at the Convent of the Holy Innocent School where the lieutenant's daughter was a student. The series opened in 1959 with *The Saint Maker* and lasted for eleven books, the last in 1977. Holton was probably more famous under his real name, Leonard Wibberly, the author of The *Mouse That Roared* and *Mouse on the Moon*, source material for two well-known British comic films.

Though he leaves "Father" off the byline of his books, Andrew M. Greeley is still a priest, as is his detective Father John Blackwood "Blackie" Ryan, rector of Chicago's Holy Name Cathedral. Introduced in 1985's *Virgins and Martyrs*, Father Ryan has appeared in nearly a dozen more novels, including *Happy Are The Meek* (1985) and *Happy Are The Oppressed* (1996). A best-selling mainstream novelist, Greeley has enjoyed great popularity, as well as controversy, for the strong sexual content of his novels.

Boy (and Girl) Detectives

By the 1920s, the literacy rate in the United States had climbed to over ninety percent, and publishers began thinking about capturing mystery readers at a younger age. Edward Stratemeyer, owner of the Stratemeyer Syndicate, helped fill that void. In *The Tower Treasure* (1929), he introduced the trouble-shooting brother team of Frank and Joe Hardy, better known as the Hardy Boys.

Prolific Stratemeyer (creator of Tom Swift, the Bobbsey Twins, and other famed juvenile series) conceived the property, then turned it over to Canadian author Leslie McFarlane, who wrote the first sixteen volumes of the series. In all—including the second series, *The Hardy Boy Files*—the brothers have solved more than two hundred mysteries without ever finding time to grow up. The Hardy Boy novels are periodically updated to keep current with new generations of young readers; to Baby Boomers who grew up on the quaint, un-updated versions written for their parents' generation—complete with rumble seats and seamed stockings— this seems somehow blasphemy. The string also inspired four television series, notably the serialized adventures on the original mid-1950s version of *The Mickey Mouse Club* starring Tim Considine and Tommy Kirk.

Realizing he had a winning formula, Stratemeyer decided to create a girl's series to compliment the Hardy Boys. Thus was born Nancy

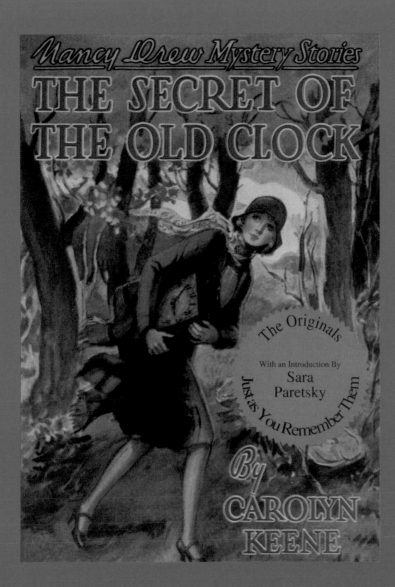

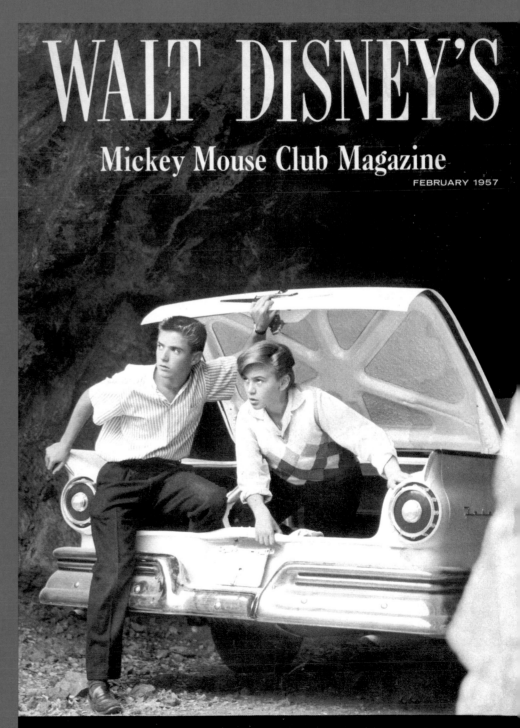

FURTHER ADVENTURES OF THE HARDY BOYS see page 18

THE SECRET OF THE OLD CLOCK

Hardcover
1991

The love of Baby Boomer readers for the vintage, un-updated Nancy Drew adventures led to facsimile editions of selected originals (like this 1930 entry) with introductions by top mystery writers, in this case Sara Paretsky.

WALT DISNEY'S MICKEY MOUSE CLUB MAGAZINE

Magazine
February 1957
Tommy Kirk as Joe Hardy and Tim Considine as Frank Hardy pose for illustrations in a fan club magazine adaptation of Franklin W. Dixon's *The Shore Road Mystery*.

Drew. Since her debut in 1930's *The Secret of the Old Clock*, Ms. Drew has aged from sixteen to eighteen. After Stratemeyer passed away in 1930, the series was turned over to his daughter, Harriet Adams, who controlled the property until her own death in 1982. Simon and Schuster purchased the syndicate in 1984.

In recent years, two other series have developed, *Nancy Drew on Campus*—featuring a college freshman Nancy on the campus of Wilder University with her two best friends Bess Marvin and Georgia Fayne—and *The Nancy Drew Notebooks*, a series aimed at beginning readers, featuring an eight-year-old Nancy as she investigates her first cases.

The daughter of a lawyer, whose cases are the inspiration of many of meddling Nancy's adventures, Nancy has solved more than three hundred cases thus far. As with the Hardy Boys books, unfortunate updatings of the text have robbed the original novels of their nostalgia. Movie and TV versions of Nancy have never matched the success of the books, though a quartet of B-movies starring Bonita Granville in the late 1930s was good, low-budget fun. A 1977 series

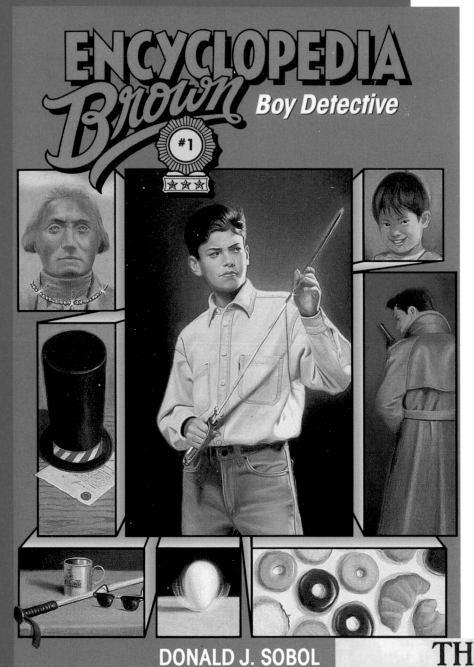

DONALD J. SOBOL

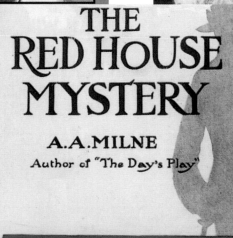

ENCYCLOPEDIA BROWN

Trade paperback
1994

How many lifelong mystery fans have been born thanks to the efforts of Don Sobol and his young sleuth, Encyclopedia Brown? Cover art copyright by Eric Velasques.

THE RED HOUSE MYSTERY

Hardcover
1922

The celebrated creator of Winnie the Pooh wrote a single mystery, once considered to be one of the top three ever written. Cover art by Frank Wright.

DIGITAL DETECTIVES MYSTERIES

Trade paperback
2000

A new generation of readers will be gained for the genre by such inventive, well-packaged Internet/interactive mysteries as these. Cover illustration copyright Mike Harper.

THE EX-MRS. BRADFORD

Laserdisc
1991

The success of MGM's *Thin Man*, derived from Hammett's novel and starring William Powell and Myrna Loy, led to imitations—including several starring Powell himself (like this 1936 effort), nudging MGM into turning Nick and Nora into the stars of what became a long-running series.

paired up both of Stratemeyer's famous teen detectives: *The Hardy Boys/Nancy Drew Mysteries*, remembered today (if at all) for the fuss when *Playboy* magazine ran a nude spread on fetching Nancy Drew, Pamela Sue Martin.

Like *The Nancy Drew Notebooks*, *Encyclopedia Brown* is aimed at very young readers. Created by Donald Sobol in 1963, ten-year-old Leroy "Encyclopedia" Brown has solved over two hundred cases, many in collaboration with his father, the chief of Idaville's Police Department. That first book, *Encyclopedia Brown, Boy Detective*, set the stage for a career that has lasted more than thirty years. Written at a third-grade level, each mystery can be solved through careful reading of the stories.

Launched in 1969, Scooby Doo and his pals in the Mystery Machine—Freddy, Daphne, Velma, and the irrepressible Shaggy—drove around solving, and debunking, paranormal activities long before *The X-Files* began the search for Mulder's sister. *Scooby Doo, Where Are You?* ran through 1971 then found new life recently on the Cartoon Network. Even the youngest viewer could figure out the mysteries without a great deal of difficulty. But one thing was sure—Shaggy would do almost anything for a Scooby snack. Discerning viewers might find these cartoons crude and clumsy, but many a kid has learned to love mysteries from this bewilderingly beloved series.

With the invention of the Internet, the trend to woo young mystery readers has continued. Jay Montavon's *Digital Detective Mysteries: The Case of the Killer Bugs* has turned juvenile mystery reading interactive. In this series, the reader joins in the investigation by going online to study clues at the Digital Detectives Website, giving the reader the opportunity to study the crime scene, interrogate witnesses, and actually accuse the suspect of the crime.

The idea was, and still is, hook the readers as kids, keep them as adults.

Wives and Lovers

After the success of Hammett's *The Thin Man* in 1934, husband-and-wife detective teams began appearing in print with some regularity. Because Hammett had not pursued a series of Nick and Nora Charles novels—although he did contribute screen stories to the first few of the enormously popular MGM sequels—the field was wide open for pretenders...several of whom became very successful.

Photographer Jeff Troy and his ex-actress wife Haila—one of the first faux Nick and Nora teams—showed up in 1940's *Made Up to Kill*. And wouldn't you just know it, the Troys were constantly getting involved in murder cases. Written by Audrey and William Roos, writing as Kelley Roos, the series lasted for nine books in the 1940s, followed by one last novel in 1966's *One False Move*.

Francis Crane's couple, Pat and Jean Abbott, met in 1941's *The Turquoise Shop*. San Francisco detective Pat, on vacation in New Mexico, stopped to investigate a Southwestern crime with the help of comely Jean, who ran a souvenir shop. The couple stayed together, not marrying until the third book in the series, *The Yellow Violet*. The mysteries—like John D. MacDonald's more famous Travis McGee adventures—each contained a color in the title. For nearly a quarter of a century, including twenty-six books and three years on the Mutual Radio Network (*The Abbott Mysteries*), the couple bounced around the world, solving crimes.

Aside from Nick and Nora, however, the most successful married couple in mysteries had to be Pam and Jerry North. Created almost by accident by Frances and Richard Lockridge, the couple was developed for noncriminous humor pieces Richard did for *The New Yorker*. A few years later, as Frances struggled with a mystery novel, Richard proposed that the already-existing Norths might relieve her character problems. Helping her flesh out the plot led to their collaboration in 1940 on *The Norths Meet Murder*.

A year later, the Norths were on Broadway in a play written by Owen Davis, followed by a movie version thereof; William Post, Jr., and Gracie Allen portrayed the couple, then came a twelve-year span on the CBS and NBC radio networks, followed by a three-year television run with the same networks. The Lockridges kept the series alive with twenty-six novels running through 1963.

British Invasion

Perhaps second only to Christie among women writers of the period was Dorothy L. Sayers. Many fans consider her a giant of the genre, and few doubt that Sayers as a wordsmith was superior to Christie.

Her creation, Lord Peter Wimsey, debuted in 1923 in *Whose Body?*, a case brought to him by his mother. Considered by many to be the love of Sayers's life, Lord Peter is equal parts gentleman, stunt man, and detective. The match of any task set before him, Lord Wimsey appeared in eleven novels and numerous short stories; in 1930's *Strong Poison*, the reader is introduced to Lord Peter's love interest, Harriet D. Vane. Not surprisingly, the heroine is a veiled reference to Sayers herself.

Two big-screen adaptations of Wimsey preceded an excellent TV series of serialized adaptations of the original novels for the BBC, with Ian Carmichael portraying the seemingly bored, actually alert sleuth. Carmichael's whimsical Wimsey offended some Sayers purists—the comic actor was not the tall, slender, athletic protagonist of the novels, after all—but it remains a classic performance, and the series of serials (aired in America on *Masterpiece Theater* in the mid-1970s) set the tone for what would become the much-loved PBS series, *Mystery*.

Not far removed from Lord Wimsey was H. C. Bailey's Reggie Fortune, a London physician referred to (in the British tradition) as Mr. Fortune, not Dr. Fortune. *Call Mr. Fortune*, a 1920 collection of short stories, served as his introduction. Intuitive and blessed with what Bailey referred to as an "old-fashioned sense of right and wrong, of sin and punishment," Mr. Fortune, like Wimsey and several others of the British aristocratic school, never seemed short of funds. Reggie's last adventure, *Saving a Rope*, appeared in 1948.

A rougher variant of this school is Hugh "Bulldog" Drummond, a former British Army officer who seeks adventure after the end of his service. The character's debut bore the unlikely title *Bull-dog Drummond: The Adventures of a Demobilised Officer Who Found Peace Dull* (1920). The hyphen disappeared almost immediately, and the adventures of this proto-James Bond continued. Though an amateur, Drummond is a two-fisted, hardboiled type.

Sapper (the pseudonym of H. C. McNeile) created Drummond and continued writing the series until his death in 1937, when a dear friend, Gerard Fairlie, took over. Along with the long-running series of novels, Drummond appeared in a Mutual Radio Network show for seven years and a long series of films, both British and American, that saw actors as diverse as Ralph Richardson, Ronald Colman, Ray Milland, and Richard Johnson portraying the wily adventurer.

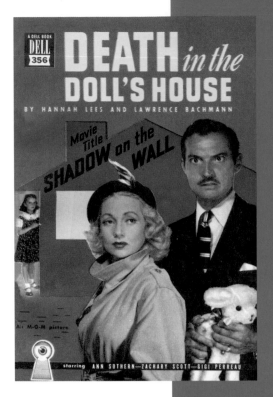

DEATH IN THE DOLL'S HOUSE

Paperback
1950

Among many *Thin Man* imitations was *Shadow On The Wall*, starring Ann Southern and Zachary Scott; this is a movie tie-in edition of the original source, *Death In The Doll House* (1943) by Hannah Lees and Lawrence Bachman.

HAVING WONDERFUL CRIME

Hardcover
1945

Jake and Helene Justus were one of the most popular Nick and Nora knockoffs, sleuthing in tandem with lawyer John J. Malone in wacky, wildly popular novels from 1940s superstar Craig Rice (Georgiana Ann Randolph). This is a movie edition of Rice's 1943 original.

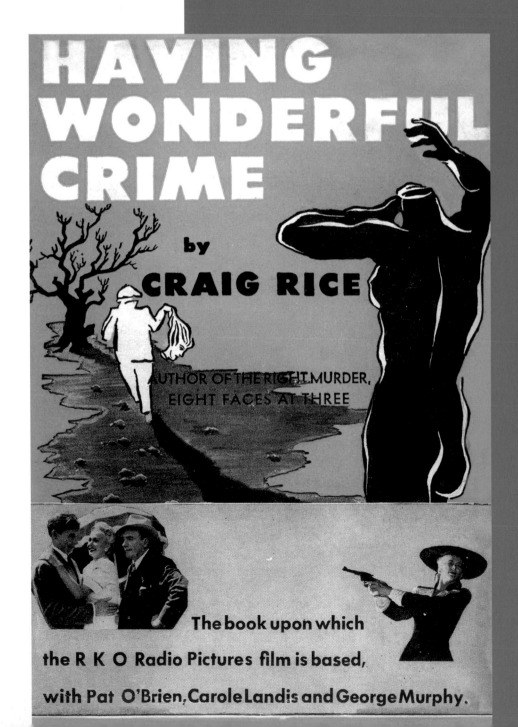

CLOUDS OF WITNESS

Hardcover (British)
1926

Over the course of eleven novels and twenty-one short stories, Sayers—so infatuated with her sleuth she later essentially wrote herself in as his sweetheart—developed Wimsey from a shallow socialite into a full-blooded character. Cover art by J. Abbey.

MURDER MUST ADVERTISE

Paperback
1967

Ian Carmichael's Wimsey appeared in BBC adaptations of *Clouds Of Witness*, *The Unpleasantness At The Belona Club*, *The Nine Tailors*, *The Five Red Herrings*, and (witness this tie-in edition) *Murder Must Advertise*, which drew upon Sayers's background in advertising.

BULLDOG DRUMMOND

VHS Tape
1996

Ronald Colman played Hugh Drummond twice on the big screen; John Howard appeared in a long-running Paramount 1930s series, many entries of which co-starred John Barrymore as a Scotland Yard inspector.

**THE SAINT AND THE
SIZZLING SABOTEUR**

Paperback
1958

**THE SAINT AROUND
THE WORLD**

Paperback
1958

**THE SAINT CLOSES
THE CASE**

Paperback
1963

Like Sherlock Holmes, Leslie Charteris's the Saint was both amateur sleuth and hardboiled dick; the Saint's American adventures—like *Sizzling Saboteur*—especially tended toward the tough. A James Meese cover dresses up the Saint's *Around The World* short-story collection, which includes a poignant last appearance from Simon Templar's perennial police adversary, Inspector Teal. Roger Moore—future movie James Bond—appeared on numerous tie-in paperback editions during the 118-episode run of the *Saint* TV series.

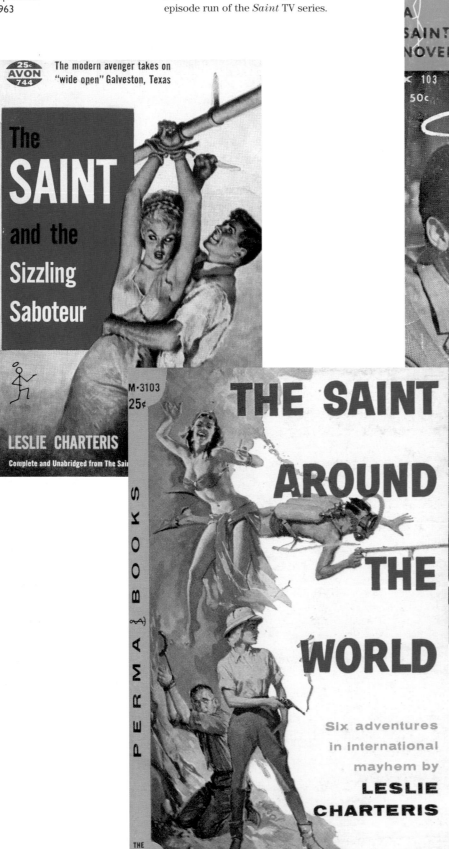

THE LONE WOLF

Paperback
1952

The Lone Wolf—another gentleman thief in the Raffles/Saint mold—appeared in eight novels by Joseph Lewis Vance. Numerous Lone Wolf films were made, including a lengthy Warren William-starring series starting in 1939. Vance coined the "lone wolf" term, now a part of our language.

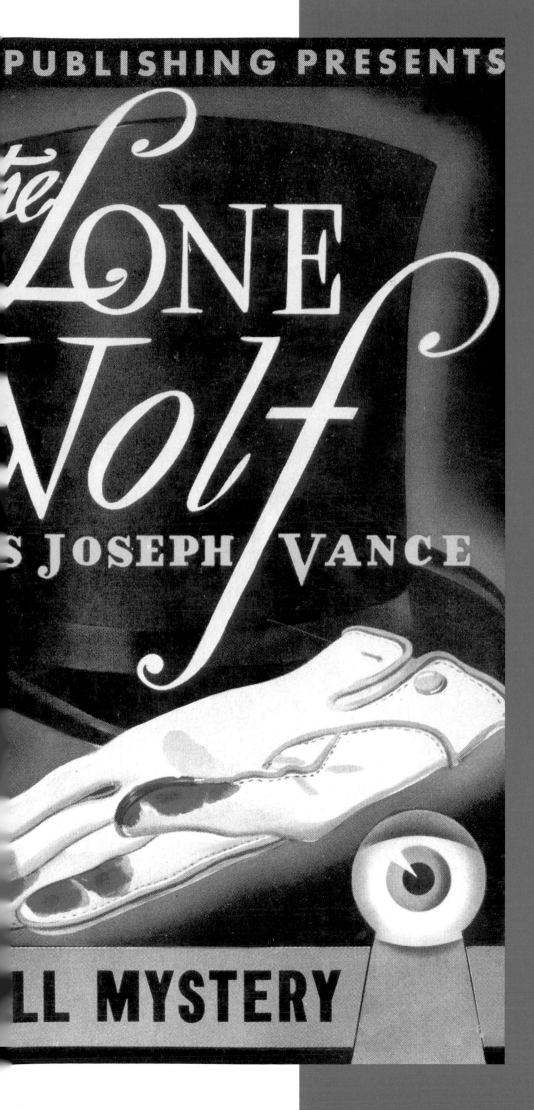

PUBLISHING PRESENTS

The LONE Wolf

AS JOSEPH VANCE

LL MYSTERY

Detecting Criminals

Also jumping into the ring as a less cerebral, more physical two-fisted adventure-seeking sleuth was Simon Templar—the Saint. Leslie Charteris unleashed "the Robin Hood of Modern Crime" in 1928's *The Saint Meets the Tiger* (a k a *Meet the Tiger*). A veritable superman, Templar could fly (well, in a plane anyway), fight, shoot, not to mention being a master of disguise and an unparalleled thief. The Saint, though considered a criminal by the police, always seemed to be on the right side of the law when it came to ending the exploits of the real gangsters. An avenger who steals only from crooks, Templar often plays amateur sleuth, though his adventures are frequently as hardboiled as anything Hammett or Chandler might have dreamed up.

Templar first appeared on film in 1938: *The Saint in New York* featured a well-cast Louis Hayward as Simon Templar, cleaning up crime in the Big Apple. The film was successful enough that RKO Studios contracted George Sanders—the smoothly villainous Sanders slightly miscast, particularly compared to the swashbuckling Hayward—to appear in a sequel. Sanders ended up appearing in five Saint films, carrying the series until 1941, before transferring to the rival, imitative Falcon series, much to Charteris's dismay. The Saint also appeared in various radio series from 1945 until 1950, notably a run with Vincent Price as Templar. In 1954 Louis Hayward returned for another spirited go round—*The Saint's Double Trouble*—but it was the last time Simon Templar would appear on film for quite some time.

Between 1962 and 1969 Roger Moore portrayed the Saint on television; scripts were often based on Charteris's real stories, though the criminous aspect of the character was watered down. One hundred eighteen episodes were shot, many in color, and the show catapulted Moore into his more famous role as James Bond. Several television failures followed, and the Saint seemed primed to disappear until he was resurrected on film one last time (to date, anyway) in an underrated 1997 outing with Val Kilmer in the title role.

Though he was a criminal who solved crimes, the Saint was not the first thief-turned-detective. Created by Conan Doyle's brother-in-law, E. W. Hornung, safecracker extraordinaire A. J. Raffles first appeared in *The Amateur Cracksman* (1899). Hornung wrote about

25

TWENTY-FIVE GREAT AMATEUR DETECTIVE NOVELS

MARGARY ALLINGHAM	*Death of a Ghost (1934)*
E.C. BENTLEY	*Trent's Last Case (1913)*
ANTHONY BERKLEY	*The Poisoned Chocolates Case (1929)*
NICHOLAS BLAKE	*The Beast Must Die (1938)*
ANTHONY BOUCHER AS H.H. HOLMES	*Rocket to the Moon (1942)*
SIMON BRETT	*So Much Blood (1976)*
JOHN DICKSON CARR	*The Crooked Hinge (1938)*
AGATHA CHRISTIE	*The ABC Murders (1936)*
CLYDE B. CLASON	*The Man from Tibet (1938)*
EDMUND CRISPIN	*Bured for Pleasure (1948)*
HARRY KEMMELMAN	*Friday the Rabbi Slept Late (1964)*
EMMA LATHEN	*Accounting for Murder (1964)*
FRANCES AND RICHARD LOCKRIDGE	*The Norths Meet Murder (1940)*
STUART PALMER	*The Penguin Pool Murder (1931)*
ELIZABETH PETERS	*Crocodile on the Sandbank (1975)*
ELLIS PETERS	*A Morbid Taste for Bones (1977)*
ELLERY QUEEN	*Cat of Many Nine Tails (1949)*
PATRICK QUENTIN	*A Puzzle for Fools (1936)*
CLAYTON RAWSON	*The Headlines Lady (1940)*
KATE ROSS	*The Devil in Music (1997)*
DOROTHY L. SAYERS	*The Nine Tailors (1934)*
PHOEBE ATWOOD TAYLOR	*Banbury Bog (1938)*
S.S. VAN DINE	*The Canary Murder Case (1927)*
MARY WILLIS WALKER	*The Red Scream (1994)*
JAMES YAFFE	*A Nice Murder for Mom (1988)*

Selected by Jon L. Breen, mystery reviewer,
Ellery Queen Mystery Magazine

BLIND MAN'S BLUFF

Hardcover
1943

Baynard Kendrick's Dunclan Maclain started a sub-genre of blind detectives; Kendrick was instrumental in the founding of the Mystery Writers of America (he carried card #1). Cover art by E.H. Hart.

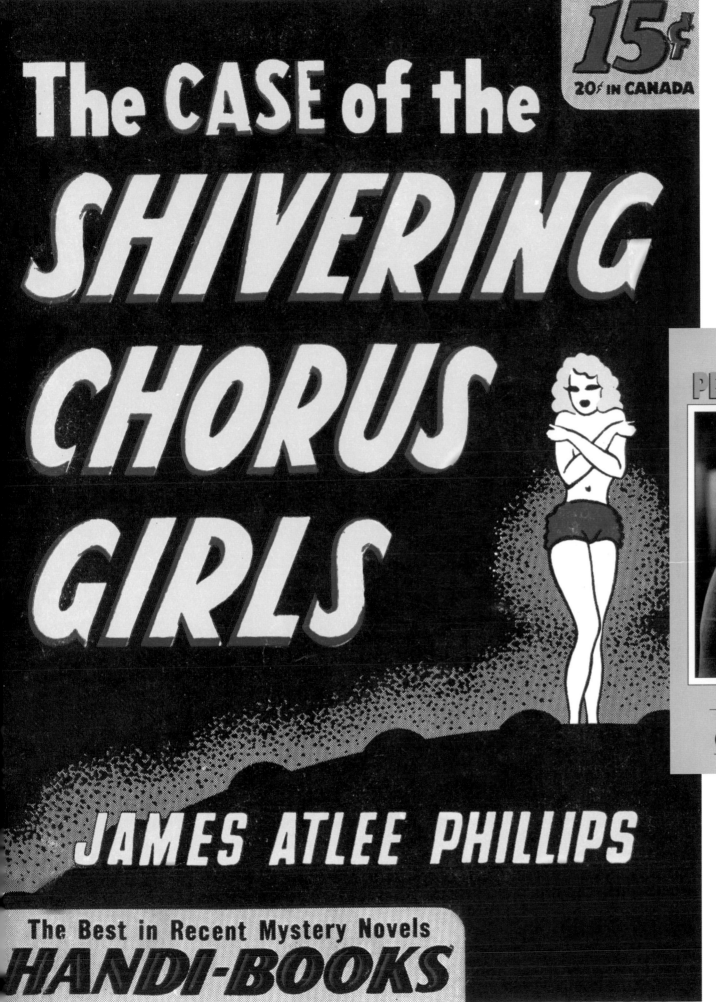

THE CASE OF THE SHIVERING CHORUS GIRLS

Paperback
1943

James Atlee Phillips combined elements of Kendrick's Maclain and Stout's Nero Wolfe in blind ex-ambassador Henry Morton Wardlaw. The author, as Phillip Atlee, had greater success with his long-running Gold Medal paperback original series about hardboiled spy, Joe Galt.

PENGUIN POOL MURDER

Laserdisc
1990

Edna May Oliver made a memorable Hildegarde Withers in this 1932 film from Stuart Palmer's novel. Palmer collaborated with Craig Rice on a series of stories involving his snoopy schoolmarm and Rice's skirt-chasing shyster, John J. Malone.

the Devil's Stronghold

Leslie Ford

A NEW COLONEL PRIMROSE MYSTERY

THE DEVIL'S STRONGHOLD

Hardcover
1948

Leslie Ford (pen name of Zenith Jones Brown) also wrote as David Frome. Her Colonel Primrose (technically a private eye) and his amateur sleuth partner, Grace Latham, were great favorites of readers of the *Saturday Evening Post*, where their adventures were often serialized.

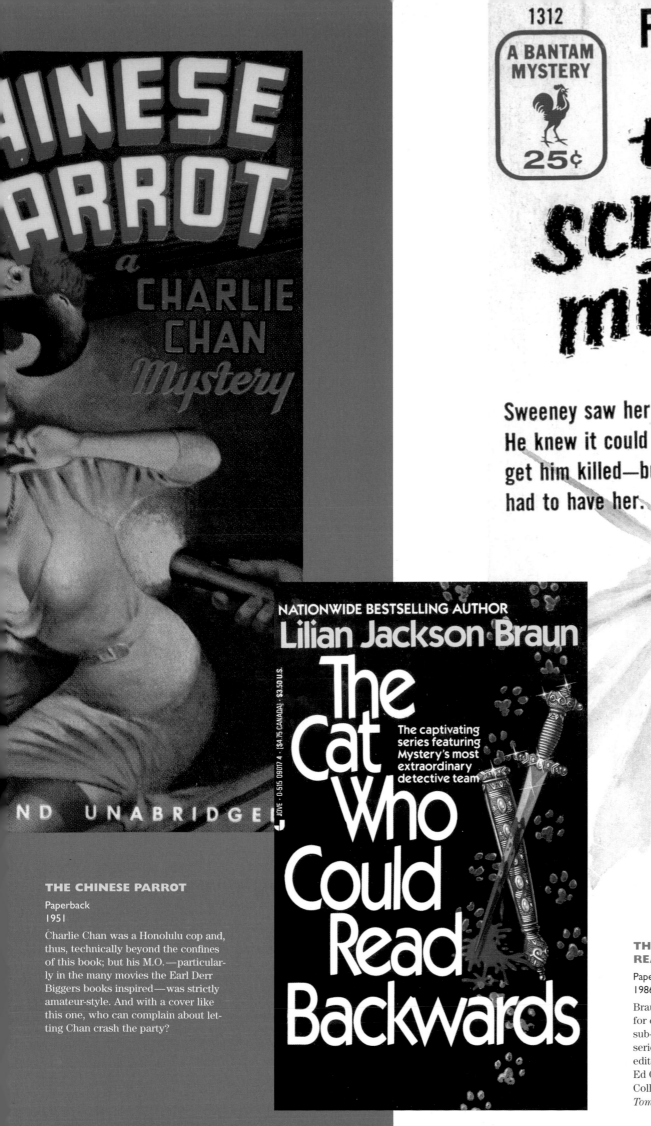

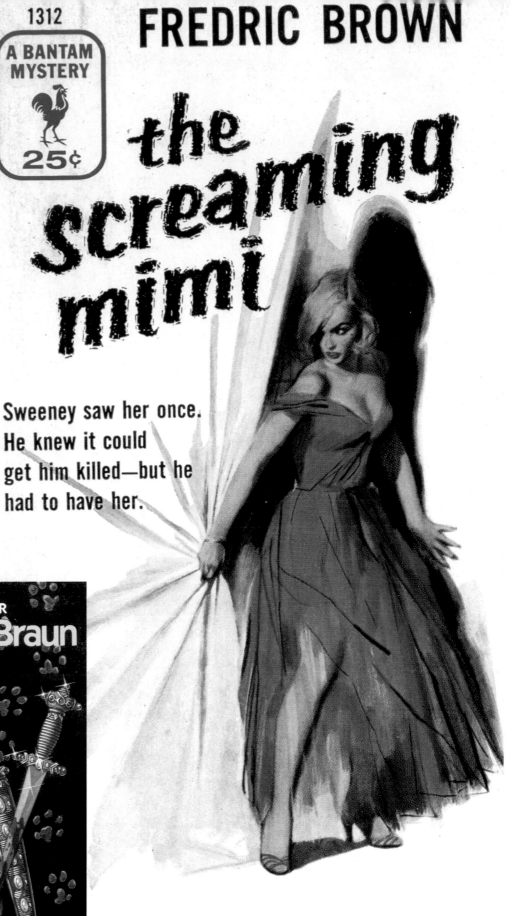

THE CHINESE PARROT

Paperback
1951

Charlie Chan was a Honolulu cop and, thus, technically beyond the confines of this book; but his M.O.—particularly in the many movies the Earl Derr Biggers books inspired—was strictly amateur-style. And with a cover like this one, who can complain about letting Chan crash the party?

THE CAT WHO COULD READ BACKWARDS

Paperback
1986

Braun ignited the enthusiasm for cat-oriented mysteries. The sub-genre includes a long- running series of *Cat Crimes* anthologies edited by Martin H. Greenberg and Ed Gorman, as well as Barbara Collins's collection, *Too Many Tomcats* (2000).

THE SCREAMING MIMI

Paperback
1955

Fredric Brown—master short-story writer—saw this reporter yarn made into a movie (1958). Famed for his science fiction, Brown also wrote a father-and-son P.I. series, Ed and Am Hunter.

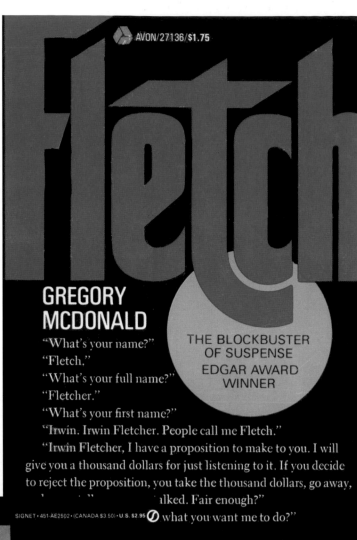

FLETCH

Paperback
1976

As good as McDonald's books are—and they are very good —the unique, modern cover design, highlighting the author's dialogue-driven style, had much to do with the initial success of the series.

TRACE

Paperback
1983

Though the publisher "borrowed" the *Fletch* cover concept, Trace and his Asian ex-hooker girlfriend are unique products of the wonderfully warped mind of Murphy, who also co-created the long-running *Destroyer* series.

the crime-solving thief through 1909. After the creator's death in 1921, the series was revived twice by Barry Perowne, first in the 1930s, bringing Raffles into that time period, then in the 1940s when Ellery Queen commissioned Perowne to again write about Raffles, this time in Hornung's original time period.

Raffles appeared in silent movies as early as 1905. John Barrymore portrayed the thief in 1917 and, in a 1930 talkie, Ronald Colman took over the role of the suave thief. David Niven had his shot at the character in 1940, and a 1945 radio program lasted less than a year.

A skillful safecracker, Blackshirt's first magazine appearance was in 1923. Creator Bruce Graeme (pseudonym of Graham Montague Jeffries)—who surprisingly got the inspiration for his knight errant from his mother—penned ten short-story collections between 1925 and 1940. Mystery writer Richard Verrell, Blackshirt's secret identity, had a seventeenth-century ancestor, Monsieur Blackshirt, who appeared in four novels of his own in the 1930s, with Graeme taking the first name of David on the byline. Three more collections of stories appeared from 1941 to 1943, featuring Blackshirt's never-before-seen son, Anthony (Verrell had retired!). Then Bruce Graeme himself retired, and writing the Blackshirt stories fell to his son, Rodric Jeffries. Twenty novels followed, and Blackshirt ended up enjoying a forty-six year-run of popularity; only the Saint had lasted longer.

A bold-faced knockoff of the Saint, the Toff appeared in 1933 in a British magazine called *The Thriller* (where Charteris had been a contributor). Created by John Creasey, Richard Rollinson (a k a the Toff) is pretty much a straight copy of the Saint, all the way down to his leaving behind a calling card. Copy or not, the Toff managed a career that lasted forty years, including fifty books and two British films.

The Baron, also created by the staggeringly prolific John Creasey (this time writing as Anthony Morton), was actually retired jewel thief John Mannering. The Baron starred in forty-seven books over forty-two years, starting with *Meet the Baron* in 1937. With his thieving days behind him, Mannering married and became an antiques dealer, though he frequently solved crimes. For some unknown reason, the Baron's first American publisher, Lippincott, changed the character's name to the Blue Mask.

The rogue-turned-hero was also the basis for the 1955 Alfred Hitchcock film *To Catch a Thief* (based on a David Dodge novel), starring Cary Grant as a retired cat burglar who must solve a string of burglaries that mirror his own M. O. A TV variation, *It Takes a Thief* starring Robert Wagner, ran on ABC from 1968 to 1970.

The modern torchbearer for the good-hearted thief is Lawrence Block's Bernie Rhodenbarr. Truly a thief with the heart of gold, Bernie is continually trying to give up his burgling ways and just as continually falling back into them. When he's not stealing or solving crimes, he spends his time in the secondhand bookstore he owns. Bernie has been featured in eight novels, many short stories, and one ill-conceived 1987 film, *Burglar*, in which Bernard was changed to Bernice and Whoopi Goldberg played the burglar who stumbles over a dead body in the closet.

Blind Justice

Mystery fiction has seen physically challenged detectives sleuths of every stripe, including the aforementioned bizarre "defective detectives" of the pulps. But the first was probably Ernest Bramah's blind detective, Max Carrados. Featured in three short-story collections and a novel, Carrados debuted in 1914 and made his farewell appearance in *The Bravo of London* (1934). Carrados might be viewed as a private eye, although—as the blind detective had inherited a fortune from a relative—he never charged his clients, which preserves his amateur standing.

Following Carrados was Captain Duncan Maclain. A New York detective blinded in World War I, Maclain appeared in more than a dozen books from 1937's *The Last Express* through 1961's *Frankincense and Murder*. Maclain's creator Baynard Kendrick, in a departure from the Carrados yarns, only used actions blind persons had accomplished in reality, such as shooting a gun by tracking the sound of a target. The more credible Maclain even managed to make it to movies; in the first attempt, an adaptation of his debut, he was played as sighted by Kent Taylor. Edward Arnold then portrayed Maclain as blind in two more films.

Appearing on television from 1971 to 1972, the title character of *Longstreet* (played by James Franciscus) was an insurance investigator blinded while working on a case that also cost the life of his wife. Consumed by vengeance, Longstreet fought back and stayed in business with the help of an electronic cane, a seeing-eye dog named Pax, and his assistant Nikki (Marlyn Mason). To keep in shape, Longstreet had a martial arts trainer played by occasional guest star Bruce Lee. While Longstreet owed a debt to the Carrados and Maclain stories, the real inspiration was the success of wheelchair-bound TV detective, *Ironside* (played by television's definitive Perry Mason, Raymond Burr).

Deadline Chasers

Sorting through the amateurs and professionals can be a tough call. Reporters are paid for their efforts, but it's fair to say editors would prefer journalists who cover the news, rather than make it. For our purposes, let's say the reporter playing gumshoe is no private eye.

Featured in more than twenty novels by Lillian Jackson Braun, Jim Qwilleran—former big-city reporter turned features writer for the small-town *Daily Fluxion*—solves mysteries with the assistance of Koko and Yum Yum, his pet cats.

Premiering in *The Cat Who Could Read Backwards* in 1966, Sir Kao K'o Kung (Koko), a show-quality Siamese, helps Qwilleran solve the mystery and ends up with a new home. Playing Oscar to Koko's Felix, the somewhat less refined Yum Yum doesn't show up until book two, *The Cat Who Ate Danish Modern* (1967). Much as some readers may regard "cat mysteries" with disdain, many others adore this sub-genre, in which Braun was a pioneer.

Also crossing the media line was photographer Kent Murdock. Originally called Jack "Flash" Casey in a series of 1934 pulp stories, George Harmon Coxe changed his character's name and made Murdock more urbane and professional than Casey for his novel premiere in 1935's *Murder With Pictures*. This was not uncommon among writers "graduating" from the pulps: Erle Stanley Gardner, in shifting from his tough *Black Mask* tales to a hardcover publisher, sought a slick-magazine style with his urbane Perry Mason, who combined elements of several Gardner pulp heroes.

Murdock, the chief photographer for the *Boston Courier-Herald*, though married in the beginning—notably 1941's *Mrs. Murdock Takes A Case*—wound up a bachelor, appearing in nearly two dozen books through 1973. In 1936, Lew Ayres portrayed the ace photographer in a film adaptation of the first novel. Coxe, a two-time president of the Mystery Writers of America, also received that group's Grand Master Award.

Ironically, "Flash" or "Flashgun" Casey also made it to the silver screen in 1936. The 1934 short stories, which had run in *Black Mask*, proved popular enough to inspire two films. Casey went hardback when he appeared in 1942's *Silent Are the Dead*, and Coxe was in the unique position of writing separate series about what he had conceived as a single character. A brawler and drinker, Casey lived alone but he managed to find his share of trouble. Casey also enjoyed a nine-year run on radio, the show going through several name changes, although Staats Cotsworth was the only actor to portray Casey. A television series in the early 1950s had a brief run, first with Richard Carlyle, then Darren McGavin (pre-*Mike Hammer*) playing the cameraman.

Gregory McDonald introduced newspaper reporter/gumshoe Irwin M. Fletcher in his 1974 novel, *Fletch*. Funny, cynical books, they bear little resemblance to the two films that came along later, the character retooled for former SNL star Chevy Chase's broad comedic presence. The novels, more than ten now, reveal McDonald an author to be reckoned with and Fletch to be a keen observer of the American condition. McDonald is also one of only three authors to win Edgars from the Mystery Writers of America for adult novels in consecutive years. The other two are Warren Murphy and William D'Andrea.

Media Mavens

Radio and television versions of literary sleuths have been commonplace, though the private eyes and cops have far outnumbered the amateurs. While such noted amateurs as Ellery Queen, the Thin Man, Mr. and Mrs. North, and the Saint have all enjoyed series in both radio and TV, few original creations have had much impact (a notable exception is *Murder, She Wrote*, as we'll see). Most Golden Age "mystery" radio anthology series—*Suspense, The Inner Sanctum Mysteries, Lights Out, The Whistler*—told tales of suspense and horror, rarely if ever a mystery (and television's

Alfred Hitchcock Presents would follow that pattern); more general anthology series—*Lux Radio Theater*, Orson Welles's *The Mercury Theater on the Air*—produced an occasional whodunit. But, with the exception of a handful of obscurities—*Murder by Experts*, Anthony Boucher's *The Casebook of Gregory Hood*—radio was not the province of the amateur sleuth. Occasionally, however, broadcasting has provided the backdrop for fictional sleuthing.

The late William D'Andrea's Matt Cobb, who debuted in 1978's *Killed in the Ratings*, held the title "vice president in charge of special projects" for a major television network. A troubleshooter, Cobb considered his duties to include "everything too delicate for security and too nasty for public relations." He appeared in half a dozen novels, and D'Andrea also penned the outstanding reference work, *Encyclopedia Mysteriosa* (1994).

Matt Cobb's spiritual father was a Hollywood troubleshooter, Bill Lennox. First appearing in a 1933 *Black Mask* story entitled "A Little Different," Lennox was supposedly a publicist for General Consolidated Studios, but instead his duties usually involved investigating murders somehow related to the studio's stars. Created by Willis Todhunter Ballard, a cousin of Rex Stout, Lennox appeared in numerous short stories and novels.

Among the newest of the media-related detectives is Sparkle Hayter's Robin Hudson. A reporter in the New York office of the All News Network, Hudson describes herself as a "slightly rumpled third-string reporter in Rita Hayworth's body." Hayter, a stand-up comic and former Afghan War reporter, introduced her gutsy, comic detective in 1994's *What's A Girl Gotta Do?*

This is only a sampling of the wide array of amateur sleuths—and their assorted sub-genres—that have entertained mystery readers for more than one hundred years. Scores of other talented storytellers and unpaid snoops have made their contributions as well, and, while some of the above are undoubtedly superstars, others have been chosen to represent the variety and breadth of the field.

And while their characters might be amateurs, the gifted mystery writers who have created these sleuths—and concocted so many intriguing, often baffling mysteries—are clearly professionals.

SIGNET 25¢ BOOKS

EDGAR BOX

Death likes it Hot

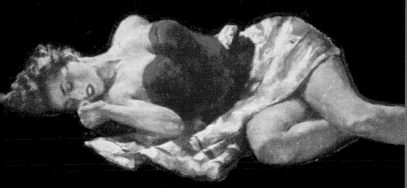

"SPILLANE IN MINK"
Saturday Review

A SIGNET B...
Complete and Unc...

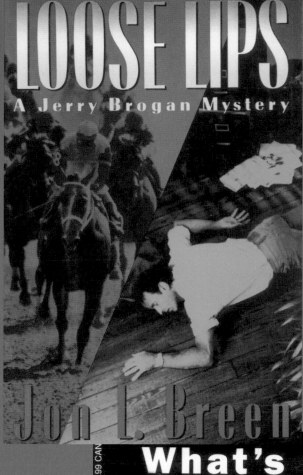

LOOSE LIPS
A Jerry Brogan Mystery

Jon L. Breen

LOOSE LIPS
Hardcover
1990

Racetrack announcer Jerry Brogan is
Jon Breen's amateur sleuth in several
witty, Golden Age- school mysteries.
Breen has also made a name for himself
as a reviewer and parodist.

WHAT'S A GIRL GOTTA DO?
Paperback
1994

Sparkle Hayter's mysteries have been
described as "sexy, funny, raunchy," as she
carries the screwball comedy torch passed
by Craig Rice. Cover designed by Paul
Buckley, illustrated by Mark Zingarelli.

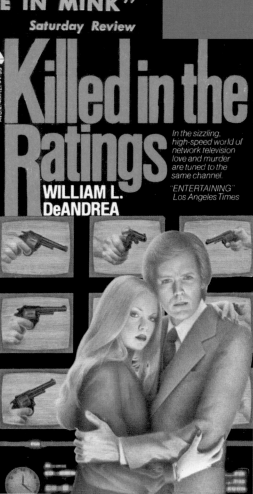

AVON/43612/$1.95

Killed in the Ratings

*In the sizzling,
high-speed world of
network television
love and murder
are tuned to the
same channel.*

*"ENTERTAINING"
Los Angeles Times*

WILLIAM L. DeANDREA

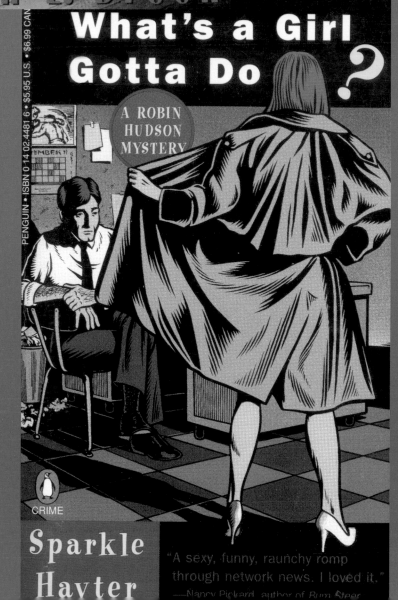

PENGUIN • ISBN 0 14 02.4481 6 • $5.95 U.S. • $6.99 CAN.

What's a Girl Gotta Do?

A ROBIN
HUDSON
MYSTERY

CRIME

Sparkle Hayter

"A sexy, funny, raunchy romp
through network news. I loved it."
—Nancy Pickard, author of *Bum Steer*

DEATH LIKES IT HOT
Paperback
1958

Even Gore Vidal got the
Spillane treatment from
Signet Books in the 1950s.
Writing as "Edgar Box,"
Vidal produced a handful
of sharp mysteries about
amateur sleuth/press agent,
Peter Cutler Sargeant II.

KILLED IN
THE RATINGS
Paperback
1978

DeAndrea's Matt Cobb
mysteries shrewdly update
the Ellery Queen approach,
adding wiseguy humor to
Golden Age-style fair-play
puzzles.

ELLERY QUEEN

Frederick Dannay, left, and Manfred B. Lee,
right, collaborated as Ellery Queen. Dannay
plotted the mysteries, providing a detailed
outline, and Lee did the writing.

Frederic Dannay (1905–1982)

Manfred Lee (1905–1971)

The rule is the original is better than the knock-off—except in the case of Ellery Queen. Originally a younger version of Philo Vance, detective Ellery Queen grew to be far more popular, with a much longer shelf life, than S.S. Van Dine's somewhat snottier character. Queen, however, was not just a fictional detective who solved mysteries to aid his police inspector father, Richard Queen; Ellery Queen was also the pseudonym under which his adventures were penned.

Cousins Manfred B. Lee and Frederic Dannay—a P.R. flack and ad copywriter, respectively—entered a novel writing contest sponsored by *McClure's*, magazine and Lippincott Publishing. Their byline, "Ellery Queen," fulfilled the contest rule that stated novels had to be submitted under a pseudonym. The pair also decided that since mystery readers seemed to remember the names of characters better than authors, their detective would be Ellery Queen as well. Winning the $7,500 prize in 1928 led to the publication of *The Roman Hat Mystery* in 1929. Yearly, Van Dine-esque novels followed, though by the late 1930s, the Philo Vance mannerisms had vanished.

A long-running radio show began in 1939, and in 1941 *Ellery Queen's Mystery Magazine* debuted. Over the years, Queen made numerous appearances in movies, on radio and television, and in anthologies. The well-known magazine, which is still published, has kept the character's name synonymous with the mystery genre, although among major names in the field, Queen is the least read today. The 1975–1976 television show featured Jim Hutton as an absent-minded, warmly human Ellery and David Wayne as a sharply intelligent, just a little cranky Inspector Queen. Set in 1940s period, the well-produced, low-rated show established the "all-star suspect" format followed by *Murder She Wrote*.

In response to the hardboiled writers of the day, whose works were attracting serious critical attention (Hammett and Chandler, both of whom "Queen" admired), the cousins took steps to elevate the literary quality of the field, moving their books to the next level. Even though the public liked the series as it was, Dannay and Lee risked making their plots more adult, their characterizations deeper, and their issues more contemporary. Ellery, himself, changed as well; he became less like the aloof Vance and actually showed an interest in the human side of the mysteries he solved. These elements are illustrated best in the Wrightsville novels which followed 1942's *Calamity Town*. Queen's popularity was only enhanced by this more adult approach; however, in the last period of Queen novels, the cousins reverted to lighter-hearted, less naturalistic fare. No less an authority than Anthony Boucher, stated, "Ellery Queen is the American detective story."

THE FOUR
OF HEARTS

Hardcover
1938

Dannay and Lee had
a brief screenwriting
fling, reflected in their
character Ellery turn-
ing to screenwriting
himself, as in this fine
evocation of late
1930s Hollywood.

ELLERY QUEEN

960

POCKET BOOK
25¢

THE
COMPLETE
BOOK

POCKET
BOOKS
INC.

THE
FOUR of HEARTS

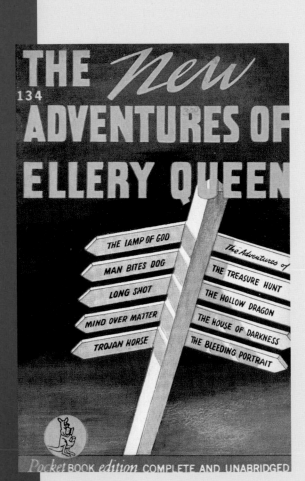

THE *New*
134
ADVENTURES OF
ELLERY QUEEN

THE LAMP OF GOD
MAN BITES DOG
LONG SHOT
MIND OVER MATTER
TROJAN HORSE

The Adventures of
THE TREASURE HUNT
THE HOLLOW DRAGON
THE HOUSE OF DARKNESS
THE BLEEDING PORTRAIT

Pocket BOOK *edition* COMPLETE AND UNABRIDGED

THE NEW ADVENTURES
OF ELLERY QUEEN

Paperback
1941

A typically eye-catching deco
cover from Pocket Books provides
a literal signpost to adventure.

THE TRAGEDY OF X

Paperback
1942

This strong Pocket Books cover reveals
the identity of Barnaby Ross as a pseudonym of Ellery Queen, also a pseudonym!
The well-named sleuth Drury Lane is, of
course, an actor.

ELLERY QUEE
125

The Tragedy
of

Now it can be told: Barnaby Ros
original author of "The Tragedy
is really Ellery Queen.

Pocket BOOK *edition* COMPLETE AND UN

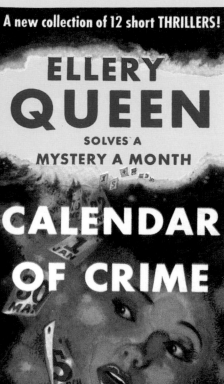

CALENDAR OF CRIME
Paperback
1953

This short story collection sports a dizzingly beautiful Richard Powers cover.

THE KING IS DEAD
Hardcover
1952

A prime example of the mature Queen (both writer and detective), *The King Is Dead* combines classic Golden Age mystery techniques with postwar political themes.

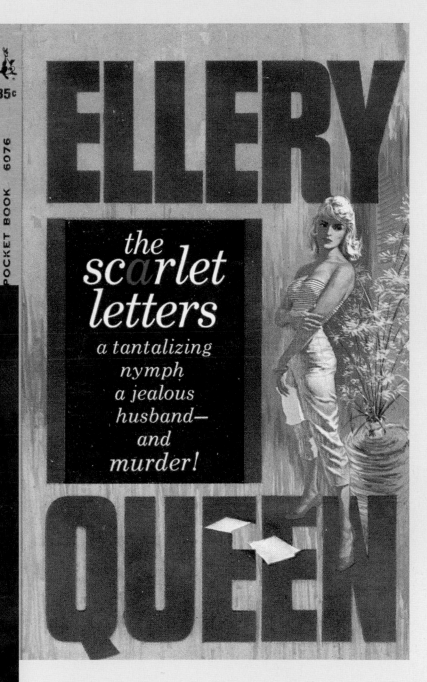

THE SCARLET LETTERS
Paperback
1961

A love interest was part of many Queen novels, but the pensive blonde (Richard Powers, again) on *The Scarlet Letters* seems to be longing for a spot on a tough P.I. cover.

A SIGNET MYSTERY • Q4907 • 95¢

Ellery Queen

Ten Days' Wonder

NOW A THRILLING FILM, DIRECTED BY **CLAUDE CHABROL**
SPECIAL 8-PAGE MOVIE INSERT!

ELLERY QUEEN

NBC publicity still
1975

Suspect Bert Parks seems peeved by the attention of amateur sleuth Jim Hutton, portraying Ellery on the first-rate though short-lived Levinson and Link TV series.

TEN DAYS' WONDER

Paperback
1972

This movie tie-in of an all-star Claude Chabrol version of this particularly adult, dark Queen novel made a minor change: the character of Ellery Queen was eliminated.

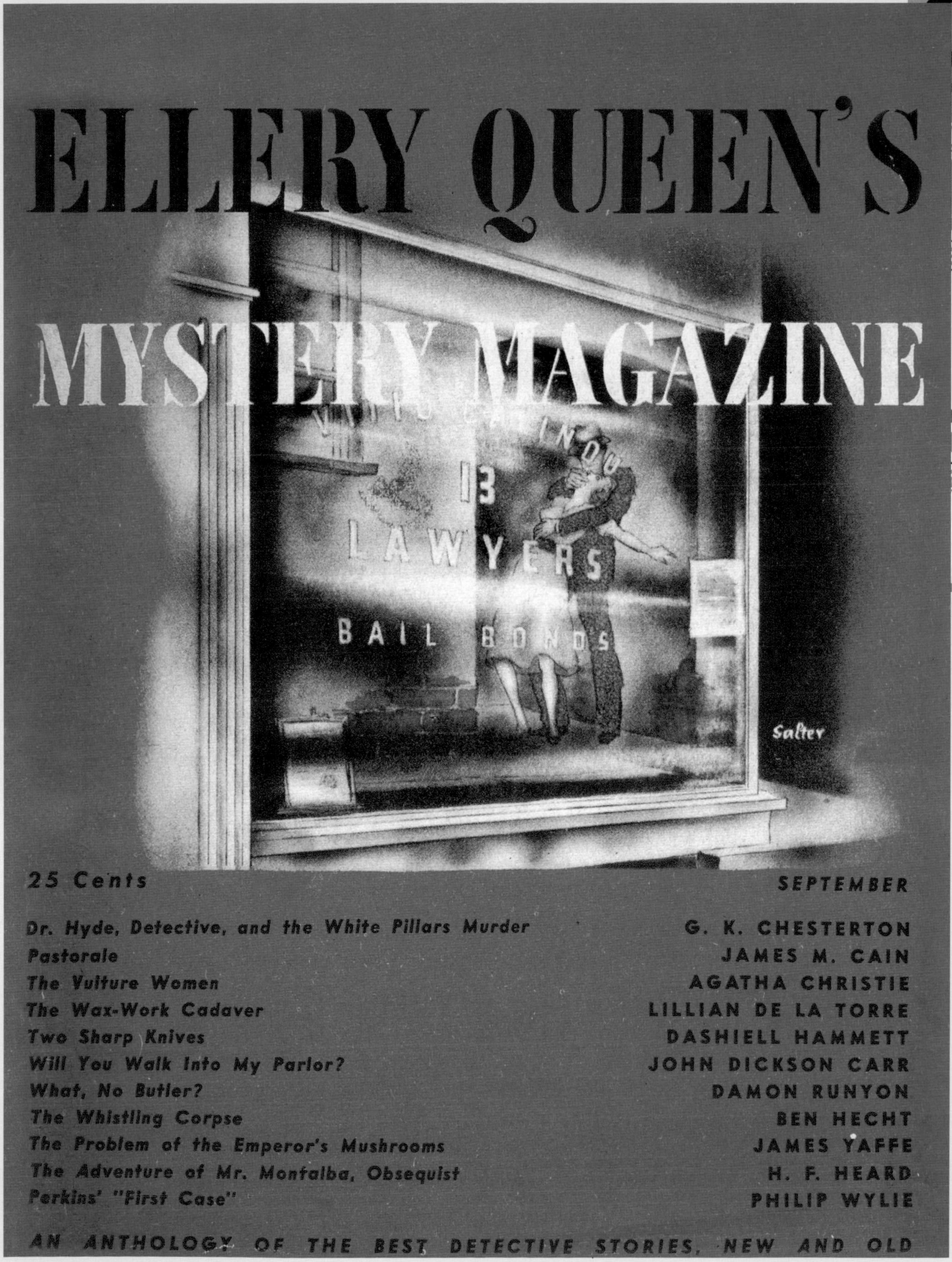

ELLERY QUEEN'S
MYSTERY MAGAZINE
13
LAWYERS
BAIL BONDS
Salter
25 Cents
SEPTEMBER
Dr. Hyde, Detective, and the White Pillars Murder G. K. CHESTERTON
Pastorale JAMES M. CAIN
The Vulture Women AGATHA CHRISTIE
The Wax-Work Cadaver LILLIAN DE LA TORRE
Two Sharp Knives DASHIELL HAMMETT
Will You Walk Into My Parlor? JOHN DICKSON CARR
What, No Butler? DAMON RUNYON
The Whistling Corpse BEN HECHT
The Problem of the Emperor's Mushrooms JAMES YAFFE
The Adventure of Mr. Montalba, Obsequist H. F. HEARD
Perkins' "First Case" PHILIP WYLIE
AN ANTHOLOGY OF THE BEST DETECTIVE STORIES, NEW AND OLD

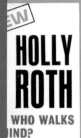

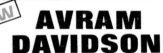

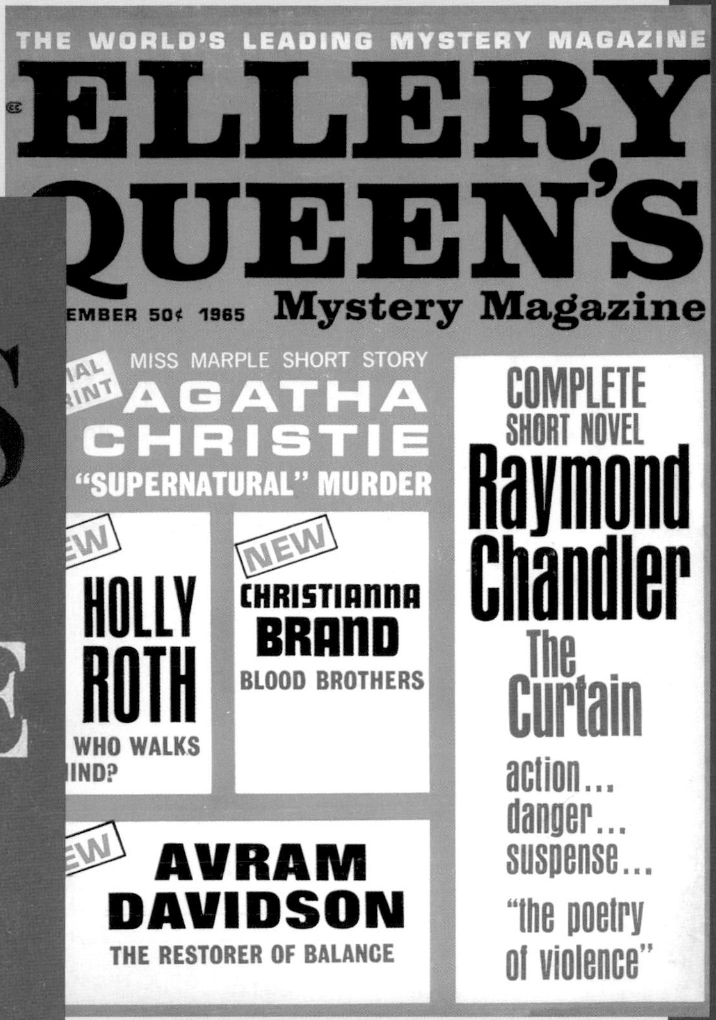

THE WORLD'S LEADING MYSTERY MAGAZINE
ELLERY QUEEN'S
EMBER 50¢ 1965
Mystery Magazine
MISS MARPLE SHORT STORY
AGATHA CHRISTIE
"SUPERNATURAL" MURDER
COMPLETE SHORT NOVEL
Raymond Chandler
The Curtain
action... danger... suspense...
"the poetry of violence"
HOLLY ROTH
WHO WALKS
IND?
NEW
CHRISTIANNA BRAND
BLOOD BROTHERS
AVRAM DAVIDSON
THE RESTORER OF BALANCE

ELLERY QUEEN'S MYSTERY MAGAZINE

Magazine
September 1965

ELLERY QUEEN'S MYSTERY MAGAZINE

Magazine
1945

The long-running *EQMM* has helped keep Ellery Queen's name a symbol of detection, and the roster of contributors is a Who's Who of mystery fiction.

RAYMOND CHANDLER

(1888–1959)

Born on July 23, 1888, in Chicago, Raymond Thornton Chandler grew up in England, becoming a naturalized British subject as a teenager (he restored his American citizenship in 1956). This master of the American hard-boiled idiom received a classical education at Dulwich College, London (1900–1905), and studied further in France and Germany. After several years as a freelance journalist, he enlisted in the Canada's Gordon Highlanders, serving with distinction in France during World War I. Afterward, he settled in Los Angeles, returned to re-porting, became an accountant, then began a successful career as an executive with several oil companies. The oil industry's collapse during the Depression sent the journalist (and poet, back in his college days) into writing for the pulp magazines, which had become a favorite source of light reading for the oil exec.

Enter Philip Marlowe, the compassionate urban knight whose wisecracks are intermingled with evocative language—that is, enter early, otherwise-named (or unnamed) incarnations of Marlowe, making pulp appearances start-ing in 1933. A frequent *Black Mask* contributor, Chandler followed Dashiell Hammett's lead, "cannibalizing" several novelettes into *The Big Sleep*, which Knopf—publisher of the now missing-in-action Hammett—brought out in 1939. Though the author was not an overnight sensa-tion, reviewers took note of his vivid, metaphor-strewn language, and Hollywood took to his exciting, if haphaz-ardly plotted yarns, peopled with colorful characters from the underworld up to high society.

If Marlowe's creator lacked the real-life private-eye background of Hammett, Chandler's world of big-shot gangsters, troubled socialites, and wacko doctors is no less wonderful a place for not being a real one. And if it seems real, that's because the author's descriptions of Los Angeles are so effective—a city with the personality, Marlowe tells us, of "a paper cup." Chandler's enduring contribution is a more compassionate, recognizably human (yet no less tough) urban knight—that, and a passion for language, laced with masculine humor, in the most distinc-tive first-person American voice since Huckleberry Finn.

Of the screen Philip Marlowes, the best is probably Dick Powell in the definitive *noir* directed by Edward Dymtryk, *Murder, My Sweet* (1944); also strong are James Garner, a proto-Rockford in *Marlowe* (1969), and Robert Mitchum in two 1970s features. As Chandler said, Bogart in *The Big Sleep* (1946) is a better Bogart than Marlowe. Radio and television Marlowes have been routine, though in the 1980s Powers Boothe appeared in a British TV series taken directly from Chandler, a well-produced pe-riod rendition.

Chandler did not adapt his own work, though he had a stormy Hollywood screenwriting career that includes two masterpieces: Billy Wilder's *Double Indemnity* (1945, from James M. Cain, whom Chandler looked down upon) and Alfred Hitchcock's *Strangers on a Train* (1951). His later years were a lapse into sad alcoholism after the death of his beloved wife, Cissy.

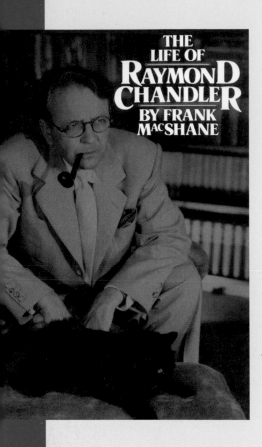

THE LIFE OF
RAYMOND CHANDLER

Hardcover
1976

Raymond Chandler—who
managed to make the hard-
boiled medium accepted as a
literary form—has generated
numerous biographies and
studies; several collections
of his lively (if cranky) letters
make great reading.

THE BIG SLEEP

Paperback
1943

FINGER MAN

Paperback
1950

THE HIGH WINDOW

Paperback
1945

Chandler's early paperbacks received star treatment at Avon Books, where this haunting deco image of a beautiful blonde skeleton ranks among the most memorable of all mystery covers. Its cover more prosaic but still handsome, *Finger Man* is one of the rarest Chandler books. Pocket Books gave Chandler strong presentation as well—witness the air-brushed abstraction of E. McKnight Kauffer's cover for *High Window*.

MURDER, MY SWEET

Radio show LP
1979

This album presented a 1945 radio version of *Murder, My Sweet* (based on Farewell, My Lovely), with Dick Powell reprising his role. Powell also played Marlowe on a now-lost early 1950s TV adaptation of *The Long Goodbye*.

THE BIG SLEEP

Hardcover
1946

This movie edition of the famous Howard Hawks film shows the emphasis on the Bogart/Bacall relationship that, in part, caused a substantial portion of the film to be re-shot when the public took a shine to Bogie and Baby in Hawks's *To Have And Have Not* (1944). The first draft of the Hawks masterpiece of style over content is now available on DVD as a double feature with the more confusing final version.

Pocket Book № 154,632,137

389

Raymond Chandler

Another Philip Marlowe Mystery

The **LADY IN THE LAKE**

COMPLET
UNABRID

THE LADY IN THE LAKE

Paperback
1946

This reprint makes no mention of the concurrent Montgomery film, for which Chandler wrote an early draft of the screenplay…a rarity, as he (inexplicably) was usually called upon to adapt other writers' work…and his solo screenplay, *The Blue Dahlia* (1946), was a non-Marlowe mystery.

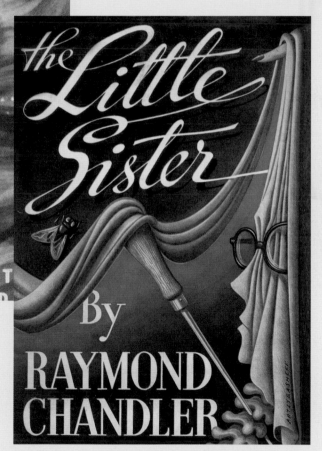

the Little Sister

By **RAYMOND CHANDLER**

The Lady in the Lake

RAYMOND CHANDLER

A METRO-GOLDWYN-MAYER PICTURE

starring **ROBERT MONTGOMERY**

with **AUDREY TOTTER** and **LLOYD NOLAN**

THE LADY IN THE LAKE

Hardcover
1946

Robert Montgomery as Marlowe looms large on the jacket of this movie tie-in edition, but in the experimental film itself (which Montgomery directed) he's rarely seen…and then mostly in mirrors. A noble failure, *The Lady In The Lake* is an extended exercise in subjective camera, with the viewer "seeing" through Marlowe's eyes, hearing Montgomery's dialogue and voice-over.

THE LITTLE SISTER

Hardcover
1949

Famed illustrator Boris Artzybasheff provides notably surrealistic cover art for Chandler's acidly funny Hollywood novel.

TROUBLE IS MY BUSINESS

Paperback
1951

PICK-UP ON NOON STREET

Paperback
1957

THE BIG SLEEP

Paperback
1958

PLAYBACK

Paperback
1960

Chandler allowed his pulp tales involving prototypes of Philip Marlowe to take the detective's name in various editions (all flowing from the massive collection, *The Simple Art Of Murder*, 1950); Chandler held back the stories he had cannibalized for such novels as *The Big Sleep* and *Farewell, My Lovely*. *Trouble Is My Business* (with a bizarre cover by Herman Geisen) gathers some of these "sort of" Marlowe tales, while *Pick-Up On Noon Street* (with its sublime sex-and-violence cocktail of a cover by Robert Maguire) gathers non-P.I. crime yarns. The Spillane influence —a masculine detective with his back to the camera, facing a lush, dangerous dame—is at work on the Darcy cover of the classic *Big Sleep*. William Rose provides a glamorous, tastefully sexy cover for Chandler's unfortunate final novel, *Playback*.

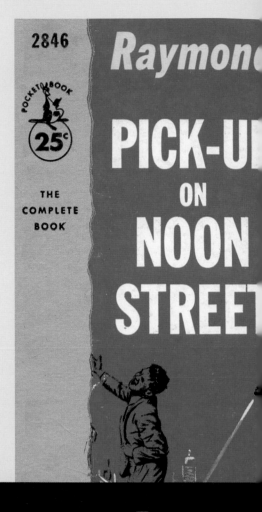

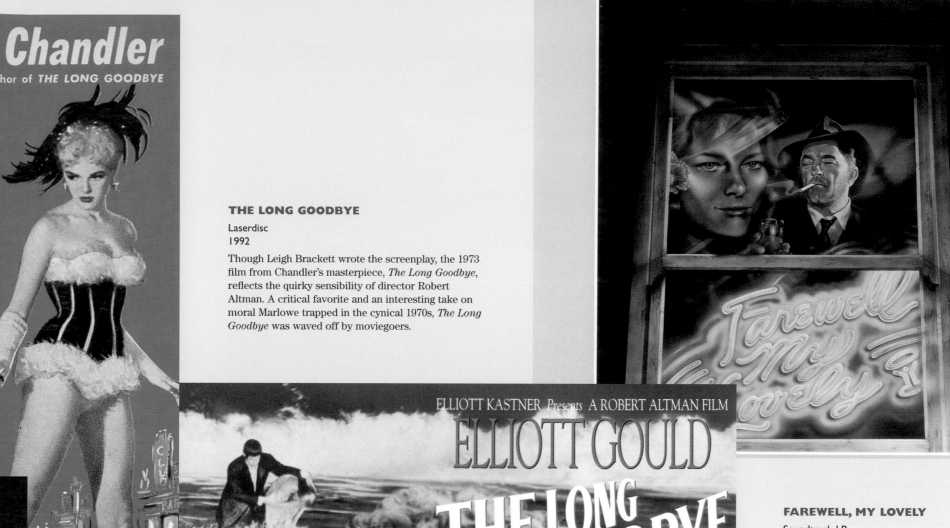

Chandler

thor of *THE LONG GOODBYE*

FAREWELL, MY LOVELY

THE LONG GOODBYE

Laserdisc
1992

Though Leigh Brackett wrote the screenplay, the 1973 film from Chandler's masterpiece, *The Long Goodbye*, reflects the quirky sensibility of director Robert Altman. A critical favorite and an interesting take on moral Marlowe trapped in the cynical 1970s, *The Long Goodbye* was waved off by moviegoers.

ELLIOTT KASTNER *Presents* A ROBERT ALTMAN FILM

ELLIOTT GOULD

THE LONG GOODBYE

FAREWELL, MY LOVELY

Soundtrack LP
1975

Just two years after Altman's folly, in the aftermath of the Chandler-esque *Chinatown*, director Dick Richards's period-piece version of *Farewell, My Lovely* appeared, starring the rumpled, world-weary Robert Mitchum. Slightly stilted, the film argued for Mitchum as the definitive screen Marlowe, though a follow-up—directed by Michael Winner—moved Mitchum's Marlowe to modern-day London, a bewildering misjudgment in an otherwise faithful version of *The Big Sleep* (1978).

CHAPTER

5

PEEPERS

Thinking 'Tecs

If the amateur who solved crimes for his own pleasure was the province of the rich, then the private detective belonged to the working man. The private dick was the last bastion of justice and honesty in a corrupt world. If the wealthy held the police in disdain for being just working men, and bumblers at that, the police were held in equal contempt by the less privileged, because they were seen as corrupt, bribeable, and lackeys for the rich. The private eye stood for the intriguing notion that the "little guy" didn't have to be at the mercy of the wealthy. • To be sure, there were thinking detectives of the private variety, those eccentrics who used deduction and psychology to ferret out the culprits. Sherlock Holmes, of course, is the prototype and certainly the greatest private (consulting) detective in the history of fiction. Though not the only private detective in the deductive school, Holmes is easily the most famous, with only a handful of real rivals ... Hercule Poirot, perhaps, and certainly Nero Wolfe. • Rex Stout's rotund detective debuted in 1934's *Fer de Lance*, along with his assistant Archie Goodwin, in a canny blend of the thinking detective and the working-class tough guy. A behemoth with expensive taste in most everything, Nero Wolfe is the consummate armchair detective, unwilling to leave his beloved brownstone unless absolutely necessary. He prefers, instead, to spend his time with his "children"—the pampered orchids of his rooftop greenhouse.

Any legwork is taken on by Archie. A decent detective in his own right, Archie is not the average Dr. Watson-style narrator. He gets deeply involved in cases, investigating clues, fighting thugs, and cajoling Wolfe into working. Wolfe himself would examine Archie's evidence, then sit in his chair for hours mulling over the different possibilities before gathering the suspects and employing one of his "charades"...to name the culprit.

Rex Stout is the only American mystery novelist who consistently, effectively wedded the drawing-room school to the hardboiled. The wonderfully glib, out-of-the-corner-of-a-wise-guy's-mouth narration of Archie Goodwin gets taken for granted simply because it's so well done; as a wordsmith, Archie Goodwin is in a class with Raymond Chandler's Philip Marlowe—only Archie isn't as arch. And Stout's dialogue is crisp and wry, comparing favorably with Dashiell Hammett or James M. Cain.

Two films based on the series appeared in 1936 and 1937; however, Stout disliked them and thereafter refused to license his characters for the screen. Radio was a different story, and between 1943 and 1950, three Nero Wolfe programs came and went, one of which featured an admirably cast Sidney Greenstreet. In 1981, Nero Wolfe finally came to American television with William Conrad as the portly detective and Lee Horsley as Archie in an underrated series reminiscent of the Jim Hutton version of *Ellery Queen*. In the late 1990s, the A&E network mounted a production of *The Golden Spiders* based on Stout's 1953 novel. Maury Chaykin portrayed Wolfe, and Tim Hutton was featured as Archie. A series has followed.

Stout wrote the novels until his death in 1975. In the 1980s, Robert Goldsborough added five more books to the string.

Much has been made of female private detectives in recent years, but too seldom mentioned is Patricia Wentworth's Maud Silver. A logician of a different stripe, Silver is a retired governess who operated as a private detective to supplant her pension. In *Grey Mask* (1927), Silver already has a thriving practice, one that even Scotland Yard occasionally turns to for help. Miss Silver appeared in an impressive thirty-two novels between 1927 and 1961.

Carolyn Wells's creation of Fleming Stone brought another non-tough-guy, larger-than-life thinker into the private detective field. Introduced in 1909 in *The Clue*, Stone proved to be one of those detectives who solved crimes as if they were merely childish jigsaw puzzles. The last book in the series, *Who Killed Caldwell*, appeared in 1942, the year of Wells's death.

Most private eyes, however, are not chiefly thinkers: like Nero Wolfe—they are men (and women) of action.

Hard Dicks

The twentieth century brought with it an over ninety percent literacy rate in the United States, better economic times (which meant more money for more people), and, right after the end of World War I, a new type of private detective.

Race Williams, the invention of pulp writer Carroll John Daly, changed private eye fiction forever. Dishing out justice from the two guns he toted, Race Williams first appeared in *Black Mask* on June 1, 1923, in "The Knights of the Open Palm." Not only did Daly practically single-handedly invent the modern hardboiled detective genre, in this first Race Williams story he took on no less than the organized evil of the Ku Klux Klan.

Due at least partially to his upping the ante on violence in his stories, Daly was never a darling of the critics; like his disciple Mickey Spillane, Daly pleased only his fans...but for a time, they were legion. Issues of *Black Mask* featuring his work typically sold an extra fifteen percent. Though falling into obscurity later, Daly was the star performer of *Black Mask* and rival pulps, easily outselling his contemporaries Chandler and Hammett.

The hero of numerous short stories and eight novels (patched together compilations of previously published pulp novelettes), Race Williams put the tough guy detective on the map. A redheaded criminal beauty, the Flame—his Dragon Lady-like nemesis—was the only woman who really interested the detective. For her part, the Flame tried on numerous occasions to recruit Williams to become her lover and ally, but he always managed to avoid falling completely under her evil spell.

Daly also brought a second, less significant tough guy private eye into the world, Vee Brown. Vee moonlighted as both private detective and songwriter, a job he maintained under his real name Vivian Brown. A writer of great energy, Daly, who worked best in the short-story form, did not evolve and grow and never really learned to craft a novel. His innovation, the tough private eye, took off like a rocket, leaving him behind.

What Daly began, Hammett and Chandler refined. With Sam Spade, the Continental Op, and Philip Marlowe leading the way, the private-eye field began to grow.

Jonathan Latimer's nearly forgotten 1930's Bill Crane series followed the hard-drinking formula of Hammett's *The Thin Man*, and similarly mingle mystery and screwball comedy; Latimer's handful of Bill Crane novels are also the only real rival to Rex Stout's Nero Wolfe series as first-rate, hardboiled drawing-room mysteries.

Latimer's second Crane novel, *Headed for a Hearse* (1935), includes a locked room puzzle right out of John Dickson Carr; but it also features vivid if understated violence of the Hammett variety. Gut-wrenching scenes of daily life on death row alternate with scenes of partying, as the detective moves from one bar, one restaurant, one penthouse to another. In the latter quarter of the novel, when Chicago op Bill Crane decides to sober up and put his mind to the case, some frantic and hardnosed detecting ensues. All of this is delivered with casual brilliance—snappy dialogue and sharp (pre-Chandler) imagery: a cup of coffee is "excellent, as black as tar, as pungent as garlic, as clear as dry sherry, as hot as Bisbee, Arizona." Latimer has it both ways: he masters the style he mocks.

Three of the five Crane novels made it to the silver screen with Preston Foster portraying the often inebriated shamus. Latimer traded mystery writing for screenwriting, relinquishing his position as one of the few true peers of Hammett and Chandler. His later career included writing many scripts for the *Perry Mason* TV show.

Brett Halliday (pseudonym of Davis Dresser) introduced red-headed Mike Shayne in 1939's *Divided on Death*. A big guy with concrete fists, Shayne seldom used a gun and relied more on his detecting abilities to solve cases. Shayne is a typical private eye, with all the conventional trappings: loyal secretary girlfriend, cop confidant, cop enemy; but the Miami setting was unique for its day and helped establish that corner of America as a prime *noir* setting. In the mid-1940s the well-characterized Shayne worked in New Orleans for a time, moving there after the death of his wife Phyllis (both the private eye's marriage and the death of this sympathetic recurring character were unusual for the genre in that era).

Halliday wrote the Shayne books until his retirement in 1958, and from then until the demise of the series in 1976, ghost writers filled Halliday's shoes. *Mike Shayne's Mystery Magazine* ran from

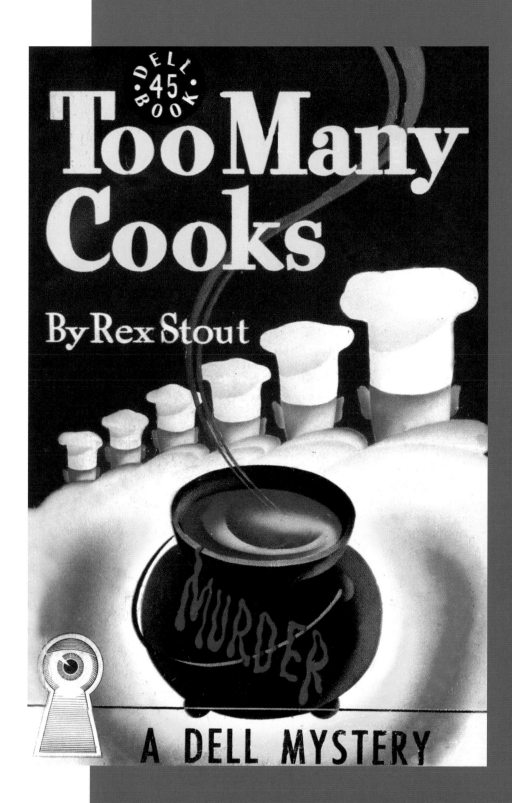

TOO MANY COOKS

Paperback
1938

This Dell paperback, with its wonderful deco cover, indicates how well Stout's mix of soft and hardboiled styles served as a recipe for suspenseful entertainment.

BLACK ORCHIDS

Paperback
1963

Stout's rotund detective often does not appear on the covers of his own book jackets, even paperbacks like this blandly surreal depiction of Wolfe's trademark orchid and a rigged revolver.

THE CLOCK STRIKES TWELVE

Paperback
1944

Little remembered today, Miss Silver—done proud by this striking art deco cover—foreshadowed female private eyes, despite her cozy, little-old-lady M.O.

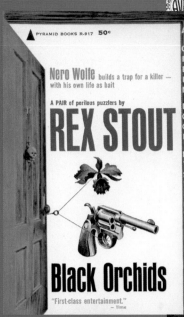

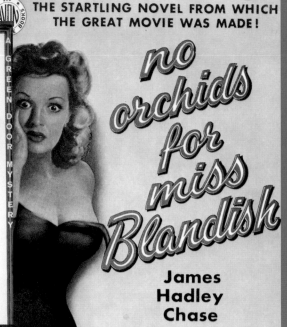

NO ORCHIDS FOR MISS BLANDISH

Paperback
1951

No Orchids For Miss Blandish —Britisher James Hadley Chase's notorious, sexy-for-its-time chiller —is one of two books featuring P.I. Dave Fenner. Several movies have been made from *Orchids*, including Robert Aldrich's *The Grissom Gang* (1971), the director's only other P.I. movie after his classic *Kiss Me, Deadly* (1955). Note the wide-eyed, face-clutching terror, indicating the horrific undertones of Chase's then-potent work.

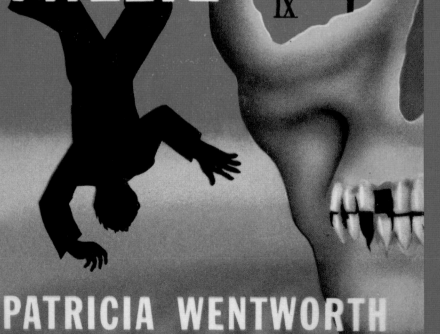

THE LADY IN THE MORGUE

Paperback
1943

No writer combined screwball comedy with hardboiled fiction better than Jonathan Latimer, a forgotten master. The eerie cover is by Leo Manso.

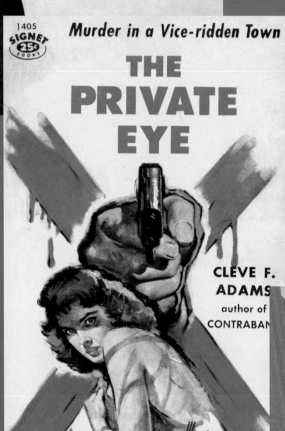

THE PRIVATE EYE

Paperback
1951

Pulpster Adams—a former detective himself—moved into hardcovers with hard-hitting tales of brutal detectives, including Rex McBride and (in this novel) J.J. Shannon. The magnificent cover art by Robert Maguire combines romantic realism with abstract design.

MISTRESS MURDER

Paperback
1951

Cheyney, like Chase, was more popular overseas, where the Britisher's tin ear for American idiom went unnoticed. Terry O'Dey stars in this one, but Slim Callaghan and especially Lemmy Caution (hero of Jean-Luc Godard's *Alphaville*, 1965) were better known.

A TASTE FOR VIOLENCE

Paperback
1949

Few would argue that Brett Halliday was a wordsmith in a league with, say, Rex Stout or Raymond Chandler. Yet Halliday's novels consistently outsold many better (and better-remembered) authors—partly because Dell Publishing provided him with wonderful covers, like this early one by Robert Stanley.

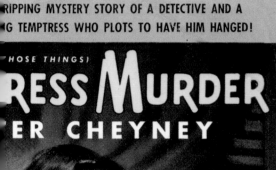

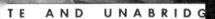

THE YELLOW OVERCOAT

Paperback
1942

Pulp veteran Gruber added a twist of screwball comedy to his tough mysteries. Rudolph Belarski is recycling a wonderful pulp cover here.

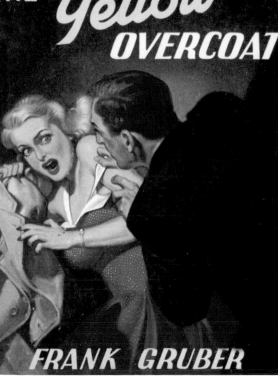

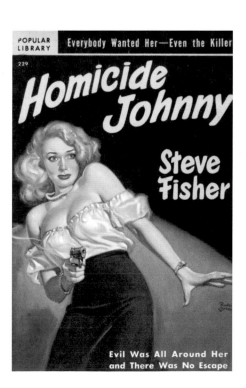

NO GOOD FROM A CORPSE

Paperback
1944

Leigh Brackett became a screenwriter, because director Howard Hawks thought this tough P.I. novel had surely been written by a man. Ms. Brackett co-wrote (with William Faulkner) the screen version of *The Big Sleep* (1946), as well as (unaided by Faulkner) *Rio Bravo* (1959) and *The Empire Strikes Back* (1979), a few examples from a mind-boggling list of credits.

HOMICIDE JOHNNY

Paperback
1940

Screenwriter Steve Fisher—former pulpster—published the occasional tough, melodramatic mystery. Belarski contributes another glorious cover.

25

TWENTY-FIVE CLASSIC PRIVATE EYE NOVELS

Selected by Gary Warren Niebuhr, author of
A Reader's Guide to the Private Eye Novel,
(G.K. Hall & Co., 1993)

1956 until 1990, and the Shayne novels themselves led to a popular, long-running film series. The first eight, all released between 1941 and 1942, featured Lloyd Nolan as the two-fisted private eye in a star-making performance. The second group, produced post-World War II, featured the future Ward Cleaver, Hugh Beaumont, as Shayne for another five lesser, low-budget installments. Mike Shayne radio and television shows also appeared over the years. Enormously popular in their day, Shayne and Halliday have not endured.

Spillane Opens the Door

Through the 1930s and well into the 1940s, the private detective had found a niche in the reading habits of Americans, with a number of genre stars—notably Hammett, Chandler, and especially Erle Stanley Gardner—enjoying strong sales and inspiring movies and radio versions of their characters. But it wouldn't be until after World War II that the private eye would make the move from genre hero to pop-cultural phenomenon.

When Mickey Spillane's 1947 *I, the Jury* appeared in paperback in 1949, the popularity of the private detective exploded, rivaling that of the frontier hero; if the shamus was a modern update of the western gunslinger, the revision of the myth was now rivaling his progenitor—John Wayne moving over to make room for Humphrey Bogart.

Just as Carroll John Daly had touched a nerve with post-World War I readers, so did Spillane, but outdistancing his role model, connecting with post-World War II readers in a much bigger way. The driving force behind the paperback explosion of the 1950s, Spillane led private-eye fiction into uncharted territory. Sex and violence had always been the spices that gave the hardboiled detective novel its pungency; but Spillane made main courses out of lust and mayhem, stirring in vengeance for that extra kick, and a horde of new fictional private eyes followed Hammer into the literary marketplace.

Imitations, variations, and even repudiations of the Spillane technique would continue well into the 1960s. Without Mike Hammer, however, the private eye might well have faded from public view.

Not long after Mike Hammer burst onto the scene, another great American detective made his less splashy yet significant debut.

In *The Moving Target* (1949), Ross MacDonald introduced Lew Archer, a compassionate tough detective stubbornly in the Marlowe tradition, rejecting the Spillane ethos (if going through the door Hammer's creator had opened for all tough P.I. characters).

Based in Los Angeles (like Marlowe), Archer spends a great deal of time in Santa Teresa, a fictionalized Santa Barbara. More introspective than the average tough P.I., Archer frequently finds himself involved in cases featuring twisted family dynamics, unearthing skeletons in one closet after another. Archer employs a fairly typical P.I. investigative technique, interviewing suspects and witnesses, digging around, following the clues, then coming up with the answer, willing to cause a little trouble along the way if that will speed up his finding the solution.

The earlier novels are tougher and more straightforward and, not surprisingly, are the Archer entries chosen for big-screen filming in Hollywood, Paul Newman portraying Archer in *Harper* (1966; from the novel, *The Moving Target*) and *The Drowning Pool* (1975). (The detective's name was changed to accommodate a successful string of Newman-starring movies beginning with the letter "H"). A television film of *The Underground Man* (1974) with a stiff Peter Graves as Archer somehow led to a short-lived TV series featuring a more aptly cast Brian Keith.

Ross MacDonald (penname for Kenneth Millar) is considered one of the best stylists in the genre by many readers and critics; others find his plots repetitious and consider him a rather forced Chandler imitator—a smaller group, but one that included Chandler himself. MacDonald described his hero as a "window" through which the world of his mysteries was viewed; only a few of the books (including the underrated final Archer, *The Blue Hammer*, 1976) delve into the detective's private life.

MacDonald and Archer—long cult figures in the genre—were discovered by serious literary critics in the late 1960s, sparking a belated popular success. MacDonald garnered the Mystery Writers of America Grand Master Award in 1973 and the Private Eye Writers of America Lifetime Achievement Award in 1981.

A more direct response to Mickey Spillane's Mike Hammer, Richard S. Prather's leering, white-haired Shell Scott, appeared in 1950, cracking yeggs and romancing frails for the next thirty-seven years. Another Los Angeles-based detective, Scott was more laid back than Mike Hammer but could be just as tough when the situation called for it. Known for his sardonic humor, Scott also shared Hammer's eye for a well-turned ankle. Enormously popular in their day, the Shell Scott books managed to spoof the genre while providing paperback fans with the requisite thrills. An underrated, influential figure, Prather has been honored by the Private Eye Writers of America with the Eye, its Lifetime Achievement award.

The textbook example of a Mike Hammer imitation, Aloysius Algernon "Rocky" Steele was a tough ex-commando and a former boxer who carried a "rod" he wasn't afraid to use (Hammer's trademark .45 automatic), with an insatiable thirst for vengeance...and, of course, irresistible to "dames." He was remarkable only because he was a white private eye whose exploits were chronicled by an African-American author, a rather distinguished one at that. John B. West, M.D., who resided in Liberia, was a prominent businessman, the Liberian Broadcasting Company only one of his ventures. Steele walked Mike Hammer's mean New York streets in six ridiculous, fun novels between 1959 and 1961—all published by Spillane's publisher Signet Books.

Rejecting Phillip Marlowe's Los Angeles and Mike Hammer's Manhattan, Carney Wilde roamed the streets of Philadelphia after World War II. Beginning with a one-man office, Wilde had built his agency into one employing hundreds by the time of his last appearance in *Exit Running* in 1960. Bart Spicer's Wilde mysteries were always well-crafted, as was the dialogue, but Wilde, who debuted in 1949's *The Dark Light*, is unfortunately little remembered.

William Campbell Gault—writing the first volume as Roney Scott—introduced Los Angeles private eye Joe Puma in 1953's *Shakedown*; the tough, entertaining series spanned seven books over eight years. Gault's second P.I. series proved more enduring. Brock "The Rock" Callahan, ex-Los Angeles Rams football player, took his first case in 1955's *Ring Around Rosa*; after a seven-year-run, however, Gault put Callahan out to pasture.

In 1982, the former football player returned in *The Bad Samaritan* and chalked up another half-dozen adventures, including 1982's *The Cana Diversion* in which—in a unique genre twist—Callahan investigated the murder of Gault's other dick, Joe Puma. For this strong effort, Gault received the Shamus Award from the Private Eye Writers of America for best paperback original. In 1952, Gault received the Edgar for best first novel and he also won the Private Eye Writers of America Lifetime Achievement Award.

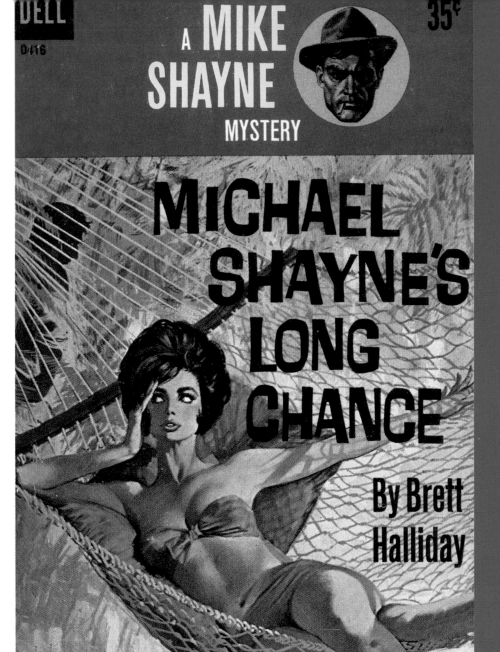

A MIKE SHAYNE MYSTERY

DELL D416 35¢

MICHAEL SHAYNE'S LONG CHANCE

By Brett Halliday

A NEW MIKE SHAYNE MYSTERY

DELL D374 35¢

Date With A Dead Man

BRETT HALLI

A MIKE SHAYNE MYSTERY

DELL D425 35¢

Stranger in Town

by Brett Halliday

A NEW MIKE SHAYNE MYSTERY

DELL D437 35¢

The Homicidal Virgin

BY BRETT HALLIDAY

A DELL BOOK
DELL 316

MICHAEL SHAYNE'S LONG CHANCE

Paperback
1961

STRANGER IN TOWN

Paperback
1961

DATE WITH A DEAD MAN

Paperback
1960

THE HOMICIDAL VIRGIN

Paperback
1961

If the Mike Shayne mysteries weren't as outrageously sexy as those of Mickey Spillane or Richard S. Prather, the covers—particularly these examples from a stunning run by James Bond movie poster artist, Robert McGinnis—certainly were. If few Halliday collectors are around these days, many McGinnis ones certainly are. These covers were also used for foreign editions of Spillane.

THE BLUE HAMMER

Hardcover
1976

MacDonald's final Archer novel—written when the once-cultish author was routinely appearing on best-seller lists— finds the P.I. personally involved, a relative rarity in the series.

CRIME MAP ON BACK COVER

DELL MYSTERY

THE DROWNING POOL

Paperback
1950

Early Lew Archer novels were by "John" Ross MacDonald (the name dropped when John D. complained). James Meese provided the strong cover.

ARMCHAIR IN HELL

Paperback
1948

Henry Kane's Peter Chambers was one of the most resilient post-Spillane P.I.s surviving (if never quite thriving) into the 1970s as softcore porn. The sexy nature of even the earlier books is indicated by this fine deco cover.

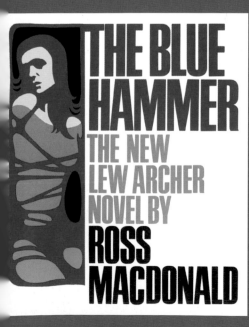

THE DROWNING POOL

VHS jacket
1984

The second HARPER movie was not a hit, but interestingly —coming ten years later—it picked up where the first film left off, adapting the second Archer novel.

DARLING, IT'S DEATH

Paperback
1952

THE WAILING FRAIL

Paperback
1960

THE SCRAMBLED YEGGS

Paperback
1959

DOUBLE IN TROUBLE

Paperback
1960

THE KUBLA KHAN CAPER

Paperback
1967

Richard S. Prather's tough, tongue-in-cheek Shell Scott series was a paperback sensation, rivaling Spillane's Mike Hammer. The witty Prather's storytelling acumen had much to do with that success—note the deliriously campy titles (not shown: *Slap Happy*; *Dig That Crazy Corpse*)—but the sexy cover art by Barye Phillips put it over the top. When Prather moved from Gold Medal Books to Pocket Books, in a big money deal, Phillips soon stopped doing the covers. Times had changed, and even "dames" like the one on *Kubla Khan Caper* (by Bob Lesser) couldn't help Prather maintain his incredible streak.

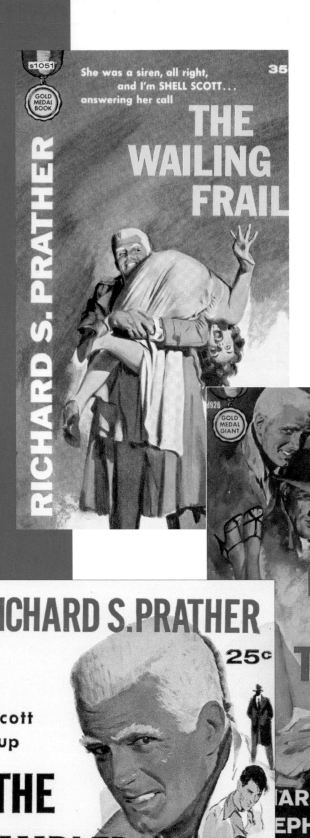

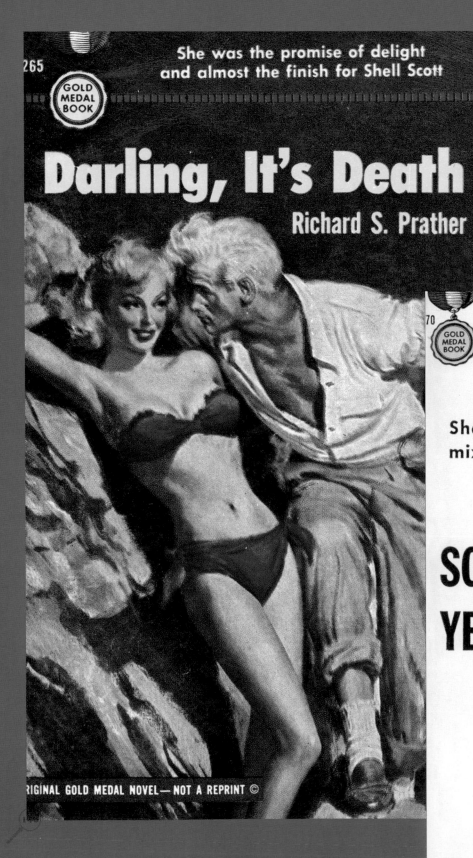

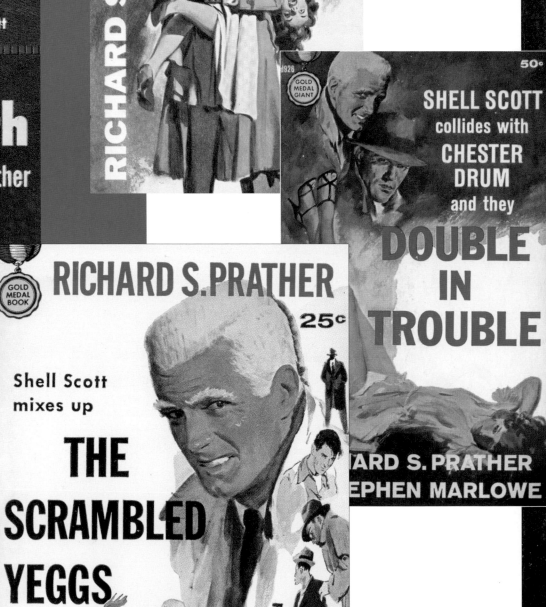

a SHELL SCOTT novel by RICHARD S. PRATHER

The Kubla Khan Caper

Over 40,000,000 SHELL SCOTT books sold!

Like Gault, Thomas B. Dewey alternated between two P.I. series, starting in the 1950s. The first featured a Chicago investigator known only as Mac; beefy ex-cop Mac took on all comers, but seemed to specialize in youth-related problems. Introduced in 1951's *Draw the Curtain Close*, Mac continued to investigate crimes—always championing the underdog, a rumpled White Knight never seeming to age—through The Taurus Trip (1970), a career that covered sixteen books.

Dewey's second series, designed for the "girls and gats" paperback original market of the 1950s and early 1960s, features Pete Schofield, a typical fifties Los Angeles private eye with one important twist—at home he has a beautiful, smart, and very jealous wife, Jeannie. Though they are sound detective novels, Schofield's ten adventures were lighter-hearted fare; if Mac followed Marlowe's lead, Schofield was a child of Shell Scott. Schofield debuted in *And Where She Stops* in 1957, and his last case was 1965's *Nude in Nevada*. Forgotten by the general public, Thomas B. Dewey is a respected name among fans and writers of hardboiled detective fiction.

Michael Avallone's Ed Noon, a New York private eye who hit the scene in 1953 was, like his creator, an eccentric movie buff whose first-person narration was sprinkled liberally with film references. Noon appeared in thirty-four books over thirty years, and his creator alternately called himself "The Fastest Typewriter in the East" and "King of the Paperbacks." Such early Noon novels as *The Tall Dolores* (1953) and *Dead Game* (1954) were solid, well-crafted examples of the private eye form; but as his creator was given over more and more to work-for-hire freelance jobs, Noon's adventures grew ever more quirky, and the prose became as careless as it was lively. Avallone came to be considered the Ed Wood of mystery writers, but he coulda been a contender.

G. G. Fickling, actually the husband-and-wife team of Forrest and Gloria Fickling, introduced their bosomy blonde answer to Mike Hammer, Honey West, in 1957's *This Girl for Hire*. Sportswriter Forrest and fashion-writer Gloria came up with the fair-haired shamus after a conversation with Shell Scott's creator Richard S. Prather, who opined that a successful female private eye had never been written. Honey starred in eleven novels and, in the mid-1960s, was brought to life on ABC by lovely Anne Francis, a stunningly appropriate piece of casting.

Shell Scott spawned his own horde of imitators. Jack Lynn's Tokey Wedge—published as quasi-softcore porn by Novel Books of Chicago—took Shell Scott's sexual hi-jinks and violent adventures (already a spoof) to surrealistic heights. Earl Norman's Burns Bannion capers took advantage of an exotic Asian locale, and Johnny Havoc's gimmick was his small size...of course Havoc's creator, John Jakes, went on to a large career, writing epic historical fiction.

KILL ME IN YOKOHAMA

Paperback
1960

SENSUAL STENOS!

Paperback
1960

JOHNNY HAVOC

Paperback
1960

BULLETS ARE MY BUSINESS

Paperback
1960
Of Spillane's imitators, the most direct was John B. West, whose Rocky Steele made Mike Hammer seem like Liberace. That the author was a black doctor in South Africa made the mix even more bizarre.

60c
NOVEL BOOK
6083

They were big and beautiful and alone and passionate—all away from home, all in one big, wild hotel in one big, wild city!

SENSUAL STENOS!

by Jack Lynn

FOR ADULTS

...demand Tokey Wedge shocker for men

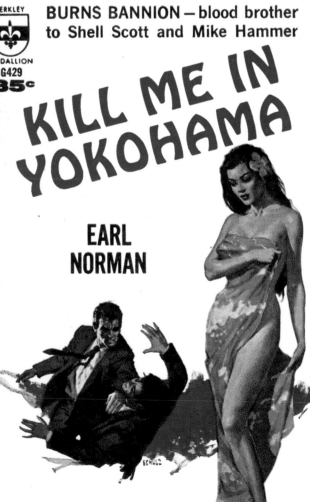

BERKLEY
MEDALLION
G429
35c

BURNS BANNION—blood brother to Shell Scott and Mike Hammer

KILL ME IN YOKOHAMA

EARL NORMAN

A BERKLEY ORIGINAL

S1852
SIGNET BOOK

A new Rocky Steele thriller by the author of
AN EYE FOR AN EYE
and **COBRA VENOM**
JOHN B. WEST

BULLETS ARE MY BUSINESS

You'll pay like I said . . . for all the blood-soaked bodies I promised wouldn't happen. And you're gonna pay my way--

Description: 5 ft. 1 in.
Weakness: Women
Business: Violence

JOHNNY HAVOC

JOHN JAKES

They called him the private eye— with a difference!

GOLD MEDAL BOOK

25c

TONY COSTAINE and BERT McCALL
are flooded with trouble
from an unfinished dam—
and a whisky mine

HOT DAM

The woods had gone wild
with murderers, salacious Scots,
and kidnapers in kilts

NEIL MacNEIL

GOLD MEDAL BOOK

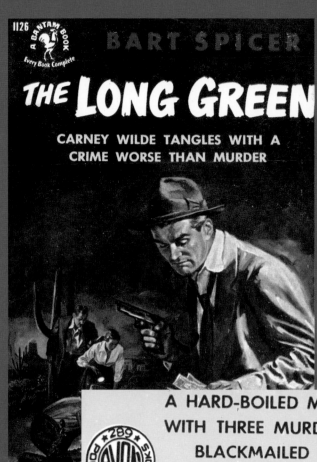

1126 · A BANTAM BOOK · Every Book Complete

BART SPICER

THE LONG GREEN

CARNEY WILDE TANGLES WITH A
CRIME WORSE THAN MURDER

Complete & Un...

HOT DAM

Paperback
1960

THE LONG GREEN

Paperback
1953

LET THEM EAT BULLETS

Paperback
1959

FRIDAY FOR DEATH

Paperback
1951

Numerous P.I.s followed in the paperback wake of Mike Hammer and Shell Scott. Neil MacNeil's wild comedies about Tony Costaine and Bert McCall, like so many Gold Medal thrillers, often sported a Barye Phillips cover. Bart Spicer's first-rate Carney Wilde mysteries suffered at the hands of Bantam's dull art department. *Friday For Death* (with an eye-popping cover from Avon's brilliant art department) features a private eye doing real P.I. work—skip tracing—prefiguring Joe Gores's DKA series. Howard Schoenfield's *Let Them Eat Bullets* features identical twins—a tough private eye and a college professor—who swap places.

...lson, a tough ...private eye, who knew what to feed a public enemy

25c

LET THEM EAT BULLETS

HOWARD SCHOENFELD

AVON 289 POCKET-SIZE BOOK
ANC

A HARD-BOILED MYSTERY OF A MAN FRAMED
WITH THREE MURDERS AND A WOMAN WHO
BLACKMAILED HIM ONCE TOO OFTEN.

FRIDAY FOR DEATH

LAWRENCE LARIAR

Eyes on TV

Honey West—like Mike Hammer, Nero Wolfe, Philip Marlowe, and Lew Archer before her—was one of numerous literary detectives enlisted for duty by radio and/or television. As the private eye became a pop-culture staple, radio and TV began developing their own characters. In the late 1940s, Jack Webb, the future Joe Friday of *Dragnet*, appeared as no less than three made-for-radio private eyes; starting in 1949, Dick Powell, an outstanding screen Philip Marlowe, starred on *Richard Diamond, Private Detective* (created by Blake Edwards), reverting to his Busby Berkeley crooning days once per episode.

Another radio show, *Yours Truly, Johnny Dollar*, featured the adventures of this freelance insurance investigator. Premiering in 1949, Dollar was portrayed by half a dozen actors over the course of the show's run. When the show finally folded its tent in 1962, *Dollar* was the last radio dramatic series to leave the air.

Another of radio's most successful originals, *Martin Kane, Private Eye*, premiered in 1949, running until 1952; success on radio, however, was overshadowed by a run on early television, initially featuring radio's Kane, William Gargan. The show remained on network TV through 1954 with several actors portraying Kane after Gargan left in 1952, among them erstwhile Mike Shayne, Lloyd Nolan, and fast-talking 1930s wiseguy, Lee Tracy. Gargan returned for a one-season syndicated run in 1957.

Once television got into the act, viewers couldn't change the channel without tripping over a private eye tripping over a corpse. The late 1950s saw the TV western fad spawned by *Gunsmoke* and *Have Gun, Will Travel* (the latter a western private eye, by the way, the idea for which was reportedly contributed gratis by Mickey Spillane) eclipsed by a wave of hardboiled private eyes.

In 1958, Los Angeles private detective Stuart Bailey made history in *77 Sunset Strip*, the first hour-long private-eye drama on television; but few remembered that the character actually first came out in the 1946 novel, *The Double Take*, and had already made one movie appearance in 1948's *I Love Trouble* (as played by Franchot Tone). Screenwriter Roy Huggins had also written a handful of *Esquire* novelettes about Bailey, though the character was hardly a household name...yet.

77 Sunset Strip featured former OSS operative Bailey in the suave form of Efrem Zimbalist, Jr. College-boy handsome Roger Smith portrayed Bailey's partner Jeff Spencer, an ex-government agent with a law degree; the pair operated an agency at the titular address next door to Dean Martin's famed restaurant Dino's, where a wannabe private eye, Gerald Lloyd Kookson III, served as parking lot attendant. While the slickly produced Warner Bros. show itself was popular as solid entertainment, "Kookie" created a national sensation; portrayed by Edd Byrnes, Kookie—who flashed a confident smile as he continually combed his hair—prompted a rise in comb sales, had teenagers mimicking his beatnik patter, and even managed to inspire a hit record or two. Byrnes had actually played a psychopath in the pilot, but when the character tested well, Kookie was born.

Despite creator Roy Huggins's hope for a straight-ahead private eye show, the Kookie factor prohibited that. Still, the show managed to stay on the air until 1964, reverting in its final season (as produced by Jack Webb) to a stripped-down format featuring Bailey operating solo out of an office in the Bradbury Building...out of which, in the 1946 novel *Double Take*, the character had originally worked.

Incidentally, Huggins—the television genius who created *Maverick*, *The Fugitive* and, with Stephen J. Cannell, *The Rockford Files*—used *The Double Take* as the basis for episodes of just about every series he produced (not an inconsiderable number).

To cash in on the popularity of *77 Sunset Strip*, Warner Bros. launched *Bourbon Street Beat* in 1959. Featuring Andrew Duggan as Cal Calhoun, Richard Long as Rex Randolph, and Van Williams as the nonalliterative Kenny Madison, the show lasted a solitary season. After its cancellation, Rex Randolph moved to Los Angeles as another operative at *77 Sunset Strip*.

Kenny Madison, still played by Van Williams, transferred to the next *77 Sunset Strip* ripoff, *Surfside Six*. Set in Miami Beach, with pretty much the same setup as its predecessors, *Surfside* also featured Lee Patterson and Troy Donahue as partners in the agency whose telephone exchange provided the title for the show, which ran two years.

Also on the Warner Bros. checklist of sunny, exciting locales for its private-eye shows was Honolulu. Its most successful *Strip* knockoff, *Hawaiian Eye*, ran from 1959 through 1963, with Robert Conrad and Anthony Eisley portraying detectives Tom Lopaka

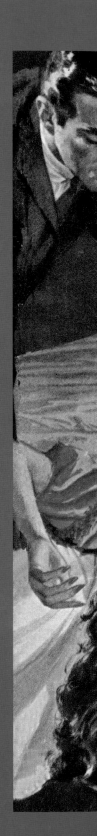

AN ORIGINAL KOZY BOOK

NEW, PRIVATE-EYE SUSPENSE NOVEL
BOLD, BRUTAL, HONEST of
WINE, WOMEN and BULLETS

K Detective K185

60¢ by NICKY WEAVER

Love Blood & Tears

A Hawaiian private eye—
a 40 million dollar heiress—
murder!

DEAD IN BED

Day Keene

A PYRAMID BO

SIGNET BOOKS 1358

He Welshed on His Debts
and Courted Murder

One Tear for my Grave

MIKE ROSCOE
author of
Death Is a Round Black Ball

"I WANTED TO GRAB, RIP AND MANGLE
THE PUNK WHO DID THIS TO DOTTY"

Lady, Don't Die on My Doorstep

JOSEPH SHALLIT

COMPLETE AND UNABRIDGED

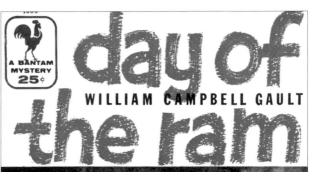

A BANTAM MYSTERY 25¢

day of the ram

WILLIAM CAMPBELL GAULT

I'm a tough private eye—
but no man alive is
tougher than a forty-five
in the hands of a killer.

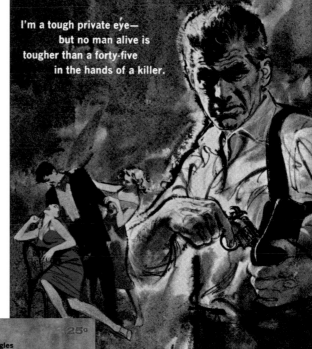

CREST BOOK 309

JOE PUMA tangles
with murder, mugs
and a man-hungry blonde

SWEET WILD WENCH

WILLIAM CAMPBELL GAULT

25¢

DEAD IN BED
Paperback
1959

**LOVE BLOOD
& TEARS**
Paperback
1963

**ONE TEAR FOR
MY GRAVE**
Paperback
1956

**LADY, DON'T DIE
ON MY DOORSTOP**
Paperback
1952

The Spillane influence even extended
to the cover art of rival P.I. novels.
Soft-core porn frequently hijacked the
Spillane approach, as in the Nicky
Weaver novels (Weaver is both author
and lead character) from "Kozy Books."
Some Spillane imitators were actually
very good—Mike Roscoe, the pen name
of a team of ex-P.I.s, wrote lean, evocative tales about hardboiled Johnny April
in Kansas City. Paperback factory Day
Keene contributed Johnny Aloha, an
early Hawaiian eye. Dramatic, strongly
designed cover art by Harry Schaare.

DAY OF THE RAM
Paperback
1956

SWEET WILD WENCH
Paperback
1959

Gault's topline P.I. was
former L.A. Ram Brock
Callahan, nicely depicted by
the stylish Mitchell Hooks.
Gault's Joe Puma was a
bottom-feeder down in the
paperback-original world,
as the title and the painting
(based on a still from a
Bardot movie) indicates.

Thomas B. Dewey's Mac never made a splash, but he endured through changing times—and changing styles of cover art. The detective is suggested by a shadow on both the bold deco cover of *Draw The Curtain Closed* and its retitled reprint (*Dame In Danger*) nine years later, as a deadly Maguire damsel holds a gun on him. Dewey's other private eye, Pete Schofield, rates a tiny portrait on the boldly colorful cover of *Go, Honeylou* (courtesy, artist Victor Kalin) with its unsmiling, nonetheless dimpled doll. Mac was still around, struggling to survive in the hippie days of the early 1970s, getting little help from somber, overly designed cover art that gives no suggestion a 1950s era P.I. lives inside.

DRAW THE CURTAIN CLOSE

Paperback
1949

DAME IN DANGER

Paperback
1958

GO, HONEYLOU

Paperback
1962

THE LOVE-DEATH THING

Paperback
1971

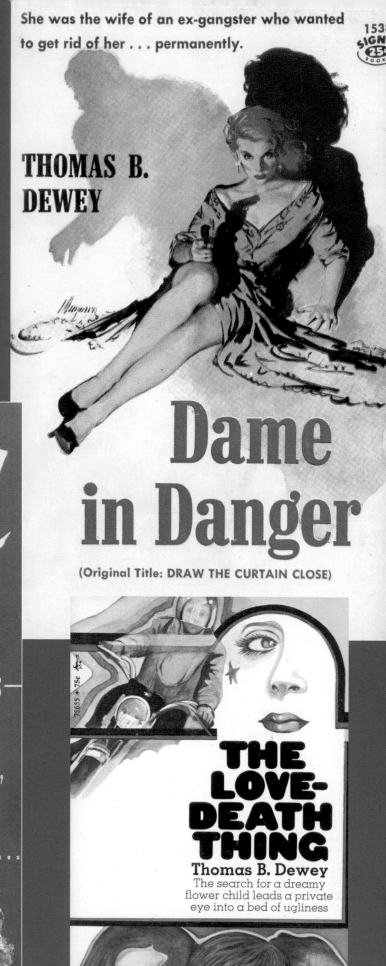

DELL
FIRST EDITION
B197

FRANK KANE'S STACKED DECK

Sizzling cases
of private-eye
Johnny Liddell
who has a passion
for redheads
and a talent
for trouble.

35¢

Chuck Merrick,
private eye, and the
girl with the .32 gun
and the 36" chest

GIRL IN A JAM

James Savage

An Avon Book—35 cents—ICD

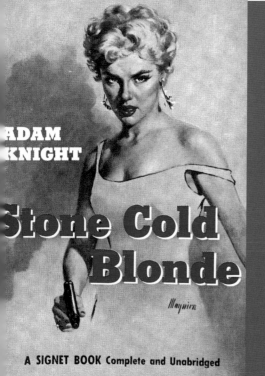

1322
The Case of the Nude Beauty's Corpse

ADAM KNIGHT

Stone Cold Blonde

Maguire

A SIGNET BOOK Complete and Unabridged

1243
SIGNET 25¢ BOOKS

BILL S. BALLINGER
Author of *Portrait in Smoke*

THE BODY in the BED

The Case of The Murdered Mistress

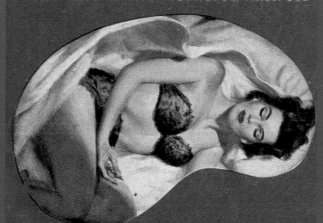

"A good rough-stuff detective story."
—Cincinnati Enquirer

A SIGNET BOOK Complete and Unabridged

STACKED DECK
Paperback
1961

GIRL IN A JAM
Paperback
1959

STONE COLD BLONDE
Paperback
1956

THE BODY IN THE BED
Paperback
1955

Frank Kane's Johnny Liddell had more in common with Shell Scott than Mike Hammer, but Kane's Liddell tales were frequently used as sources for episodes on the late 1950s *Hammer* TV series; Kane's paperback novels —like those of many Dell mysteries—benefited from the tousle-haired, big-eyed, bruised-lipped damsels of master artist Robert McGinnis. Iowa-born Bill Ballinger's lean mysteries (this one starring the unlikely named Barr Breed) got the Signet Books pseudo-Spillane treatment, as did many a paperback by journeyman suspense writer Adam Knight—the cover of whose *Stone Cold Blonde* is the work of McGinnis's only real rival, Robert Maguire. The absurd, yet strikingly designed cover of *Girl In A Jam* might be the work of Mitchell Hooks; but James Savage's Chuck Merrick was just another of an endless army of would-be Mike Hammers...still, who could resist a "girl with the .32 gun and 36" chest?"

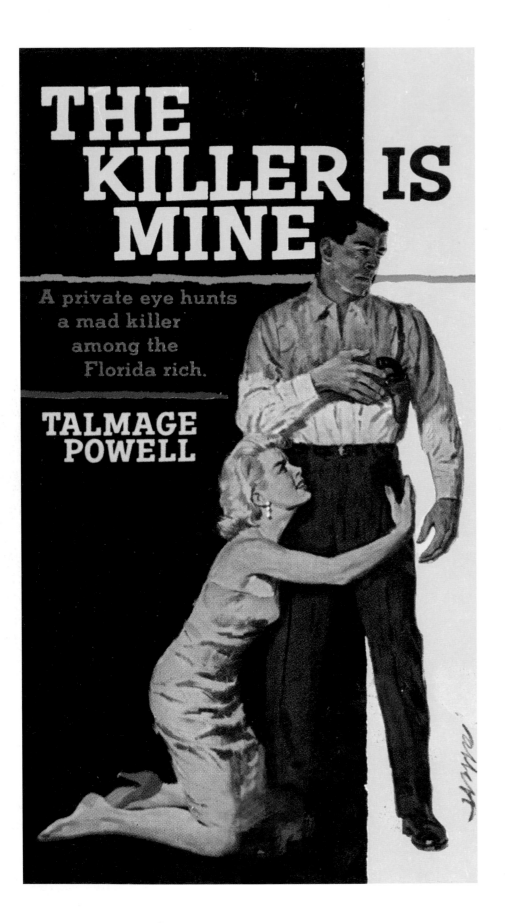

THE KILLER IS MINE

Paperback
1959

Talmage Powell's Ed Rivers staked out Florida as his stamping grounds in anticipation of the Robert B. Parker-inspired trend for writers to abandon L.A. and N.Y.C., and stake out new locations for their private eyes. Cover art by Robert K. Abbett.

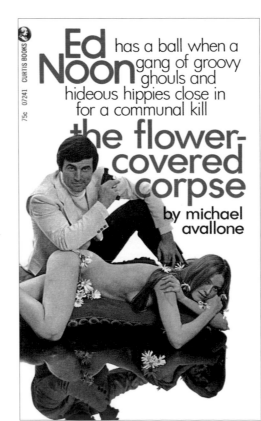

THE CRAZY MIXED-UP CORPSE

Paperback
1957

THE FLOWER-COVERED CORPSE

Paperback
1969

Like his creator Mike Avallone, Ed Noon was a survivor, spanning decades while never landing long at any one publisher. But whether courting the negligée-wearing damsel of 1957 or wooing the flower child of 1969, a private eye needed one thing to make a case worth taking: a corpse.

THE NAME IS JORDAN

Paperback
1962

The private-eye TV craze gave the paperback P.I. a second lease on life (and death); this collection of Scott Jordan (lawyer/P.I.) tales was one of a trio including a Craig Rice "John J. Malone" collection and another featuring Henry Kane's Peter Chambers. Cover by Ronnie Lesser.

A PAUL PINE MYSTERY

JOHN EVANS
HALO FOR SATAN

Twenty-five million bucks is a lot more than I can count on my fingers, but the dough, the blonde and the Bishop all added up—to murder

BANTAM MYSTERY · TWENTY-FIVE CENTS

HALO FOR SATAN

Paperback
1958

This reprint of a 1948 novel is one of a handful of Paul Pine novels by screenwriter Howard Browne. Though his mystery output was meager, Browne's reputation is major.

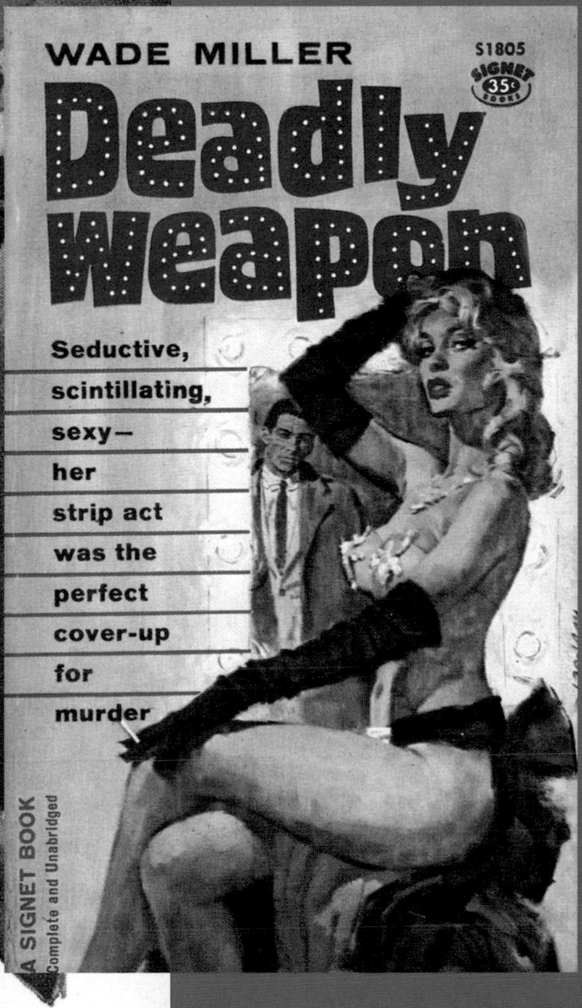

PYRAMID BOOKS   F-720   40¢

THE NAME IS JORDAN

Scott Jordan—lawyer and private eye—up to his ears in dames and danger!

Harold Q. Masur

WADE MILLER   S1805   SIGNET 35¢

Deadly Weapon

Seductive, scintillating, sexy— her strip act was the perfect cover-up for murder

A SIGNET BOOK
Complete and Unabridged

DEADLY WEAPON

Paperback
1960

Deserving rediscovery, Wade Miller's Max Thursday was one of the best tough P.I.s of the Spillane era. Miller was the pseudonym for Robert Wade and Bill Miller. Cover by Abbett.

155

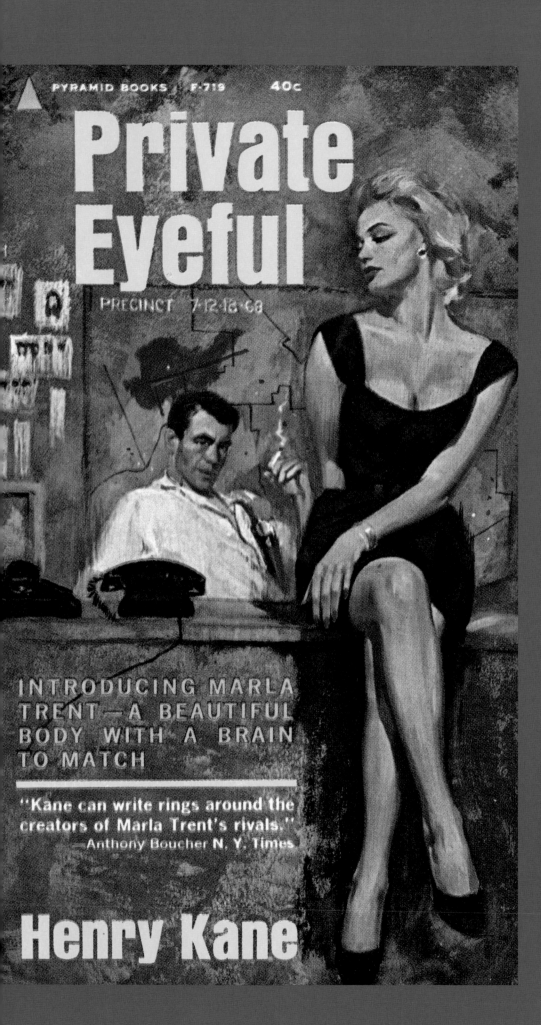

PYRAMID BOOKS F-719   40c

Private Eyeful

PRECINCT 7-12-18-68

INTRODUCING MARLA
TRENT—A BEAUTIFUL
BODY WITH A BRAIN
TO MATCH

"Kane can write rings around the
creators of Marla Trent's rivals."
— Anthony Boucher N. Y. Times

Henry Kane

GOLD MEDAL k1520   40c

NO BUSINESS FOR A LADY

Meet Miss Donovan,
the private eye
who wears mascara.
She's easily the
most beautiful
shamus living

JAMES L. RUBEL

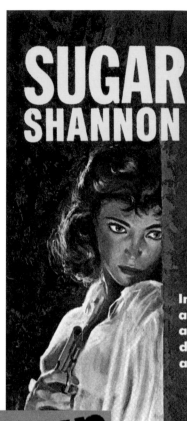

SUGAR SHANNON

In a a dra

A

AD

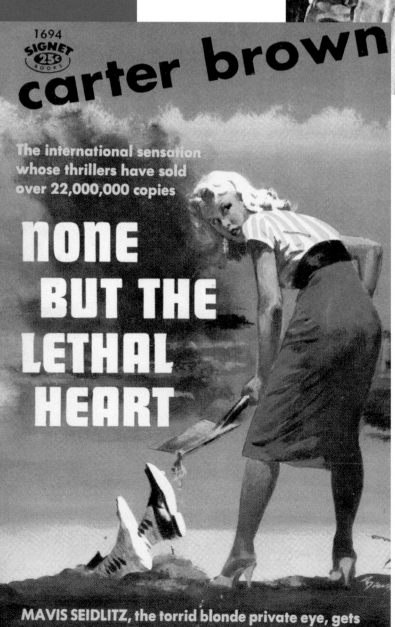

1694

SIGNET BOOKS 25c

carter brown

The international sensation
whose thrillers have sold
over 22,000,000 copies

none BUT THE LETHAL HEART

MAVIS SEIDLITZ, the torrid blonde private eye, gets
stuck with a cold corpse that's too hot to handle.

A SIGNET BOOK

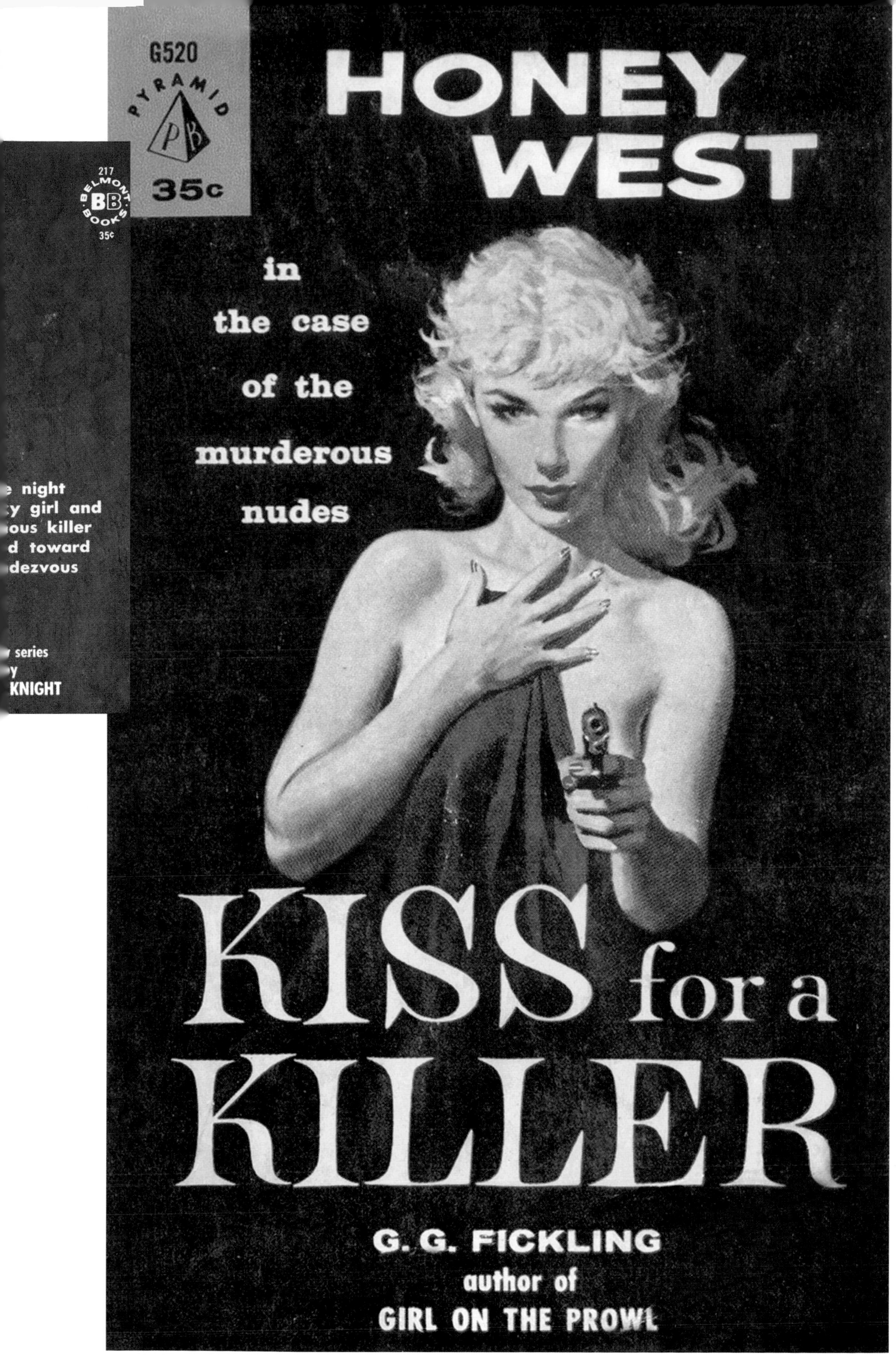
G520
PYRAMID
PB
35c
HONEY WEST
in the case of the murderous nudes
KISS for a KILLER
G. G. FICKLING
author of
GIRL ON THE PROWL
217
BELMONT BOOKS
BB
35¢
night
y girl and
ous killer
d toward
dezvous
series
y
KNIGHT

PRIVATE EYEFUL
Paperback
1962

NO BUSINESS FOR A LADY
Paperback
1950

NONE BUT THE LETHAL HEART
Paperback
1959

SUGAR SHANNON
Paperback
1960

KISS FOR A KILLER
Paperback
1960

The Spillane era saw a wave of female private eyes, the most successful of which was G.G. Fickling's Honey West (sumptuously rendered by Robert Maguire). Honey's chief competition was Australian Carter Brown's Mavis Seidlitz (seen on this wonderful Barye Phillips cover); the best-selling Brown wrote pulpy, playful thrillers and his male detectives included Al Wheeler and Danny Boyd. James L. Rubel's oddly named Eli Donovan was among the earliest tough female P.I.s, but *No Business For A Lady* is apparently her only case. Perhaps the best was Henry Kane's Marla Trent (envisioned by cover artist Mort Engle). But *Private Eyeful* is her only solo caper (she teams elsewhere with Kane's Peter Chambers). Sugar Shannon was Adam Knight's short-lived attempt to stay in the P.I. game with a Honey West imitation.

and Tracy Steele. Though not as big as the Kookie craze, Connie Stevens's portrayal of singer/photographer Cricket Blake won her a host of fans. These *Strip* knock-offs and other Warner Bros. series recycled scripts from each other, particularly during a writers' strike that had the Hawaiian eyes cracking "cases" previously handled by the likes of westerners Cheyenne and Bret Maverick.

Debuting in 1957, *Richard Diamond, Private Detective*—a non-musical re-working of the radio series—featured David Janssen as an ex-New York cop turned private eye; after nearly two years in New York, the setting shifted to Hollywood, where Diamond used an answering service manned by the sexy-voiced "Sam," an actress only seen from the waist down. Never revealed in the show's credits, leggy Sam's identity became a mystery in itself. Eventually, Sam was revealed to be none other than a very young Mary Tyler Moore, who left after that season and was replaced by Roxanne Brooks for the show's final season in 1960.

The most successful—and influential—show of the TV-private-eye craze was writer/director/producer Blake Edwards's *Peter Gunn* (premiering 1958). In 1954 Edwards had written and helmed a *Mike Hammer* pilot with Brian Keith that had been rejected as too violent by the networks; he retooled the working-class Spillane model into a hipper, slicker mode, giving his star Craig Stevens a Brooks Brothers wardrobe, a taste for jazz music, and a Cary Grant-esque smoothness. The Henry Mancini score, with that famous pulsating theme song, joined with Edwards's witty, quirky dialogue (the most distinctive since *Dragnet*) to make *Peter Gunn* the single best private-eye show of the era. No small part of that success was the tongue-in-cheek delivery of Stevens and fellow cast members Lola Albright, Gunn's thrush girl friend, and Hershel Bernardi, the detective's world-weary cop pal.

When not hanging out at "Mother's," the jazz club where his girlfriend Edie was the house singer, Peter Gunn found time to solve cases, often—in the Hammer tradition—helping out friends for no fee. Despite his cool, suave, wryly understated demeanor, Gunn was as ruthlessly violent as Mike Hammer and represents the "missing link" between Spillane's Hammer and Ian Fleming's super-spy James Bond.

When Edwards took *Gunn* (1967) to the big screen to compete with Bond, he lifted the ending of the Mike Hammer novel, *Vengeance is Mine!*, further indicating his Spillane debt. A tough, watchable, typically witty variation on the show, unfortunately minus Albright and Bernardi, the film was a box office flop. An excellent Edwards 1989 TV movie with Peter Strauss replacing Stevens unfortunately did not lead to more TV movies or a new series; interestingly, this movie update of the most modern of P.I. shows was set in period—the late 1950s.

1960s Sleuths and a Black Eye

Through the 1960s, the private-eye craze raged on, and readers of John D. MacDonald were treated to one of best detective series of the second half of the twentieth century. Already forty-three novels into his career, MacDonald—nudged by Gold Medal Books editor Knox Burger, eager to replace Richard S. Prather's departed Shell Scott series—finally bit the bullet and took a crack at a series character.

Travis McGee worked as a private detective in every respect except title and license; referring to himself as a "salvage consultant," ostensibly he recovered stolen property for half its value. What he really did was solve mysteries. Unleashed in 1964's *The Deep-Blue Goodbye* and an immediate success, McGee appeared in more than twenty books before MacDonald passed away in 1986.

McGee lived on his houseboat, "The Busted Flush," but his adventures occasionally took him away from his Florida anchorage. Being a chronic complainer didn't keep McGee from having his way with pretty much every damsel in distress he met. Somehow, no matter how deep the trouble, McGee—in true latter-day knightly fashion—would inevitably save the day and the girl. He was occasionally assisted by his best friend and next-slip neighbor, Meyer, an economist with a formidable intellect and a yen for conversation.

McGee's only big-screen appearance came in a hard-hitting 1970 adaptation of the 1966 novel, *Darker Than Amber*, with Rod Taylor right on the money as McGee. Sam Elliott played McGee in a 1978 TV movie of *The Empty Copper Sea* (1978), a less successful outing. Like the Philip Marlowe and Mike Hammer novels before them, the Travis McGee books, with their crackling first-person narration, are perhaps best played out in the theater of the mind.

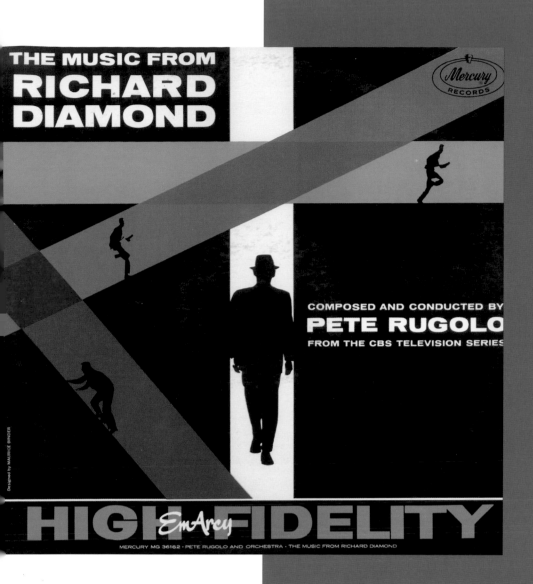

HIGH FIDELITY

Soundtrack LP
1959

This album is a true collector's item: the music is by famed jazz conductor/composer Pete Rugolo; the liner notes are by original radio Diamond (and screen Marlowe) Dick Powell; and the album cover is designed by Maurice Binder, the creative genius responsible for the James Bond credits sequences

GUNN

Soundtrack LP
1967

Though the film was a box-office failure, *Gunn* featured both TV's Peter Gunn (Craig Stevens) and the music of Henry Mancini, whose jazzy scoring for the original series had revolutionized television music.

77 SUNSET STRIP

Soundtrack LP
1959

Music was a big part of the P.I.'s world, and both the snapping-fingers theme song and several Edd "Kookie" Byrnes novelty discs made the charts.

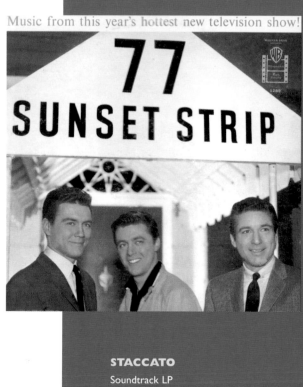

STACCATO

Soundtrack LP
1959

Even Peter Gunn's imitators got soundtracks, as the likes of Elmer Bernstein took Mancini's challenge. Moody method actor John Cassavetes made a fine musician/P.I. in a series often featuring jazz greats such as guitarist Barney Kessel and vibraphonist Red Norvo.

ORIGINAL MOTION PICTURE SOUNDTRACK ALBUM
"LADY IN CEMENT"

COMPOSED AND
CONDUCTED BY
HUGO MONTENEGRO

S4204

Anthony Rome
solves the case of the multiple murders in

MIAMI MAYHEM

A POCKET BOOK
1269
25¢

236
BELMONT
BOOKS
35¢

Ray Milland
stars in
the T.V. Series

MARKHAM

Markham was playing with
dynamite in
**"THE CASE OF
THE PORNOGRAPHIC PHOTOS"**

A SAVAGE CRIME NOVEL
by Lawrence Block

LADY IN CEMENT

Soundtrack LP
1968

Sinatra made an ideal
tough P.I., and the
Tony Rome movies—
while hardly classics
—remain at least as
entertaining today as
when they were made.

GOLD MEDAL
k1272

JOHN D.
MACDONALD

"... one of the most creative and reliable writers
of paperback originals ... Mr. MacDonald can
create a series character just as well as he does
everything else in the suspense field."
—ANTHONY BOUCHER
THE N. Y. SUNDAY TIMES BOOK REVIEW

THE
QUICK
RED FOX

Meet
TRAVIS McGEE
—and the beautiful woman
who swung a little too wild
and lived a little too free
for the lily-white reputation
McGee was supposed to protect

**THE QUICK
RED FOX**

Paperback
1964

John D. MacDonald's
Travis McGee was
envisioned as a mod-
ernized replacement
for Prather's Shell
Scott. This early
paperback includes
a blue-eyed portrait
of McGee that echoes
the recurring portrait
of Shell Scott on the
Prather covers.

MIAMI MAYHEM

Paperback
1960

Marvin Albert's trio of Tony Rome mysteries
were solid P.I. novels, but today stand out from
the pack chiefly because Frank Sinatra chose
to make films of the first two.

MARKHAM

Paperback
1961

Even an also-ran Gunn imitator like the
syndicated *Markham* got the occasional
TV tie-in novel. This is notable for its
cover portrait of star Ray Milland and as
an early P.I. entry by Lawrence Block.

KINDS OF LOVE, KINDS OF DEATH

Hardcover
1966

Tucker Coe/Donald Westlake's Mitchell Tobin was one of the first of the tough, recognizably human detectives of the modern era, and—while a descendent of Hammett, Chandler, and Spillane—not in their debt.

445-08203-075   75c

**They're not cool slick heroes.
They're worn, tough men
and that's why they're so dangerous.**

"HICKEY & BOGGS"

— BY PHILLIP ROCK —

Based on an original screenplay by Walter Hill

Now a sensational action-packed movie from United Artists
starring Robert Culp as Franklin Boggs
and Bill Cosby as Albert Hickey

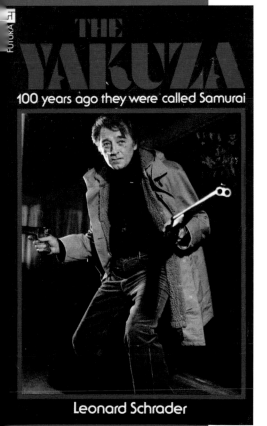

THE YAKUZA

100 years ago they were called Samurai

Leonard Schrader

THE YAKUZA

Paperback
1975

A minor classic of the private-eye form, *The Yakuza* (directed by Sydney Pollack) anticipates American interest in Japanese gangster culture, and affords Robert Mitchum his finest P.I. role in a screenplay by *Chinatown*'s Robert Towne and Paul Schrader (from Leonard Schrader's story).

HICKEY & BOGGS

Paperback
1972

This unfortunately little-seen reunion of the *I, Spy* TV team of Cosby and Culp—in an early Walter Hill screenplay—redefined the P.I. in melancholy, modern terms.

From 1960 to 1962, Marvin Albert, writing as Anthony Rome, chronicled the hard-hitting adventures of detective Tony Rome in three novels that prefigure the McGee novels with their Florida/houseboat settings. The first two, *Miami Mayhem* and *Lady in Cement*, were produced as feature films (1967 and 1968), though the former's title was changed to *Tony Rome*. Frank Sinatra, ideal for Bogart-style roles in his fifty-something years, played Rome in these fun, minor P.I. films, co-starring first with Jill St. John, then Raquel Welch.

Though Donald E. Westlake is among the giants in mystery fiction, he has only made one major foray into P.I. writing, under the pseudonym Tucker Coe. *Kinds of Love, Kinds of Death* (1966) introduced Mitch Tobin, an ex-New York cop turned private eye, whose dalliance with another woman got his partner killed. Lasting five novels, Tobin investigated crimes while, with his wife's help, he regrouped his life, even as he constructed a literal (and symbolic) wall to hide behind.

By 1972's *Don't Lie to Me*, Tobin had made the decision to get licensed; but once the character's demons were exorcised, Westlake apparently lost interest. Westlake's earliest books (prior to his more famous comic novels) rework Hammett's Continental Op tales, sometimes bordering on the private-eye tale, and his celebrated series about professional thief Parker occasionally veers into tough amateur-sleuth territory—an amoral version of the Saint.

Introduced in 1967, Dan Fortune, the one-armed New York private eye created by Michael Collins (pseudonym for Dennis Lynds), has been featured in over fifteen novels and numerous short stories. Fortune first appeared in *Act of Fear*. Writing under a host of pseudonyms, Lynds, also an acclaimed literary writer, has authored more than seventy-five novels, including entries in *The Shadow* and *Nick Carter-Killmaster* series. A thoughtful wordsmith with an eye on social concerns, Lynds is also a past president of the Private Eye Writers of America and received its Lifetime Achievement Award in 1988.

Who's the black private dick who's a sex machine to all the chicks? Ernest Tidyman's John Shaft, of course. *Shaft* (1970) introduced readers to something new: a successful, unapologetically African-American private eye, as tough as Mike Hammer, as cool as James Bond, as irresistible to women as both of 'em put together. Big and athletic, Shaft always stayed in shape. The survivor of a rough and tumble childhood in Harlem, Shaft knew the value of his body as a survival tool. He always dressed sharply, caught women with barely more than a glance, and wouldn't hesitate to kill an enemy to protect himself or his clients and friends. The working-class private eye had become an ethnic hero.

Director Gordon Parks brought *Shaft* to the big screen in 1971, one of the first and most successful of the so-called "blaxploitation" movies, finding an audience well beyond the black community. Charismatic, confident Richard Roundtree portrayed the investigator in three films, including *Shaft's Big Score* (1972, also directed by Parks from a Tidyman script) and the little-seen, first-rate *Shaft in Africa* (1973, directed by John Guillermin from a Sterling Silliphant screenplay). A watered-down TV series of TV movies followed (1973–1974), also starring Roundtree but otherwise standard network fare, effectively ending the Shaft fad.

Roundtree played his famous character in the 2000 big-screen continuation version of *Shaft*, in which a cool Samuel L. Jackson portrayed the famous detective's nephew. The original series included seven novels (some of which were paperback originals and may have been ghosted), the final one being 1975's *The Last Shaft*. That final novel, never published in the United States, is the rare P.I. novel to bring a major series to a definitive conclusion. Ernest Tidyman's contribution to the private-eye genre is a major one.

By the mid-1970s, however, the private eye seemed both a fixture of popular culture and a little used up. The short-lived Shaft craze had been the last new wrinkle the genre had seen; the private eye was a healthy if cliched presence on TV, but largely missing in action on the newsstands and bookstore shelves. Just as such pioneers as Daly, Hammett, Chandler, and Spillane had jump-started the genre with new directions, the private-eye novel needed new blood and fresh ideas.

SHAFT
ERNEST TIDYMAN

SHAFT
Hardcover
1970

SHAFT'S BIG SCORE
Paperback
1972

A breakthrough and potentially a new direction in the P.I. story, Ernest Tidyman's Shaft burned bright and fast in the popular culture, until his creator disposed of him a few years later. The Issac Hayes movie theme—and Richard Roundtree's memorable screen presence—have seen to it that Shaft has left an indelible impression. Too bad the tough, crisp books are forgotten.

N7540 ★ 95¢ ★ A BANTAM BOOK

YOU LIKED HIM BEFORE SO HE'S
BACK FOR MORE—THE BADDEST MOTHER
EVER MADE OF MUSCLE AND ICE!
A BRAND-NEW SHAFT CAPER
BY ERNEST TIDYMAN

SHAFT'S BIG SCORE

NOW A JOLTING NEW MOVIE FROM MGM!

MICKEY SPILLANE

(1918–)

Mickey Spillane, circa 1954, is seen
recording his "Mickey Spillane's Mike
Hammer Story" record album, on which
he portrayed Hammer for the first time.

Mickey Spillane was born in Brooklyn, New York, on March 9, 1918, the son of a bartender. An only child who swam and played football as a youth, Spillane got a taste for storytelling by scaring other kids around the campfire. After a truncated college career, Spillane—already selling stories to pulps and slicks under pseudonyms—became a writer in the burgeoning comic-book field, a career cut short by World War II. Spillane, who had learned to fly at air strips as a boy, became an instructor of fighter pilots.

After the war, Spillane converted an unsold comic-book project—"Mike Danger, Private Eye"—into a hard-hitting, sexy novel. The $1,000 advance was just what the writer needed to buy materials for a house he wanted to build for himself and his young wife on a patch of land in New Jersey.

The 1948 Signet reprint of his 1947 E.P. Dutton hardcover novel, *I, the Jury*, sold in the millions, as did the six tough mysteries that soon followed; all but one featured hard-as-nails P.I. Mike Hammer. The Hammer thriller *Kiss Me, Deadly* (1952) was the first-private eye novel to make the *New York Times* best-seller list.

Much of Mike Hammer's readership consisted of Spillane's fellow World War II veterans, and the writer —in a vivid, even surrealistic first-person style—escalated the sex and violence already intrinsic to the genre, in an effort to give his battle-scarred audience hard-hitting no-nonsense entertainment. For this blue-collar approach, Spillane was attacked by critics (who perceived

MIKE DANGER

Comic art
circa 1941

The unpublished cover of Spillane's comic book, *Mike Danger*, drawn by Harry Sahle.

I, THE JURY

Hardcover
1947

A memorable airbrushed cover captures the final moments of Spillane's debut novel.

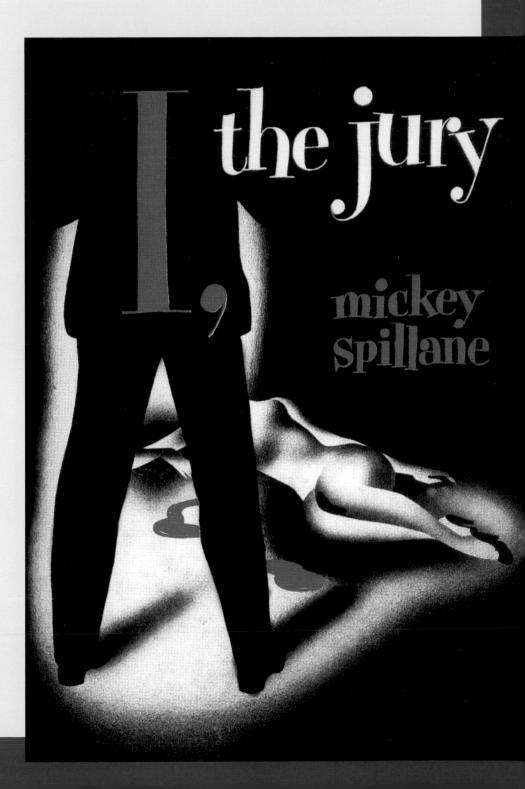

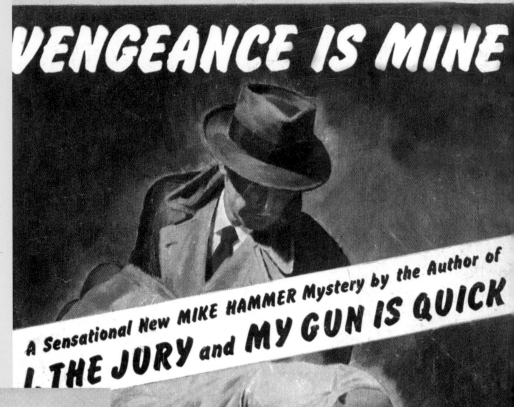

Mickey Spillane

VENGEANCE IS MINE

A Sensational New MIKE HAMMER Mystery by the Author of

I, THE JURY and **MY GUN IS QUICK**

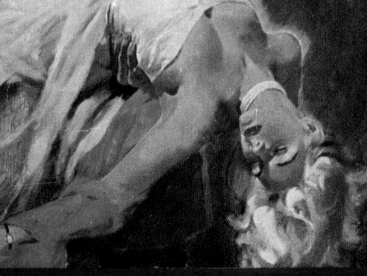

A SIGNET BOOK
Complete and Unabridged

699

Mickey Spillane

I, THE JURY

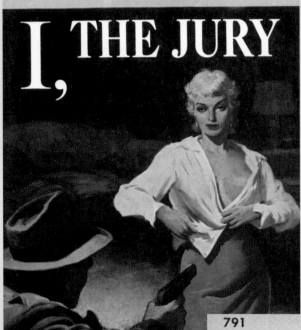

The Sensational Mike Ha...

A SIGNET BOO...
Complete and Unabri...

791

More SENSATIONAL than I, THE JURY

MY GUN IS QUICK

MICKEY SPILLANE

A NEW MYSTERY
by the Author of I, THE JURY

SIGNET BOOKS
Complete and Unabridged

I, THE JURY	VENGEANCE IS MINE	THE BIG KILL
Paperback	Paperback	Paperback
1952	1951	1951

MY GUN IS QUICK	ONE LONELY NIGHT	KISS ME, DEADLY
Paperback	Paperback	Paperback
1950	1951	1953

These six paperbacks changed mystery fiction and paperback publishing forever. As powerful a writer as Spillane is, these covers played no small role in his success. The *noir*-ish art never really reveals Mike Hammer's face, encouraging reader identification, as on Lou Kimmel's classic cover (actually, the second painting to illustrate Signet's paperback) of *I, The Jury*. The artist responsible for the bold, hyper-realistic cover to *My Gun Is Quick* is unknown; but the gifted Kimmel provided the art for *Vengeance Is Mine!*, *One Lonely Night*, and *The Big Kill*, with James Meese stepping in for the particularly memorable cover of *Kiss Me, Deadly*.

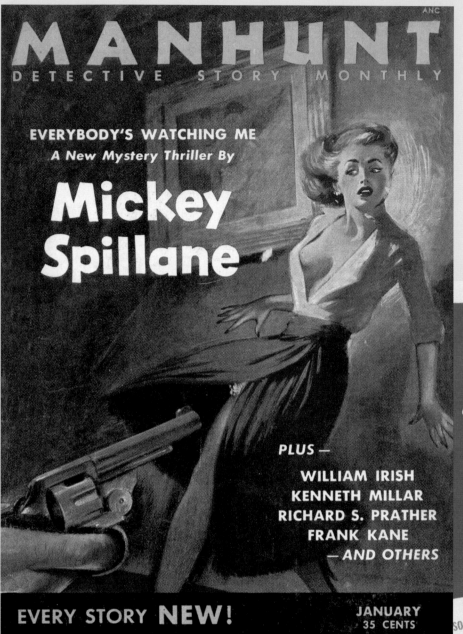

I, THE JURY

Lobby Card
1953

Spillane detested director Harry Essex's 3-D version of *I, The Jury*, starring unknown Biff Elliot as Hammer. A 1999 British Film Institute screening of a restored 3-D print revealed *I, The Jury* as an underestimated gem, with stunning *noir* cinematography by John Alton.

MANHUNT

Magazine
1953

This is the first issue of *Manhunt*, and the prominence of Spillane's name on the cover shows how valuable he was to the launch of the magazine…and compare his billing to fellow luminaries William Irish (Cornell Woolrich), Kenneth Millar (Ross MacDonald), and Richard S. Prather. Spillane's four-part *Manhunt* serial, "Everybody's Watching Me," is collected in *Tomorrow I Die* (1984).

KISS ME, DEADLY

Laserdisc
1993

Robert Aldrich and screenwriter A.I. Bezzerides intended to undermine Spillane with their nasty version of Mike Hammer (Ralph Meeker). Along the way they created one of the best private eye movies, bringing the sex and violence of the books (and their covers) to gritty life in an apocalyptic masterpiece considered by many to be the last great film *noir*.

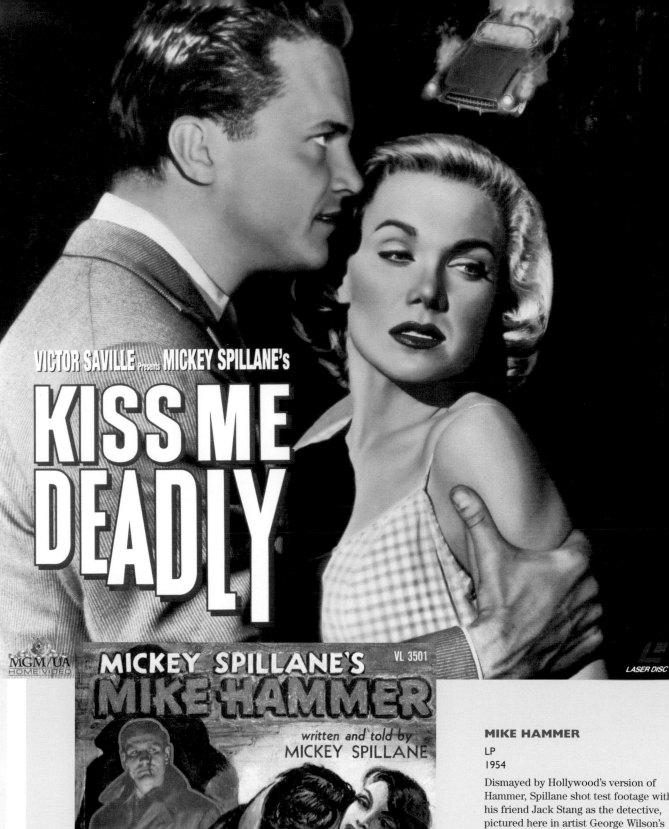

first time...
hat
MICKEY
SPILLANE

le *ice*
sts out
he screen
t you in

IENSION

OR SAVILLE Production · Released thru UNITED ARTISTS

nal Screen Service Corp. Licensed for display only in connection with his picture at your theatre. Must be returned immediately thereafter.   53 \435   3D

VICTOR SAVILLE Presents MICKEY SPILLANE's

KISS ME DEADLY

MGM/UA HOME VIDEO   VL 3501   LASER DISC

MICKEY SPILLANE'S
MIKE HAMMER

written and told by
MICKEY SPILLANE

music by STAN PURDY and his orchestra

A 33⅓ RPM LONG PLAYING RECORDING

MIKE HAMMER

LP
1954

Dismayed by Hollywood's version of Hammer, Spillane shot test footage with his friend Jack Stang as the detective, pictured here in artist George Wilson's painting/montage. But for this rare, self-produced album, Spillane played Hammer himself in "Tonight, My Love." The platter included jazzy P.I. themes that Spillane feels Mancini plundered conceptually for *Peter Gunn*.

him as a right wing, misogynistic vulgarian) and adored by readers (who perceived him as a great storyteller). His influence on the mass-market paperback was immediate and long-lasting, his success imitated by countless authors and publishers. Gold Medal Books, pioneering publisher of "paperback originals," was specifically designed to tap into the Spillane market.

Spillane's career has been sporadic; his conversion in 1952 to the conservative religious sect, the Jehovah's Witnesses, is often cited as the reason he backed away, for a time, from writing the violent, sexy Hammer novels. Another factor may be the enormous criticism heaped upon Hammer and his creator. Spillane claims only to write when he needs the money, and it's undeniable that in periods of little or no publishing, Spillane has been occupied with other pursuits—flying, travelling with the circus, appearing in motion pictures, and nearly twenty years spoofing himself and Hammer in a lucrative series of Miller Lite beer commercials.

The controversial Hammer has been the subject of a radio show, comic strip, and two television series, starring Darren McGavin (in the late 1950s) and Stacy Keach (in the mid-1980s with a 1997 revival). Numerous gritty movies have been made from Spillane novels, notably director Robert Aldrich's seminal film *noir Kiss Me Deadly*, 1955, and *The Girl Hunters* (1963), starring Spillane as his famous hero.

THE GIRL HUNTERS

Publicity photo
1963

Mickey Spillane embraces Shirley Eaton in the film *The Girl Hunters*, the script for which was by Spillane, who starred as his own famous detective—the only mystery writer ever to do so.

MICKEY SPILLANE

Trade paperback
2001

A recent—and beautifully designed—omnibus of Mike Hammer novels is poised to acquaint a new generation with the toughest of hard-boiled dicks.

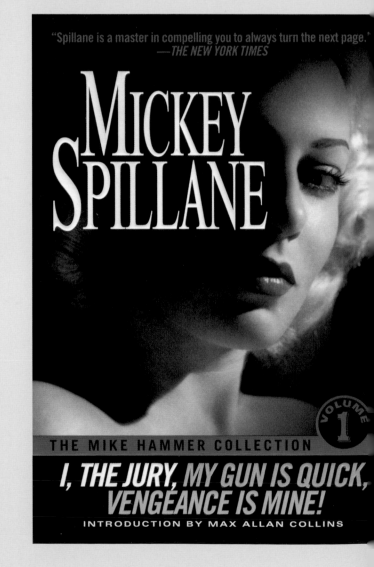

"Spillane is a master in compelling you to always turn the next page."
—*THE NEW YORK TIMES*

MICKEY SPILLANE

VOLUME 1

THE MIKE HAMMER COLLECTION

I, THE JURY, MY GUN IS QUICK, VENGEANCE IS MINE!

INTRODUCTION BY MAX ALLAN COLLINS

Publicity photo, CBS
1984

Stacy Keach starred as Mike
Hammer in several series; a fine
actor, and an effective Hammer,
Stacy's TV dick was adrift in
campy waters. Keach read audio
books of the original novels that
showed him at his Hammer best.

CHAPTER

6

FURTHER SUSPECTS

TV Detectives

In the wake of Vietnam, the trend for a postwar rise in the popularity of detective fiction continued; however, after the World Wars and the Korean conflict, the degree of violence and sex in detective fiction had tended to ratchet up a notch each time. The Ian Fleming-led spy boom of the 1960s — a Cold War phenomenon — had also spawned an escalation of violence, which spilled over into the detective field, notably the Shaft series. • But the 1970s saw the emergence of new and different detectives, few of whom were in the tradition of increasing violence associated with Race Williams, Mike Hammer, and James Bond. The TV cop shows of the period — *Starsky and Hutch*, *Hawaii Five-O*, *S.W.A.T.*, and the rest — filled that brutal bill. So did a breakout paperback action series, Don Pendleton's *The Executioner*, in which a Spillane-style hero reeks vengeance on the entire Mafia. This modern pulp series is still running, long after its creator's passing. • Only television's *Mannix* (1967–1975), starring Mike Connors as a two-fisted brawler, seemed to offer typical tough-guy detective action. The well-produced if cliched show constantly featured Joe Mannix in fist fights, getting whaled on by the bad guy before bouncing back. (Recommended listening: Bob and Ray's radio satire, *Blimmix*.) Mannix once even fought off hoods with both his hands encased in casts, and he also wasn't above

THE BIG FIX

Trade paperback
1973

Simon's Moses Wine was a refreshing attempt to bring the private eye into the Woodstock world.

occasional gunplay before showing his tender side by hugging a client's child or some equally sentimental gesture. This was standard TV fare, courtesy of producer Bruce Geller of *Mission: Impossible* fame, professional but stale, at least after its innovative first-season concept was sadly abandoned: as created by Levinson and Link, Mannix initially had been a tough P.I. employed by a huge, computerized agency.

As the country's politics leaned more left, some detective fiction turned in that direction as well. Premiering in *The Big Fix* (1973), Roger L. Simon's Moses Wine found right-wing conspiracies under every rock. In 1975, Richard Dreyfuss portrayed the counter-culture P.I. in an okay big-screen version of the first novel; but after an initial splash over the "hippie detective" gimmick, the character never really took hold, and Simon—a successful screenwriter, and first-rate mystery novelist who brings considerable wit to Wine— only sporadically followed up with further adventures.

No onslaught of counter-culture private eyes followed, though television saw its share of offbeat detectives, for which Wine and the changing times paved the way. These were gimmick detectives, less violent than *Peter Gunn* and the recently departed *Mannix*, occasionally straight-laced, often vapid.

A prime offender was *Charlie's Angels*, debuting in 1976, featuring beautiful police academy dropouts who went to work for the unseen Charlie (John Forsythe). Supposedly a great private eye himself, Charlie did no investigating, leaving that duty instead to the three jiggling "angels," initially Farrah Fawcett, Jacqueline Smith, and Kate Jackson. Braless and brainless, the series spawned numerous T & A imitators, a pop cultural phenomenon courtesy of Aaron Spelling. A recent big-budget big-screen remake treated this insipid material with campy fondness.

Tenafly featured an African-American family man (James McEachin) who worked as an operative in a large detective agency. Looking more like a corporate "suit" than a rumpled P. I., Tenafly seldom found himself meeting the same clients as Shaft or Mike Hammer.

George Peppard starred as *Banacek*, an insurance investigator who only got called in on "impossible" crimes. He would spout old Polish proverbs along the way to nabbing the bad guy, explaining how the pieces of the puzzle fit together.

One of the longest running mystery shows, *Barnaby Jones* (1973–1980) had Buddy Ebsen (the former Jed Clampett) playing a retired detective who comes back to solve the murder of his son, then decides to keep the shingle out a while longer. Thus Barnaby Jones became the "old" detective (shades of dime novels), while William Conrad as *Cannon* (1971-1976) was the resident "fat" detective...and so on.

Stellar Shamuses

No such gimmicks were found on *The Rockford Files* (1974–1980), which cast James Garner as the self-effacing and laconic detective, only slightly braver than Garner's earlier television success, Bret Maverick. Rockford, who lived in a trailer, didn't really charge ahead as much as he seemed to wobble through investigations. As he put the pieces together, he always stumbled to overcome the "help" provided by his cantankerous father (Noah Beery) and his wildly ineffective, con-man/ex-cellmate Angel (Stuart Margolin). Witty scripts, Garner's wry, irritable presence, and an extended cast of oddball characters helped make *Rockford* the quintessential 1970s TV P.I. show.

A similar series, *Harry O*, starring David Janssen—former Richard Diamond (and Richard Kimble)—ran only two seasons (1974–1976) but is much beloved by detective fans. Janssen's beach-dwelling Harry Orwell—rumpled, melancholy, forever repairing his boat, "The Answer"—carried echoes of both Philip Marlowe and Travis McGee. The series, created by Howard Rodman, who contributed several fine scripts, utilized Chandler-style, masculinely poetic voice-over narration...and very well.

A short-lived spin-off of *Rockford*, *Richie Brockelman, Private Eye* (1978), might be dismissed as just another gimmick show, this one about a "kid" private eye. Certainly Brockelman (perfectly portrayed by Dennis Dugan) is young and looks younger, trading the traditional trench coat for tennies, plaid shirt, and jeans. Affable, a con man in the Rockford tradition, Brockelman is the co-creation of Stephen J. Cannell (*Rockford's* co-creator) and Stephen Bochco (of *NYPD Blue* fame). The short-lived show was one of the best of its era.

Another blink-and-you-missed-it private-eye show—*Tenspeed and Brownshoe*—featured Ben Vereen as a con man and Jeff Goldblum as a naive would-be private eye. One of the many joys of the witty,

CHARLIE'S ANGELS
Trading cards
1977
Actresses Farrah Fawcett, Jaclyn Smith, and Kate Jackson—despite the "jiggle" nature of their popular TV series—did represent young women as heroic P.I.s for a new generation.

$1.25   445-00354-125

Based on the great new TV detective series!

THE ROCKFORD FILES #2
THE DEADLIEST GAME

Rockford finds himself on the wrong side of the law when he follows a treacherous trail of death and doublecross

a novel by Mike Jahn

$1.25   445-00337-125

Hollywood's #1 private eye in a behind-the-screams case of drugs, death and doublecross

DAVID JANSSEN
STARRING AS
HARRY O

THE HIGH COST OF LIVING
a novel by Lee Hays
Based on the smash-hit ABC-TV series!

HARRY O

Paperback
1976

Harry Orwell (David Janssen) spent the first of two well-regarded seasons in San Diego and the second in Santa Monica, living on the beach in both cases. Future Charlie's Angel Farrah Fawcett had a recurring role.

RICHIE BROCKELMAN, PRIVATE EYE

Publicity still
1978

Richie Brockelman (future film director Dennis Dugan) first appeared in a TV movie, then moved over to a *Rockford* supporting role before spinning off into a short-duration, highly regarded series.

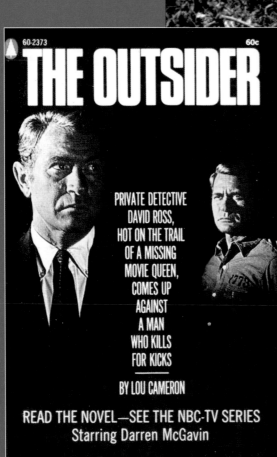

60-2373   60c

THE OUTSIDER

PRIVATE DETECTIVE DAVID ROSS, HOT ON THE TRAIL OF A MISSING MOVIE QUEEN, COMES UP AGAINST A MAN WHO KILLS FOR KICKS

BY LOU CAMERON

READ THE NOVEL—SEE THE NBC-TV SERIES
Starring Darren McGavin

THE ROCKFORD FILES #2

Paperback
1976

Jim Rockford—like actor James Garner's (and writer Roy Huggins's) earlier anti-hero, Bret Maverick— professed cowardice and was the rare P.I. who would abandon a client if the going got too rough.

THE OUTSIDER

Paperback
1969

Darren McGavin portrayed TV sleuths such as Flashgun Casey, Mike Hammer, and Carl Kolchak; but his little-seen *Outsider* (as rumpled P.I. David Ross) was a Roy Huggins dry run for Jim Rockford.

fast-paced series were the constant references to "Mark Savage" novels by a mystery writer named Stephen J. Cannell...real-life creator of the series. Goldblum's Lionel "Brownshoe" Whitney quotes such deathless passages as: "Okay, so maybe Savage was the guy on the short end. But he'd have his memories, and his scars.... He'd have his one-room apartment and his TV dinner, and—for a Hollywood tough guy—maybe, just maybe, that could be enough."

The major problem with 1970s detective shows was that the good ones simply did not last. Also, the influx of cop and private detective series seemed to delegate the amateur sleuth to the caste of second-class citizen.

Case in point: *The Adventures of Ellery Queen* (1975–1976), starring Jim Hutton as the affable amateur detective, constantly in the hair of his father, Inspector Queen (David Wayne). Set in 1947, the show also included a rival detective, Simon Brimmer (John Hillerman), who competed with Ellery to solve the mystery. Brimmer's elaborate solutions were invariably wrong, though polite Ellery would compliment his rival on his imaginative thinking. Every week, right before the last commercial, in the style of the Queen radio program of the 1940s, Ellery would ask "Have you figured it out? Do you know who the murderer is?"

The clues were always there for the careful viewer to find and interpret. Often based on the original Queen short stories, beautifully produced, well-acted by all-star casts with Hutton in the role he was born to play, the show barely lasted a season. A similar series from producer Peter S. Fischer, *The Eddie Capra Mysteries* (1978–1979), also failed in short order.

History Mysteries

Chinatown (1974), the classic film starring Jack Nicholson as P.I. Jake Gittes, helped spark another trend: the period private-eye story. Robert Towne's evocation of Chandler and Hammett, intertwined with a well-researched historical mystery, made for a flawless screenplay, which film schools now teach as an example of a perfectly constructed script. Roman Polanski's sensitive direction—and his own rewriting of the ending to invoke the tragic murder of his wife,

Sharon Tate—joined with indelible star turns from Nicholson and Faye Dunaway in what many believe to be the finest of all private-eye movies, *The Maltese Falcon* and *The Big Sleep* not excepted.

A little-known TV movie, *Banyon* (which led to a single-season series in 1972), had actually pioneered the period private-eye movie, establishing the concept that the Hammett/Chandler-era P.I. had been around long enough to exist in history. Robert Forster, in fine Bogart-ish form, portrayed the tough detective, who operated out of the Bradbury Building, in another strong series that failed.

Chinatown seemed to make it official: private eye stories set in the 1930s and 1940s were a sub-genre of their own. This was further underscored by a strong remake of *Farewell, My Lovely* (1975) starring Robert Mitchum as Phillip Marlowe and set in 1940s L.A.

Accordingly, another short-lived series, *City of Angels*, starring Wayne Rogers—fresh off his success on the M*A*S*H TV series—attempted to capitalize on the Polanski film's success. A collaboration between Roy Huggins and his protégé Stephen J. Cannell, the series used Huggins's Stuart Bailey stories as their basis, which means *City of Angels* and *77 Sunset Strip* shared the same source material. Rogers was wonderful as wise-guy private eye Jake Axminster, who also worked out of the Bradbury Building, and the series beautifully evoked a corrupt Los Angeles in the 1930s, with the toughest hardboiled detective yarns seen on TV since the heyday of *Peter Gunn*. No one noticed.

But the *Chinatown* approach soon began to show up in the world of literary detectives. Screenwriter/director Andrew Bergman contributed a pioneering pair of period private-eye novels—*The Big Kiss-Off of 1944* (1974) and *Hollywood and LeVine* (1975)—which feature nonglamorous P.I., Jake LeVine. The novels are funny but not parodies, and the detective encounters famous historical figures. In 1977, Stuart Kaminsky introduced Toby Peters, a 1940s detective-to-the-stars who debuted with Errol Flynn as a client in *Bullet for a Star*; a long series has ensued.

In 1990, Walter Mosley's semi-private eye, Easy Rawlins, entered the postwar L.A. scene in the evocative *Devil in a Blue Dress*, which eventually found its way to the big screen with Denzel Washington assaying the Rawlins role and Don Cheadle tagging along as Easy's gun-toting friend, Raymond "Mouse" Alexander. Mosley achieved fame in part due to President Clinton singling him out as his favorite mystery writer; but the novels have won critical and reader acclaim on their own considerable merits.

Traditional TV

The 1980s turned out to be a kinder, gentler time for the amateur sleuth. Led by *Murder, She Wrote*, whose first season began in 1984, the quality of amateur sleuths on television increased even if the quantity didn't. Angela Lansbury's portrayal of mystery writer Jessica Fletcher won the show—which had a similar all-star format to the unsuccessful *Ellery Queen* series—a devoted following. For twelve years, Jessica found time to write fictional mysteries which brought in enough money for her to travel the world solving "real" mysteries. Most seasons, five of the episodes would be set in Cabot Cove, Maine, the hometown of the retired teacher turned author and gumshoe; the remainder of the shows would focus on Jessica's travels.

The Father Dowling Mysteries, starring Tom Bosley as Ralph McInerny's crime solving priest, debuted in 1989 and lasted two years. In 1993, Dick Van Dyke's lightweight whodunit, *Diagnosis Murder*, following the adventures of Dr. Mark Sloan and his cop son (Barry Van Dyke), seemed to inherit the *Murder, She Wrote* audience.

The 1980s saw the nonviolent, less traditional private detective trend continue. *Riptide, Simon & Simon*, and *Matt Houston* did little to expand the P.I. genre; neither did the short-lived *Partners in Crime*, which featured Lynda Carter (*Wonder Woman*) and Loni Anderson (*WKRP in Cincinnati*) as the two ex-wives of a successful though murdered private detective. It lasted from September to December of 1984, and viewers and reviewers were wondering if the genre had been stretched to the breaking point. Other shows were coming along that would prove that theory wrong.

An impudent, innovative show that experimented with breaking the "fourth wall," *Moonlighting* (1985–1989) featured David Addison (Bruce Willis) and Maddie Hayes (Cybill Shepherd) battling their mutual attraction with the same zest they used to pursue bad guys. The same theory prevailed on *Remington Steele*, where female P.I. Laura Holt (Stephanie Zimbalist) solved cases, while trying not to fall for con man "Remington Steele" (Pierce Brosnan), who took on the identity of her supposedly fictional boss. Though *Steele* was lightweight entertainment, the role proved star-making for a future James Bond, Brosnan; and Bruce Willis has been heard from since as well.

Hart to Hart (1979–1984) brought back a variation on Nick and Nora Charles. Jonathan (Robert Wagner) and Jennifer (Stefanie Powers) Hart were a wealthy jetset couple who traveled around the world solving mysteries. The show was narrated by their chauffeur Max (Lionel Stander) and even featured a family pooch, Freeway, to supplant Asta. Though a pedestrian show, *Hart to Hart* benefited from the charm and star power of its leads.

The top-private eye series of the 1980s, *Magnum, P.I.* (1980–1988), starred magnetic Tom Selleck as the ne'er-do-well detective who would rather lounge on the beach than fight crime; with a strong family of supporting characters and its Hawaiian setting, *Magnum* was a crowd-pleaser in the *Rockford* vein and harked back to the traditional private-eye construction.

In 1985, when Robert Urich debuted as *Spenser: For Hire*, a straightforward, no-nonsense P.I. story in the tradition of Marlowe and Spade was again on American television. (A *Mike Hammer* series with Stacy Keach was also airing.) Not coincidentally, Spenser was inhabiting the best-seller list, as well.

Robert B. Parker's Boston-based private eye arrived on the scene in *The Godwulf Manuscript* in 1973, but the series was not an overnight success. The gourmet, Yuppie private eye—a sensitive brute—was the perfect updating of the traditional P.I., however, and to date, the single-named detective has appeared in twenty-seven novels, spawning the popular TV series and several TV movies starring Robert Urich and later Joe Mantegna. A monogamous lover to longtime paramour Susan Silverman, ex-boxer Spenser can also mix it up with the best of them, or he can resort to gunplay with no compunction about killing—that sensitive, he's not. He also has a cadré of allies to call upon should things become too hot for even his enviable skills; the most important of these allies is African-American Hawk, a stone-cold killer but Spenser's devoted friend.

Parker has his detractors: The Spenser novels have been called ineffective mysteries, the clipped style condemned as artificial, the use of Hawk racist, the literary references (including the detective's own name) pretentious. But no one can deny that Parker is the first private-eye writer since Mickey Spillane to explode onto the best-seller lists with such an impact that he has provided countless other mystery writers a career boost.

Armed and Feminist

The only phenomenon to compare to Parker is the emergence of the hard-boiled female private eye. The godmother of this sub-genre is Marcia Muller, whose Sharon McCone debuted in 1977's *Edwin of the Iron Shoes*. The first American tough female private-eye series written by a woman, the McCone novels garnered her author the Private Eye Writers of America's Lifetime Achievement Award in 1993. After twenty-one novels and two short story collections, blue-collar, San Francisco-based McCone has graduated from working as an operative for the All Souls Legal Cooperative to running her own agency.

Several other pioneers in the tough female P.I. sub-genre should be noted. Half of the G.G. Fickling team was female: Gloria Fickling, co-creator of Honey West; and Maxine O'Callaghan's Deliah West made her first appearance in 1975 in a short story. Several men also broke ground in the sub-genre: James D. Lawrence's black female P.I. debuted in 1975's *The Dream Girl Caper*; Arthur Kaplan's Charity Bay first appeared in 1976's *A Killing for Charity*; and the Ms. Tree comic book character, created by the Collins/Beatty team, was introduced in 1980.

In 1982 Sara Paretsky brought readers tough V.I. Warshawski in *Indemnity Only*. Known as "Vic" to her pals, Warshawski is the veteran of nine novels and a short story collection. A private eye in Chicago, V.I. has proved to be tough, stubborn, and a bulldog when she gets her teeth into something. Most of her cases deal with

10

TEN BEST PRIVATE EYE TV SERIES

THE ROCKFORD FILES

HARRY-O

PETER GUNN

CITY OF ANGELS

TENSPEED AND BROWNSHOE

PERRY MASON

MAGNUM, P.I.

RICHIE BROCKELMAN, PRIVATE EYE

77 SUNSET STRIP

MANNIX

Compiled by John Javna and Max Allan Collins from a survey of mystery writers and fans.

TENSPEED AND BROWNSHOE
Publicity still
1980

Odd couple Jeff Goldblum and Ben Vereen portrayed naive P.I. Lionel "Brownshoe" Whitney and con artist E.L. "Tenspeed" Turner in the short-lived cult-favorite TV series.

BANYON

Paperback
1971

Robert Forster—whose career would be rejuvenated by *Jackie Brown* (1997)—appeared in a pre-*Chinatown* period P.I. telefilm and series. Forster's self-produced, independent, private-eye film, *Hollywood Harry* (1985), indicated the actor's continuing affection for the genre.

HOLLYWOOD AND LEVINE

Hardcover
1975

Though Andrew Bergman's career as a screenwriter (and later director) limited his contributions to the genre, his pair of LeVine novels opened the door for Kaminsky and numerous other period P.I. writers.

CITY OF ANGELS

Publicity art
1976

Another short-lived cult favorite, *City Of Angels*, established comic actor Wayne Rogers as a first-rate TV P.I. Rogers would portray similar tough P.I.s in a TV movie (*Passion And Paradise*, 1989) and in a recurring role on *Murder She Wrote*.

CHINATOWN

Soundtrack LP
1974

Jack Nicholson's P.I. Jake Gittes would return in *The Two Jakes* (1990) in the second of what was a proposed trilogy from screenwriter Robert Towne. Unfortunately, the poor critical and popular reception for this fine film probably doomed the final chapter from ever being attempted.

STUART KAMINSKY
BULLET FOR A STAR

A stunningly authentic novel of the
Chicago gangland of the Thirties
True DETECTIVE
MAX ALLAN COLLINS

EXTRA THE NEWS EXT
MAYOR CERMAK SH

SPHERE

POODLE SPRINGS
RAYMOND CHANDLER AND ROBERT B. PARKER

BULLET FOR A STAR

Hardcover
1977

The versatile Kaminsky—a film-
school teacher and screenwriter
—has kept his funny Toby Peters
series alive for decades, inventing
wild, murderous scenarios for
Hollywood's Golden Age stars.

TRUE DETECTIVE

Trade paperback (British edition)

This Shamus-winning series
was the first hybrid of private-eye
fiction and true-crime subjects.
Nathan Heller has "solved" the
Lindbergh kidnapping, the Huey
Long assassination, and the
Roswell incident, among others.

POODLE SPRINGS

Hardcover
1989

Robert B. Parker joined the
historical P.I. brigade with
his completion of Raymond
Chandler's final fragment of
a Marlowe novel. A sequel to
*The Big Sleep, Perchance To
Dream*, followed in 1990.

DEVIL IN A BLUE DRESS

Paperback
1990

One of the most popular and critically successful of the period P.I. writers, Walter Mosley pays careful attention to the characterization of his hero, Easy Rawlins, well-portrayed by Denzel Washington in the 1995 film.

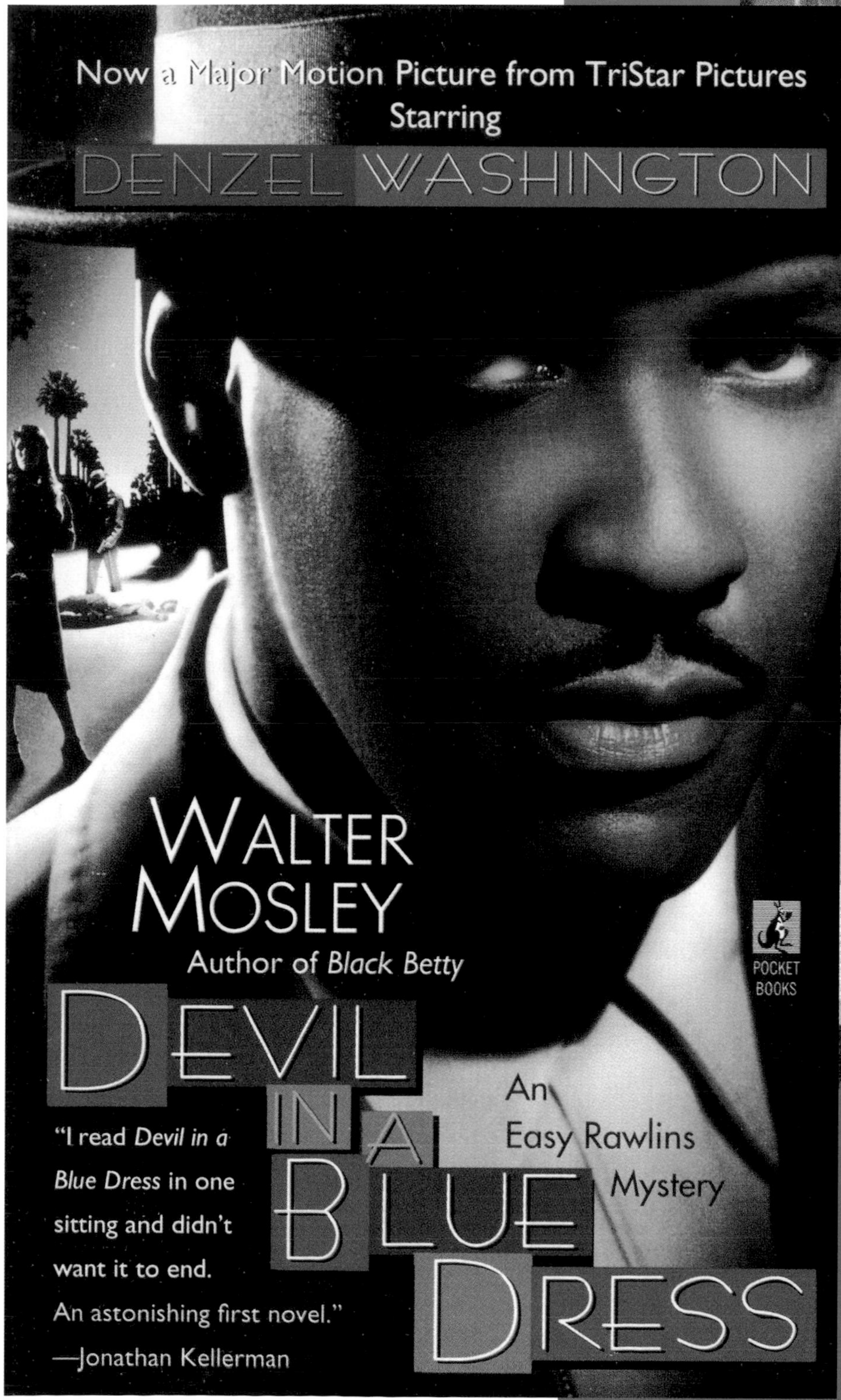

Now a Major Motion Picture from TriStar Pictures
Starring
DENZEL WASHINGTON

WALTER MOSLEY
Author of *Black Betty*

POCKET BOOKS

An Easy Rawlins Mystery

"I read *Devil in a Blue Dress* in one sitting and didn't want it to end. An astonishing first novel."
—Jonathan Kellerman

DEVIL IN A BLUE DRESS

MURDER, SHE WROTE
A DEADLY JUDGMENT

BY JESSICA FLETCHER & DONALD BAIN

Based on the Universal television series
Created by Peter S. Fischer, Richard Levinson & William Link

MURDER, SHE WROTE

Paperback
1996

Angela Lansbury (the erstwhile Mrs. Lovett of *Sweeney Todd*) portrays a character equally informed by Agatha Christie's Miss Marple and Dame Agatha herself.

V.I. WARSHAWSKI

VHS jacket
1991

The best-selling Paretsky saw her tough Chicago P.I. reach the screen in the form of Kathleen Turner, a seemingly good choice. The film was a weak representation of Paretsky's crisp, feminist approach, though its box-office failure has not impaired the ongoing success of the novels.

"F" IS FOR FUGITIVE

Paperback
1990

Paretsky's chief competitor, former screenwriter Grafton, conveys a Southern California sensibility in a first-person style, as compelling as it is chatty. She is the daughter of respected mystery writer, C.W. Grafton.

SUE GRAFTON
author of 'E' IS FOR EVIDENCE

'F' IS FOR FUGITIVE
A KINSEY MILLHONE MYSTERY

HARD EVIDENCE

Paperback
2000

Cat Marsala and her creator D'Amato are among the best of the new breed of tough female-detective fiction. Chicagoan D'Amato is also a respected true-crime author—and a former trainer of leopards (the only one in this book!).

KATHLEEN TURNER

V. I. WARSHAWSKI

"She's As Sexy As She Is Smart!"
— The New York Times

"[The] wittiest food mystery of the season."
—*Kirkus Reviews*

AWARD-WINNING AUTHOR OF *HARD BARGAIN*
BARBARA D'AMATO

HARD EVIDENCE
A CAT MARSALA MYSTERY

Author of CONFESSION

NANCY PICKARD

POCKET STAR BOOKS

A JENNY CAIN MYSTERY

BUT I WOULDN'T WANT TO DIE THERE

"Vintage Nancy Pickard. [She is] universally considered a mystery master...."—*Jackson* (MS) *Clarion Ledger*

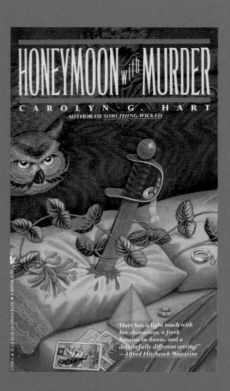

HONEYMOON WITH MURDER

CAROLYN G. HART

AUTHOR OF *SOMETHING WICKED*

"Hart has a light touch with her characters, a fresh heroine in Annie, and a delightfully different setting!"—*Alfred Hitchcock Magazine*

HONEYMOON WITH MURDER
Paperback
1989

Oklahoman Hart—also the author of the popular Henrie O. series—mines *Thin Man* territory with a light, suspenseful touch with mystery bookstore owner Annie Laurance and her eventual husband, detective Max Darling.

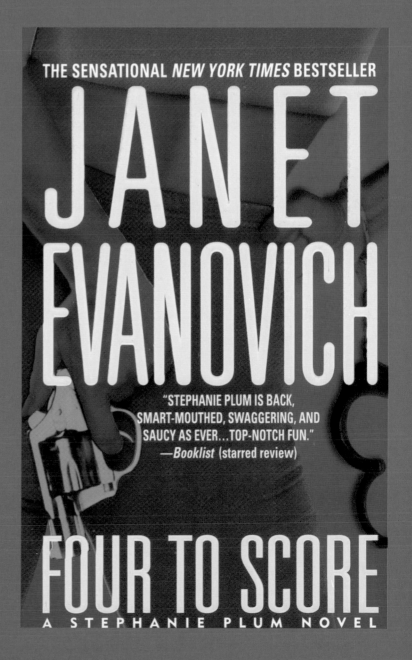

THE SENSATIONAL *NEW YORK TIMES* BESTSELLER

JANET EVANOVICH

"STEPHANIE PLUM IS BACK, SMART-MOUTHED, SWAGGERING, AND SAUCY AS EVER...TOP-NOTCH FUN."
—*Booklist* (starred review)

FOUR TO SCORE

A STEPHANIE PLUM NOVEL

BUT I WOULDN'T WANT TO DIE THERE
Paperback
1994

Nancy Pickard's Jenny Cain operates on a New England beat, though this case takes her to the mean streets of Manhattan. Pickard has won numerous awards for her lively fiction.

FOUR TO SCORE
Paperback
1999

Among the new tough P.I.s are the occasional bounty hunter, including popular Evanovich's Stephanie Plum, a witty, gritty protagonist.

Ed Gorman, the editor of *Mystery Scene* magazine, has used his hometown, Cedar Rapids, Iowa, as the backdrop for a series of novels featuring ex-cop turned private eye, Jack Dwyer. A wannabe actor, Dwyer frequently deals with social issues; the homeless are a concern of the particularly impressive *A Cry of Shadows* (1990). Gorman tempers a melancholy view of the world with sharp wit and a lean style honed as a writer of literary short fiction.

Working all over the world, but centered originally in New York, S.J. Rozan's private eyes, Bill Smith and Lydia Chin, have found themselves in cases as far away as Hong Kong. The pair first appeared in 1994's *China Trade* and have alternated narrative duties ever since. Along the way, Rozan has captured both Shamus and Anthony (presented by the Bouchercon) awards.

Seattle is home base for Earl Emerson's Thomas Black. A private eye who used to be a police officer, Black has appeared in nearly a dozen novels since 1985's *The Rainy City*. Unlike many of his contemporaries, Black doesn't get to fall in bed with every woman he meets and finally ends up marrying Kathy Birchfield. Emerson also writes a series featuring firefighter and sheriff Mac Fontana, which more closely mirrors Emerson's own career as a Seattle firefighter.

Working out of his office in San Francisco, Bill Pronzini's Nameless Detective—who predates Parker's Spenser—has appeared in more than two dozen novels, as well as two short story collections since his introduction in *The Snatch* (1971). A San Francisco cop for fifteen years, Nameless—the lack of a name is a reference to Hammett's Continental Op, courtesy of pulp fan Pronzini—prefers not to carry a gun. The first president of the Private Eye Writers of America, Pronzini received its Lifetime Achievement Award in 1987.

Also writing about San Francisco and bringing a realism due to his experience there as a P.I., Joe Gores has written a half-dozen private-eye novels featuring repo man and skip tracer Daniel Kearney, starting with *Dead Skip* (1973). He has also authored *Hammett: A Novel* (1975), mirroring Hammett's own real-life detective experiences. That book was made into a feature film starring Frederic Forrest as Hammett, but only slightly resembled Gores's strong novel, another pioneer in the "period" private-eye sub-genre. Edgar-winner Gores has also written for many mystery TV shows over the years, including *Remington Steele* and *Mickey Spillane's Mike Hammer*.

Another real-life private eye—Jerry Kennealy—brings that added authenticity to his Nick Polo series, which began with 1987's *Polo Solo*, featuring a San Francisco P.I. who initially was serving time in a federal penitentiary. After being aided by a powerful politician and completing a dangerous mission on his behalf, Polo finds himself out of jail and in possession of both a private investigator's license and a gun permit. Polo has appeared in almost a dozen novels since.

Perhaps closest in style to Parker himself are Robert Crais and Jeremiah Healy (Walter Mosley also closely follows the Spenser pattern). Crais, whose private eye, Elvis Cole, first met readers in *The Monkey's Raincoat* (1987), has received numerous nominations and awards, including the 1996 Shamus Award for Best Novel for *Sunset Express*. To date, the Disney-loving smartass Cole and his Hawk-like partner, Joe Pike, have appeared in eight novels. Crais has also written for TV series such as *Hill Street Blues*, *Quincy*, and *L.A. Law*.

Sharing Boston with Parker as a setting for his P.I. tales, Healy—a former law professor at the New England School of Law and past president of the Private Eye Writers of America—introduced former M.P.-turned-P.I. John Francis Cuddy in 1984's *Blunt Darts*, named one of the best mysteries of the year by *The New York Times*. His second book, *The Staked Goat* (1986), earned him a Shamus for Best Private Eye Novel. Cuddy has appeared in more than a dozen novels.

The founder of the Private Eye Writers of America and creator of the Shamus Awards, Robert Randisi has worked hard to see private-eye fiction recognized as an art form. Along the way, he has created several continuing private detectives himself, notably Manhattan's ex-boxer Miles Jacoby and Brooklyn's Nick Delvecchio. Jacoby, whose career begins with *Eye in the Ring* (1982)—literally the ex-boxer's first case—has learned from mistakes he's made along the way. Delvecchio debuted in 1987's *No Exit From Brooklyn*. An underrated writer, Randisi is the creator of the best-selling, long-running western series, *The Gunsmith*.

One of the finest writers in the genre, John Lutz is perhaps best known as the author of *SWF Seeks Same* (1990), which became the hit movie *Single White Female*; but he has also carved out an enviable niche in the detective field. His Florida private eye, Fred Carver, is an ex-Orlando cop who has appeared in half a dozen novels, beginning with 1986's *Tropical Heat*. Lutz's other series character,

41-706-3 • A PINNACLE BOOK • $2.75

"ne of the most notable mysteries of the year"
—*The New York Times Book Review*

It takes more than brains to be a private eye;
it takes guts.
Amos Walker is heavy on both.

Motor City Blue
Loren D. Estleman

THE WRONG CASE

Paperback
1978

Though the author of only a handful of novels, Crumley is one of the most widely praised writers of private-eye fiction in the post-Vietnam period. A dissenting minority has criticized the lowlife, "loser" nature of his characters, detectives included.

MOTOR CITY BLUE

Paperback
1983

Loren Estleman's Amos Walker is a 1940s-style sleuth in very contemporary situations; his turf is (as the title of this, his first appearance, indicates) Detroit. Estleman also writes historical crime fiction and is a highly regarded writer of western fiction.

02399-3 ✳ $1.95 ✳ A BANTAM BOOK

The powerful shocker of a tough private eye on the trail of corruption and brutal murder.
The Wrong Case
A novel by
James Crumley

JOSEPH HANSEN
FADEOUT
A DAVE BRANDSTETTER MYSTERY/1

e most exciting and effective writer of the classic
te-eye novel working today." —*The L.A. Times*

FADE OUT

Paperback
1980

Hansen's gay insurance investigator, Dave Brandstetter, is as rugged and masculine as any modern P.I., and both he and his creator handle the detective's sexual preference in an appealingly matter-of-fact manner. Gay topics occasionally take center stage but do not dominate the series.

A CRY OF SHADOWS
A JACK DWYER MYSTERY

ED GORMAN

ACT OF GOD

Hardcover
1994

An ex-captain of the Military Police, as well as a former practicing attorney, Healy outranks many of his contemporaries in drawing upon his own experience in the writing of detective fiction.

Dead Letter
JONATHAN VALIN

DEAD LETTER

Hardcover
1981

One of the finest and most highly praised of post-Parker P.I. writers, Jonathan Valin has not enjoyed the popular success he deserves. His Harry Stoner is both tough and humane, and Valin paints a gritty, real-world portrait of midwestern America in the1980s and 1990s.

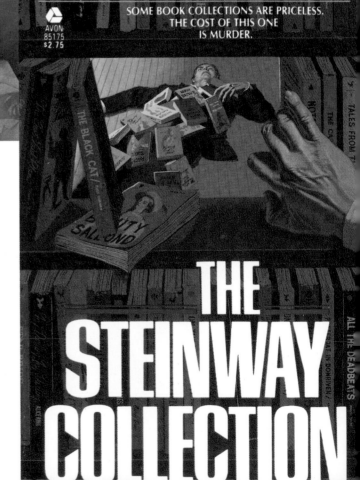

Jeremiah Healy
Act of God
A John Cuddy Mystery

THE NEW MILES JACOBY MYSTERY

SOME BOOK COLLECTIONS ARE PRICELESS.
THE COST OF THIS ONE
IS MURDER.

AVON
85175
$2.75

THE STEINWAY COLLECTION
ROBERT J. RANDISI
Author of EYE IN THE RING

A CRY OF SHADOWS

Hardcover
1990

Gorman rejects yuppie trendiness in his sad, literate novels, some of the best of which feature Jack Dwyer. A master of the short story, the somewhat reclusive Gorman is also an acclaimed writer of western fiction.

YELLOW DOG PARTY

Hardcover
1991

Noted for his dark humor and fast pacing, Washington state firefighter Emerson has been compared to both Raymond Chandler and Ross MacDonald.

A THOMAS BLACK MYSTERY

YELLOW DOG PARTY

EARL EMERSON

Author of *Help Wanted: Orphans Preferred* and *Deviant Behavior*

THE STEINWAY COLLECTION

Paperback
1983

Randisi's founding of the Private Eye Writers of America—whose Shamus Award rivals the Edgar in prestige—unfortunately tends to overshadow his own considerable body of work in the genre.

ODDS AGAINST

Paperback
1975

A typical Francis hero, Sid Halley suffers physical distress in *Odds Against*, his already crippled hand battered until amputation is needed. Francis has made racing itself his "series," though Halley does star in a handful of novels.

83350·2 · $2.25 · POCKET

ODDS AGAINST
THE GRIPPING THRILLER THAT INSPIRED
THE PBS MYSTERY! TV PRODUCTION...
———— THE ————
RACING GAME

DICK FRANCIS

Alo Nudger, is a St. Louis private eye who is both sullen and, to tell the truth, not terribly brave. Even his name is a wink at the genre: Mike hammers his cases, Alo nudges his. Nudger first appeared in 1976's *Buyer Beware* and has appeared in seven novels since.

Although the private eye has mostly disappeared from network television and the big screen—even Shaft was a cop in the 2000 update of the classic story—today's mystery novels have continued to branch out in new and interesting directions.

While most writers within the genre have recurring characters, Dick Francis has a recurring setting. Though two books feature jockey Kit Fielding and three more feature jockey turned private eye Sid Halley, Francis has written over thirty-five mysteries somehow related to the sport of horse racing. A former jockey himself, Francis' first novel was *Dead Cert* (1962), and that led to a career that has included three Edgar Awards for Best Novel and a Mystery Writers of America Grand Master Award in 1996.

With the exception of Perry Mason, lawyers have been ruled out of order for this book. But one rule-breaking lawyer is simply too fine and interesting a detective to ignore. Created for British TV (Thames Television) in 1980, John Mortimer's Horace Rumpole is a barrister like none other. Married to a wife he refers to constantly as "She Who Must Be Obeyed," he is also not above referring to a judge as "old darling." Leo McKern simply *is* Rumpole. He has cast such a shadow over the role that its creator has stated that when McKern grows weary of the role, Mortimer will stop writing the stories. Though the TV show came first, the books of Rumpole's adventures have proved to be equally satisfying over the years. In the United States, the show airs on PBS as *Rumpole of the Bailey* as part of the *Mystery* series.

Like Dashiell Hammett, Carolina Garcia-Aguilera has worked as a private investigator herself, lending credibility to her Lupe Solano series. Steven Saylor has taken the hard-boiled period piece beyond the 1930s and 1940s, his hero, Gordianus the Finder, investigates crimes in Ancient Rome.

Amateurs as well have seen new horizons. Thomas Perry's Jane Whitefield is a Native-American woman who helps people in trouble disappear. Along the way, she solves the mystery behind the need to disappear. Dana Stabenow's Kate Shugak is a former investigator for the D.A.'s office in Anchorage, who has since returned to her

Aleut roots and digs into crime in the Great White North. Jonathan Kellerman's Alex Delaware, a Los Angeles child psychologist, is constantly embroiled in mysteries detailed in more than a dozen novels, including his 1985 debut, *When the Bough Breaks*, which won both the Edgar and Anthony awards.

Harlan Coben's Yoo-Hoo swilling sports agent, Myron Bolitar, has starred in a half-dozen mysteries that show him to be lovable, wry, and a good detective. After debuting in 1995's *Deal Breaker*, Bolitar earned his creator both a Shamus and an Edgar for the third book in the series, *Fade Away* (1996).

Also returning to popularity has been the unlicensed P.I. in the tradition of Travis McGee, but with a twist. Living on the edges of society, these investigators solve cases and frequently mete out their own brand of justice without the benefits, or hindrances, of police aid and sanction. Andrew Vachss's Burke and Lawrence Block's Matthew Scudder both fit this Spillane-influenced mold.

Vachss, a child-abuse attorney in New York City, centers all of his Burke books around that theme. The product of a lifetime spent in institutions, Burke regularly finds himself investigating the seamy underside of the Big Apple. With the help of an esoteric bunch of allies, his "family," he was introduced in *Flood* (1985).

A recovering alcoholic, at least in the later books, Matt Scudder is an ex-cop who first appears in 1976's *The Sins of the Fathers*. In that novel, explaining his unlicensed status, Scudder says, "Sometimes I do favors for people. They give me gifts." Block—who broke into the field in the early 1960s, writing soft-core porn with his friend Don Westlake—is a longtime professional who has slowly built himself into a major genre figure. By cultivating the mystery-bookstore market and making appearances at fan conventions, Block climbed to the top. That he is a terrific writer, adept at humor and suspense, a master of dialogue and action also helped.

Surprise Ending

Over a century and a half after Poe's first efforts, detective fiction—exploring the mysteries of life and death, while resolving the nastiest conflicts by the final page—continues to compel and entertain. No end seems in sight for the possibilities of the genre invented by Poe, refined by Doyle, and developed by forgotten hack writers back in the days of dime novels and pulps.

Whether your cup of cyanide is the genteel Ms. Christie or the two-fisted Mr. Spillane—whether you prefer the clipped prose stylings of Dashiell Hammett or the breezy voice of Sue Grafton—this book has attempted to provide you with the story of the genre's beginnings and an overview of its growth and various trends that have arisen in the context of an array of fun, exciting, often nostalgic images. Many a fine mystery novel, movie, and TV or radio show has gone unnoticed in these pages, however; and numerous talented mystery writers have not even rated a mention here.

No mystery why—the genre is too big, too intriguing, too wide, too wonderful to be explained and encompassed within the limitations of these covers. The sleuths reading this book need to take over the case, now...to track down those missing persons, and—if your interest has been piqued by descriptions of mysteries and/or mystery writers herein—it's time to grab your trench coat, choose between a deerstalker cap and a fedora, select a magnifying glass, and by all means pack a trusty gat...and search out those suspects.

THE TRIALS OF RUMPOLE

Paperback

1981

Horace Rumpole's interior-monologue description of his wife, Hilda, as "She Who Must Be Obeyed," is a typically tongue-in-cheek reference to H. Rider Haggard's fantasy novel, *She*.

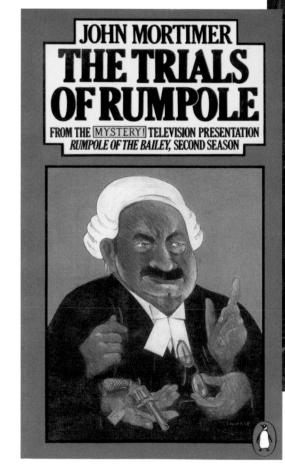

STEVEN SAYLOR

of *The Venus Throw*, *Catilina's Riddle*, and *Roman Blood*

A MURDER ON THE APPIAN WAY

A MYSTERY OF ANCIENT ROME

"Steven Saylor's lively imagination, Rome— glorious and grimy—is revived." —*Seattle Times*

A MURDER ON THE APPIAN WAY

Paperback
1997

The acceptance of Saylor's Roman detective, Gordianus the Finder, has encouraged other mystery writers to imagine new times and settings for their detectives.

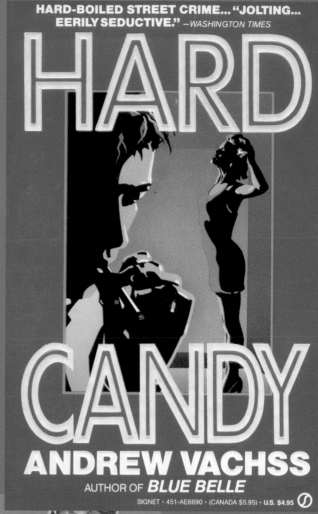

HARD-BOILED STREET CRIME... "JOLTING... EERILY SEDUCTIVE." —*WASHINGTON TIMES*

HARD CANDY

ANDREW VACHSS

AUTHOR OF *BLUE BELLE*

SIGNET • 451-AE6690 • (CANADA $5.95) • U.S. $4.95

DELL• 8701 •1.25

**Matt Scudder—
New York's answer
to Lew Archer**

TIME TO MURDER AND CREATE

Lawrence Block

HARD CANDY

Paperback
1990

Vachss is one of the few post-Parker P.I. writers to openly display the influence of Mickey Spillane and Mike Hammer with graphically violent tales of righteous revenge.

TIME TO MURDER AND CREATE

Paperback
1977

Block's P.I. Scudder began in a handful of poor-selling paperback originals and yet returned in hardcover with frequent appearances on best-seller lists. Most writers would have abandoned their character after so inauspicious a start, but Block's persistence matches his talent.

ACKNOWLEDGEMENTS

All materials in this review are included solely for artifactual and representative purposes. We have made every effort to trace the ownership of any copyrighted material and to secure permission from copyright holders. In the event of any question arising as to the ownership of any material, we will be pleased to make the necessary correction in future printings. Again I would like to thank my research associates, George Hagenauer and Matthew V. Clemens. Among those who aided in clearances were Keith Alan Deutsch and Robert Weinberg; thank you, gentlemen.

Black Mask copyright 2001, Keith Alan Deutsch. *Blue Book* copyright 1954, McCall Corporation/RedBook Publishing Company. Copyright by Conde Nast Publications, Inc.: *The Avenger*, 1939; *Detective Story Magazine*, 1929, 1930, 1931, 1932; *Nick Carter*, 1935, 1945; *The Shadow*, 1933, 1935, 1942; *The Whisperer*, 1941. Copyright and Trademark by Argosy Communications, Inc., all rights reserved (Argosy Communications is the successor in interest to Popular Publications, Inc., Fictioneers, Inc., The Frank A. Munsey Company, and The Red Star News Company): *Argosy*, 1933, 1942; *Detective Fiction Weekly*, 1938, 1940, 1941; *Detective Tales*, 1940; *Dime Detective*, 1933, 1935, 1936; *Dime Mystery*, 1940, 1941; *New Detective*, 1948; *The Spider*, 1937, 1939, 1941; *Strange Detective Mystery*, 1938. *Weird Tales* copyright 1938 by Weird Tales; *Weird Tales* is a registered trademark owned by Weird Tales, Limited. *Ellery Queen Mystery Magazine* copyright 1945, 1965, Davis Publications. *Alfred Hitchcock Mystery Magazine* copyright 1969, Davis Publications. *Mike Shayne Mystery Magazine* copyright 1980, Renown Publications, Inc. *Charlie Chan Mystery Magazine* copyright 1974, Renown Publications Inc. *Dick Tracy* copyright 2001, Tribune Media Services. *Ms. Tree*, copyright 1986, Max Allan Collins and Terry Beatty. *Johnny Dynamite* copyright 1994, 2001, Max Allan Collins and Terry Beatty. *Detective Comics* copyright 2001, DC Comics; *Batman* copyright 1987, DC Comics. *Rip Kirby* copyright 2001, King Features Syndicate. *Kerry Drake* copyright 2001, Publishers Syndicate.

SELECTED BIBLIOGRAPHY

Detectionary, Mill Roseman (The Overlook Press, 1977)

Encyclopedia Mysteriosa, William L. DeAndrea (Prentice Hall, 1994)

Encyclopedia of Mystery & Detection, Chris Steinbrunner/Otto Penzler (McGraw Hill, 1976)

The Murder Book, Tage la Cour/Harald Mogensen (Herder and Herder New York, 1971)

Murder For Pleasure, Howard Haycraft (D. Appleton-Century Co. Inc., 1941)

101 Years' Entertainment, Ellery Queen (The Modern Library, 1941)

The Book of Sleuths, Janet Pate (Contemporary Books, (Herder and Herder New York, 1971)

TV Detectives, Richard Meyers (A.S. Barnes Company, Inc., 1981)

Twentieth Century Crime and Mystery Writers, John M. Reilly (St. Martin's Press, 1985)

Tune in Yesterday, John Dunning (Prentice-Hall, Inc., 1976)

The Whodunit, Stefano Benvenuti/Gianni Rizzoni (Collier Books, 1981)

Page numbers in parentheses refer
to images or their captions